No Litmus Test

No Litmus Test

Law versus Politics in the Twenty-First Century

Michael C. Dorf

ROWMAN & LITTLEFIELD PUBLISHERS, INC.
Lanham • Boulder • New York • Toronto • Oxford

ROWMAN & LITTLEFIELD PUBLISHERS, INC.

Published in the United States of America
by Rowman & Littlefield Publishers, Inc.
A wholly owned subsidiary of The Rowman & Littlefield Publishing Group, Inc.
4501 Forbes Boulevard, Suite 200, Lanham, Maryland 20706
www.rowmanlittlefield.com

PO Box 317
Oxford
OX2 9RU, UK

British Library Cataloguing in Publication Information Available

Library of Congress Cataloging-in-Publication Data

Dorf, Michael C.
No litmus test : law versus politics in the twenty-first century / Michael C. Dorf.
p. cm.
Includes bibliographical references and index.
ISBN-13: 978-0-7425-5029-2 (cloth : alk. paper)
ISBN-10: 0-7425-5029-X (cloth : alk. paper)
ISBN-13: 978-0-7425-5030-8 (pbk. : alk. paper)
ISBN-10: 0-7425-5030-3 (pbk. : alk. paper)
1. Political questions and judicial power—United States. 2. United States—Supreme Court. 3. Constitutional law—United States. 4. United States—Politics and government—21st
century. I. Title.
KF5130.D67 2006
342.73—dc22 2005029160

Printed in the United States of America

∞™ The paper used in this publication meets the minimum requirements of American National Standard for Information Sciences—Permanence of Paper for Printed Library Materials, ANSI/NISO Z39.48-1992.

For Meena and Amelia

Contents

Acknowledgments

This book would not exist but for the help and encouragement of numerous friends and colleagues. At the height of the dot-com revolution, Julie Hilden asked me to write a column for *Writ*, a new online journal published by FindLaw. At the time, FindLaw was a California startup providing legal documents on the Internet free of charge. It is now a subsidiary of West Group, the country's leading publisher of legal texts. Julie has been my editor from the beginning, always helping me keep my writing free of legal jargon. Thanks also go to FindLaw's Diahann Reyes and her successor, Larry Haveson, who have made writing my columns a joy rather than a chore.

I had for some time thought that I ought to package some of my columns as a book, but it was not until Chris Anzalone of Rowman & Littlefield proposed the idea that I figured out that despite writing on nominally different topics every two weeks, in fact I was making a larger point with each of these. Bringing out that larger point proved harder than I expected, but I am very grateful to Chris and to the board of Rowman & Littlefield for prodding me to make the effort.

Three people were critical in the actual production of the book. My administrative assistant Gabriel Soto handled all of the tricky formatting requirements with his customary aplomb, and two of my students, David Crowley and Adam Schleifer, provided invaluable research assistance in documenting the claims made throughout this book.

Numerous people provided help at one stage or another with various columns collected here, especially those that ventured outside my main areas of expertise. These include: Benjamin Alpers, Jose Alvarez, Richard Briffault, Neil Buchanan, Lori Damrosch, George Fletcher, Samuel Issacharoff,

Vicki Jackson, Marty Lederman, Benjamin Liebman, James Liebman, Neysun Mahboubi, Nate Persily, Andrzej Rapaczynski, Charles Sabel, William Simon, Jeremy Waldron, and especially Sherry Colb, who gave me the ideas for many of the topics addressed in these chapters and helped me develop those ideas through every stage.

Note on Sources

Citations in the endnotes generally conform to the styles set forth in *The Bluebook: A Uniform System of Citation*, 18th edition (Cambridge, MA: Harvard Law Review Association, 2005). For accessibility for a general audience, in some instances, I have omitted information, such as parenthetical descriptions of cases or works of scholarship, which the *Bluebook* rules require. Citations of statutes include the year in which the relevant code section contained the material quoted or otherwise described, rather than referring to the year of publication of the bound volume. Citations of materials on websites were verified during the summer of 2005 and webpage images are on file with the author.

Introduction: The Relative Autonomy of Law

On July 1, 2005, Sandra Day O'Connor announced her intention to retire from the United States Supreme Court. Almost immediately, politicians, interest groups, journalists, and ordinary citizens focused on the question of who would be named to fill the seat of a Justice who for years had cast the decisive vote on such questions as abortion, affirmative action, school prayer, and states' rights. For his part, President Bush quickly asserted that he would use "no litmus test" in deciding whom to nominate for the position.[1]

Although religious conservatives who want to see *Roe v. Wade*[2] overturned have been among President Bush's strongest supporters, his renunciation of a "litmus test" placed him firmly in the company of that decision's author, the late Harry Blackmun. In December 1992, Justice Blackmun gave some private advice to then-President-elect Bill Clinton. In selecting a successor to Blackmun—who would announce his retirement from the Court a year and a half later—Clinton should "not use a litmus test . . . but just pick good judges."[3] The term "litmus test" is something of a code word for abortion, and so the advice must have been arresting, coming as it did from Blackmun.

Indeed, earlier in 1992, in another landmark abortion decision, *Planned Parenthood v. Casey*,[4] a bare 5–4 majority of the Court had voted to retain the core of the *Roe* decision. At that time, with the first President Bush still looking likely to secure re-election, Blackmun had written an impassioned concurrence that concluded: "I am 83 years old I cannot remain on this Court forever, and when I do step down, the confirmation process for my successor well may focus on the issue before us today."[5] That was in early July. But now in December, Blackmun seemed to have such little regard for his own legacy that he was inviting the new President to cast it aside.

What mischief was the old Minnesotan inviting by seeming to give the Arkansan triangulator carte blanche to compromise a principle that was so vital to so many of the people who had voted for him? Likewise, what was the second President Bush suggesting when he announced what must have seemed like an attitude of indifference to the people so passionately on the other side of the very same issue, who, in turn, had voted for him? To answer these questions we must look more closely at what Blackmun, Bush, and others might mean when they condemn a litmus test.

To begin, no sensible person could really mean that absolutely no litmus test should be applied in the nomination or confirmation of judges. What if an otherwise highly qualified lawyer or scholar held truly retrograde views on some issue beyond the pale of reasonable disagreement? Suppose, for example, that a prospective judicial nominee thought that state-enforced racial segregation was permissible under the Fourteenth Amendment, notwithstanding the 1954 decision to the contrary in *Brown v. Board of Education*.[6] Or worse, suppose an otherwise qualified nominee thought that the Fourteenth Amendment itself was not part of the Constitution because the congressional vote to propose the Amendment did not include delegates from the former Confederate States. Surely it would be appropriate to apply a litmus test that says in effect: If you don't accept the Fourteenth Amendment, you're unfit to be a Supreme Court Justice.

Accordingly, Blackmun probably did not mean for Clinton to take his advice literally, nor did Bush mean his statement categorically. Other things being equal, Blackmun certainly would have preferred to be succeeded by a pro-choice Justice, and Bush almost certainly would have preferred a pro-life nominee. (Blackmun's preference was satisfied when Clinton named Stephen Breyer to the seat Blackmun vacated in the summer of 1994; whether President Bush's nominee, Judge Samuel Alito, proves willing to overturn *Roe* remains to be seen.) Yet in disavowing a litmus test, Blackmun and Bush were both saying that they wanted a Court made up of judges—men and women who would decide each case according to the law as they saw it—rather than ideologues who would come to the Court with an agenda on particular issues.

To be sure, Bush's conception of judging differs substantially from Blackmun's. In his statements about judicial appointments, Bush has praised judges who go by such names as "strict constructionists," "textualists," and "formalists." Broadly speaking, the motto of this camp is that judges should apply the law rather than make it. In recent years, political conservatives have tended to adopt this position, objecting to what they regard as liberal judicial activism reflected in decisions involving abortion, gay rights, the death penalty, and other divisive social controversies. However, in other periods of American history, political liberals have used the same arguments to attack what they regarded as conservative judicial activism reflected in decisions protecting slavery, laissez-faire economics, states' rights, and other traditional institutions. Strict constructionism is a judicial philosophy that may or may not have particular consequences for particular political issues during particular periods; it is not, in itself, a political philosophy.

Accordingly, although public debate in the early twenty-first-century United States tends to portray strict constructionists as occupying one end of a spectrum, and to portray liberal judicial activists as occupying the other, in fact, the polar opposite of strict constructionism is a philosophy one frequently finds championed by academics, but which judges almost never espouse. Where the strict constructionists say that judges should simply follow the law rather than reading their own values into the law, their opposite numbers in the academy say that law itself is bunk, or more precisely, that law is politics. Beginning in the early twentieth century with a scholarly movement called "legal realism," such critical voices have long contended that in the sorts of contested cases that grab the most attention, a plausible legal argument can be made for either side, so that the real determinants of any judicial decision will be found in the judges' politics rather than the conventional legal materials. Some of these "realists"—who might better be called cynics—content themselves with debunking law, but others go so far as to say that because law is just politics, judges should feel liberated to pursue their political vision from the bench.[7]

In recent decades, the realist view of courts has been bolstered by statistical research in political science purporting to show that individual judges' political attitudes are a more reliable predictor of outcomes in contested cases than is expert analysis of the law. That claim seemed to gain further support from a 2003 experiment in which the statistical model was matched against a battery of legal experts (including yours truly) and asked to predict the outcomes of cases then pending before the Supreme Court. The results of this legal version of the chess matches between human champion Gary Kasparov and IBM's Deep Blue were, at first blush, equally dispiriting: We legal experts were soundly thrashed; the statistical model correctly predicted the outcome in 75 percent of the cases, while the human team was right in only 59 percent.[8]

Yet whatever else it may show, that result does not confirm the critical claim that law is just politics. We legal experts were not asked, after all, what was the legally correct outcome in the cases before the Court. We were asked to *predict* how the individual Justices of the Rehnquist Court would vote. It is not really surprising that a computer program designed to predict the voting pattern of those nine people would do a better job at that task than would scholars whose particular expertise lies in the field of evaluating legal arguments rather than in guessing how other people will evaluate legal arguments.

Moreover, from a certain perspective, the very design of the contest between statisticians and legal scholars assumed the correctness of the legal realist viewpoint. Oliver Wendell Holmes Jr., who was in some respects the first legal realist, once wrote that the law is simply nothing more than "prophecies of what the courts will do in fact. . . ."[9] Other legal realists practically made this aphorism their credo.[10] Of course, if you think that the law really consists of nothing but predictions of how courts behave, then it is perfectly reasonable to design a contest that aims to discern the most accurate mode of prediction.

Suppose, however, you think that law is not a matter of predictions but of discerning the meaning of authoritative texts, following the logic of prior precedents, and achieving just and sensible results. If that's your view, then you will be less interested in whether some procedure accurately predicts how five Justices of the Supreme Court will resolve the cases that come before them than in how those cases ought—all things considered—to be resolved.

Students of jurisprudence may see in the contrast I have posed echoes of a familiar debate between two great legal philosophers, Ronald Dworkin and the late H. L. A. Hart. According to Hart, in hard cases—those in which reasonable minds can differ as to the import of the conventional legal materials—judges exercise discretion, albeit discretion constrained by the range of views of the law a reasonable mind could entertain.[11] Dworkin disagrees, observing that judges certainly don't act as though their decisions are discretionary; in all cases, he notes, they write opinions that purport to explain why the legal materials justify one result rather than another. Thus, Dworkin says that there are uniquely right answers even in hard cases.[12]

I do not mean to take a position in this abstruse debate. Whether or not there are right answers in hard cases, there certainly are *better and worse answers*. Those who follow Dworkin may think that legal answers are better insofar as they approach the real right answer, while those who follow Hart may think that they are better insofar as they reflect the sound exercise of discretion, which undoubtedly should be guided, if not uniquely determined, by authoritative texts, prior precedents, justice, and common sense.

The notion that there are better and worse answers to legal questions gets at what Blackmun had in mind by urging Clinton to appoint "good judges," for judges, we do well to remember, are people who are expected to exercise judgment—and good judges exercise good judgment. Judgment, of course, is needed precisely where objective materials *do not* clearly prescribe an answer. We would not say, for instance, that it takes judgment to determine the answer to a question of mathematics. Intelligence and training, yes, but not judgment.

If not needed to solve purely mathematical questions, neither is good judgment a quality to be prized solely in matters of law. Politicians, military and business leaders, educators, and others must frequently choose one among several plausible courses of action based upon their own evaluation of a wide range of factors that cannot be reduced to an algorithm. Yet to recognize that good judgment is both partly subjective and not uniquely the province of judges raises the legal realist's question once again: In what sense do judges exercising judgment engage in a legal as distinct from political task?

The legal realists themselves—or at least the most radical among them—answer: not at all. For them, law simply is politics, and depending on the disposition of the realist in question, this observation either delegitimates most judicial decision making or liberates judges to do whatever they please.

By contrast, the formalists (some of whom dislike the term "strict constructionism," but we can put that semantic detail aside), seem to think that legal questions really can be resolved algorithmically. Judges who "make" rather than "interpret" the law, in the formalist view, do so through willfulness rather than necessity. If only judges would hew close to the formal written texts, the formalists say, they would have no excuse for imposing their subjective value choices.

This book offers a middle position between the extremes of realism and formalism. The realists do us an important service by correcting the formalists' overly mechanical picture of law. But they go too far in suggesting that there is nothing distinctly *legal* about the decision-making methodology employed by courts and other legal actors. Just as we can say of some military judgment that it was a good one in light of the particular desiderata of military affairs—it gained vital ground or struck a crippling blow against the enemy's offensive capability, say—so we can say of some legal judgment that it was a good one in light of the desiderata of the law—fidelity to authoritative text and precedent, substantive justice, and sensible policy.

I make an argument here for what might be called the *partial autonomy of law*. Recognizing our debt to the legal realists, I accept that the sorts of factors that go into a legal decision often overlap with the sorts of factors that might go into a different kind of decision, such as a political, moral, or scientific one. So the methodology of legal decision making is not entirely distinct from other kinds of decision making.

But neither are legal judgments simply reducible to judgments in other fields. To give a straightforward example, suppose that a judge is persuaded by the writings of those economists who claim that minimum wage laws either do no good (because the employers were willing to pay the minimum wage anyway) or that they cause affirmative harm (because they lead employers to relocate jobs to lower-wage locales or go bankrupt); the judge would nonetheless be wholly unjustified in ruling that a firm that failed to pay the legally mandated minimum wage could escape liability for its conduct. Economics may be relevant to the law, but it is not the whole of the law.

To be sure, in the foregoing example, the law is clear: Covered firms must pay the minimum wage to covered employees.[13] Yet the basic point holds even where the law is ambiguous. Consider, for example, the question of state payments to parochial schools. Under governing Supreme Court precedent interpreting the First Amendment's Establishment Clause, states can subsidize the secular portions of these schools' programs, such as mathematics textbooks, lunch, and bus transportation, but not the religious aspects, such as Bibles and crucifixes.[14] Should this line of precedent be overruled because, as economics teaches, money is fungible? After all, state subsidies for secular items enable the parochial schools to spend money on Bibles that would otherwise have gone for math books. Accordingly, an economist might advise a rule that either prohibits all payments to religious institutions or a rule that prohibits none.

The economist's observation should indeed give judges pause but it is not dispositive, for the Establishment Clause is concerned (or at least may plausibly be thought to be concerned) not only with the concrete financial effects of government policies but also with the symbolic meaning of those policies. When the state pays for wholesome meals for schoolchildren attending parochial schools to the same extent that it pays for such meals for schoolchildren in public schools, it typically sends only the unobjectionable signal that children should not be made to suffer a detriment to their health because their parents want them to receive a religious education. By contrast, when the state pays for Bibles or crucifixes, it impermissibly endorses religious doctrines.

Accordingly, the insights of economics—or history, moral philosophy, or any other discipline relevant to sound legal decision making—cannot simply be adopted by judges. Law is at least partly an autonomous discipline with its own tools and methods. The insights of other disciplines must be translated and integrated into the law's own language.

If the foregoing discussion makes this claim about the nature of law plausible, how shall I put more flesh on the skeletal sketch? My methodology in this book is generally indirect. Each of the chapters that follows began as a column I wrote commenting on newsworthy legal events of the last several years, and I hope the reader will find them interesting in their own right. But collectively, the chapters also serve a larger purpose. In my praise or criticism of particular legal decisions or reforms, I try to give the reader some feel for what counts as distinctly *legal* argument. I show the courts deciding cases based on factors other than the mere political, and I take them to task when their arguments fall short. I also emphasize that law's autonomy from other fields is only partial, frequently calling attention to the social or political context of important legal decisions.

In making my indirect case for the partial autonomy of law, I have included the columns more or less as I originally wrote them. With the exception of corrections of factual errors, editing for style, and the addition of endnotes, supplemental material appears mostly in section introductions and individual chapter postscripts. Had I taken a different approach, I might well have substantially revised at least some of the individual chapters to correct what I now regard as my own errors of judgment. But because my core claim is that law involves judgment, I thought it would be gilding the lily to present my own judgments as invariably sound. Hence, in a number of the chapter postscripts I apply to my own earlier expressed views the same critical analysis to which I subject the courts and other legal actors throughout the chapters.

In the end, of course, I do not expect any reader to agree with all of my judgments, and not simply because some of them contradict others! My more modest hope is that readers will find in these pages a window into how the law really works. Too often in public debate and press coverage of legal affairs, one sees either a naïve formalism or a cynical realism. The antidote to these mirroring mistakes is in the details of the good-faith (and occasional bad-faith) struggle of judges and other legal actors with the vexing problems they must confront.

Encompassing as it does all of life's messy complexity, the law undoubtedly spawns its share of hard questions. But it is the very difficulty of these questions that cries out for good judgment. This book's burden is to show that such a thing is possible.

NOTES

1. *See* Warren Vieth, *Tone of Court Debate Decried; Bush Objects to Groups' Efforts to Sway His Choice for Vacant Seat, Citing Attacks on Gonzales. President Promises He Won't Use a 'Litmus Test,'* L.A. Times, July 7, 2005, at A1.

2. 410 U.S. 113 (1973).

3. Anthony Lewis, Op-Ed., *Abroad at Home; The Blackmun Legacy*, N.Y. Times, Apr. 8, 1994, at A27 (ellipsis in original).

4. 505 U.S. 833 (1992).

5. *Id.* at 943 (Blackmun, J., concurring in part, concurring in the judgment in part, and dissenting in part).

6. 347 U.S. 483 (1954).

7. *See* Joseph Singer, *The Player and the Cards: Nihilism and Legal Theory*, 94 Yale L.J. 1, 62–63 (1984); Mark Tushnet, *The Dilemmas of Liberal Constitutionalism*, 42 Ohio St. L.J. 411, 424 (1981).

8. *See* Theodore W. Ruger et al., *The Supreme Court Forecasting Project: Legal and Political Science Approaches to Predicting Supreme Court Decisionmaking*, 104 Colum. L. Rev. 1150, 1151–52 (2004). I am proud to say that I personally did slightly better than the statistical model in predicting the result of the cases I was asked about.

9. Oliver W. Holmes, *The Path of the Law*, 10 Harv. L. Rev. 457, 461 (1897), *reprinted in* Oliver W. Holmes, Collected Legal Papers 173 (1920).

10. *See* K. N. Llewellyn, The Bramble Bush 12–14 (New York: Oceana, 3d ed. 1960); Joseph W. Bingham, *What Is the Law?*, 11 Mich. L. Rev. 1, 15 (1912); Jerome Frank, *Are Judges Human? Part Two: As Through a Class Darkly*, 80 U. Pa. L. Rev. 233, 236 (1931).

11. *See* H. L. A. Hart, The Concept of Law 124–36, 272–75 (New York: Oxford University Press, Penelope A. Bulloch & Joseph Raz eds., 2d ed. 1994).

12. *See* Ronald Dworkin, Law's Empire viii–ix, 6, 412 (Cambridge, Mass.: Belknap Press, 1986); Ronald Dworkin, Taking Rights Seriously 279 (Cambridge, Mass.: Harvard University Press, 1977) ("My arguments suppose that there is often a single right answer to complex questions of law and political morality.").

13. 29 U.S.C. § 206 (2005).

14. *See* Mitchell v. Helms, 530 U.S. 793, 822 (2000) (plurality opinion); *id.* at 857 (O'Connor, J., concurring in the judgment).

I

THE DIFFERENCE BETWEEN LAW AND POLITICS

The following question poses a simple test of the legal realist claim that law is just politics: Is it possible to think that some policy is desirable on moral and political grounds but not mandated on legal grounds? Phrased this way, the question answers itself. Anyone who has ever cursed a "stupid law" or, conversely, thought that there "oughtta be a law against" some practice, knows that the law is not always as one would wish. And indeed, the legal realists—who are not fools—do not claim that the law is always as everyone wished it were.

What the realists do say is that in hotly contested cases—the sorts of cases that give rise to appellate litigation—the factors that judges use to resolve the contests cannot be meaningfully distinguished from political factors. But if this is true, then it should also be true that at least with respect to hard cases, nobody can find a divergence between his political judgment and his legal judgment. And yet that claim seems manifestly false.

Take the matter of the juvenile death penalty. In March 2005, the Supreme Court confronted the question of whether the Eighth Amendment's bar on cruel and unusual punishment prohibits the government from executing criminals who committed their crimes when younger than age eighteen. Sixteen years earlier, by a vote of 5–4, the Court had upheld the juvenile death penalty in a case called *Stanford v. Kentucky*.[1] The question in 2005 was whether, in the interim, the "evolving standards of decency that mark the progress of a maturing society"[2] had rendered the death penalty disproportionate to the culpability of juvenile offenders. The vote in *Roper v. Simmons* was again 5–4, but this time the Court invalidated the juvenile death penalty.[3] The closeness of the vote in both instances, and the fact that the issue had reached the nation's highest court, show that this was indeed a hard case. Accordingly, if the legal realist view is right, the explanation for the decision in each case must be the Justices' political views about the juvenile death penalty.

And yet that account cannot explain the actual tally. For one thing, Justice Anthony Kennedy, who wrote the Court's 2005 opinion invalidating the juvenile death penalty in *Roper*, had been a member of the majority that upheld the juvenile death penalty in *Stanford*. It's possible that Kennedy's political views about the juvenile death penalty changed in the intervening sixteen years, but a more straightforward explanation is that his view of the *law* changed, and that is exactly what his opinion said.[4] One can think that Kennedy's legal judgment was incorrect, but something more like a conspiracy theory is required to show that Kennedy was secretly exercising political rather than legal judgment.

Indeed, Justice Sandra Day O'Connor, who dissented in *Roper*, expressly distinguished between law and politics. She wrote: "[W]ere my office that of a legislator, rather than a judge, then I, too, would be inclined to support legislation setting a minimum age of 18" for eligibility for the death penalty.[5] But finding that the legal materials on which the majority relied were not, to her mind, sufficiently compelling, O'Connor drew a line between what she thought was politically sound and what she thought was legally required.

The legal realists are aware that judges sometimes vote against their political preferences, even in hard cases, and they have an explanation for this phenomenon: The judges, the realists say, are either lying to the public or to themselves (or perhaps both). This is of course possible, but it begins to strain credulity when no motive for such systematic deception (even if only self-deception) is offered. The best that the realists can do in this regard is to say that judges deceive themselves because it is in their professional interest to believe that they are in fact engaged in the dignified determination of legal questions, rather than simply imposing their will—much in the way that a shaman might suppress doubts about the efficacy of his rituals for fear of cognitive dissonance.

At some point, however, the legal realist account loses its bite, for if judges really do decide cases based on what they sincerely regard as legal reasoning, then we have a direct test of whether they are engaged in law as opposed to politics: We can evaluate the strength of the legal arguments they provide. To do so, however, we must first move beyond familiar labels that take for granted either the naïve formalist view or the radical legal realist view of the relation between law and politics.

NOTES

1. 492 U.S. 361 (1989).
2. Trop v. Dulles, 356 U.S. 86, 101 (1958) (plurality opinion).
3. 125 S. Ct. 1183 (2005).
4. 125 S. Ct. at 1194, 1198.
5. 125 S. Ct. at 1217 (O'Connor, J., dissenting).

• 1 •

They Are All Activists Now

May 2000

George W. Bush has stated that if he were elected President, he would appoint "strict constructionists" to the federal bench.[1] With this promise, Bush courts social conservatives within the Republican Party—who praise conservative judges' "strict constructionism" at the same time they decry liberal jurists' "judicial activism." Ironically, however, on the Supreme Court, accusations of "judicial activism" have been flying in precisely the opposite direction: There, "judicial activism" has recently become a term used by *liberal* Justices to critique *conservative* Justices' views. It is time that we recognize that judicial activism is not ideological. Rather, in our current constitutional discourse, it is inevitable.

For conservatives, "judicial activism" is epitomized by the leading liberal Supreme Court decisions. The most prominent, of course, is *Roe v. Wade*,[2] recognizing abortion rights. Some other leading targets are *Miranda v. Arizona*,[3] requiring that warnings precede custodial interrogation of criminal suspects; *Engel v. Vitale*,[4] prohibiting organized prayer in the public schools; and *Romer v. Evans*,[5] invalidating a Colorado referendum that withdrew the protection of local anti-discrimination law from gays and lesbians. Each of these decisions (and others) has become a bête noire of judicial conservatives—who claim each is illegitimately grounded in the Justices' personal morality rather than in the Constitution. Vote for me, George W. signals, and I will see to it that liberal judges stay out of politics.

Within the Supreme Court, however, it is the (moderate to) liberal Justices who have lately been accusing their conservative colleagues of judicial activism. The 2000 decision in *Kimel v. Florida Board of Regents*[6] provides a prime example. There, the Court issued a 5–4 ruling that states could not be sued for age discrimination because of a general principle of state sovereign immunity.[7] *Kimel* is a conservative decision in two senses. It expands states' rights (here, the right of the state not to be subject to private lawsuits) and constricts anti-discrimination (here, age-discrimination) law. *Kimel* is also an activist decision—going far beyond the text of the Constitution.

The Constitution does not expressly say, as *Kimel* held, that citizens cannot sue the states. On the contrary, it implies that they can. The Eleventh Amendment expressly prohibits only those lawsuits "commenced or prosecuted against one of the United States by Citizens of another State, or by Citizens or Subjects of any Foreign State"—and thus implicitly *authorizes* a lawsuit against a state by one of its *own* citizens. Accordingly, in his dissent in *Kimel*, Justice Stevens angrily declared that "the kind of judicial activism manifested in [such cases] represents such a radical departure from the proper role of th[e] Court that it should be opposed whenever the opportunity arises."[8]

This is hardly the first time a liberal Justice has accused a conservative majority of the Court of activism in the state sovereign immunity context. Far from it. Dissenting in one case recognizing state sovereign immunity, Justice Souter faulted the majority for relying on principles of "natural law."[9] In a similar dissent,[10] Justice Breyer compared the Court's reasoning to the infamous decision in *Lochner v. New York*[11]—a case whose very name has become synonymous with judicial overreaching. And in a third such dissent,[12] Justice Stevens derisively described the majority as locating rules of law in the "penumbras" of the Eleventh Amendment—a reference to Justice Douglas's opinion in *Griswold v. Connecticut*,[13] in which the Court found a right to contraception in the Fourteenth Amendment's Due Process Clause.

It may be tempting to think that we are witnessing the latest swing in the pendular path of attitudes toward judicial review. A case for that viewpoint could be made. In the first half of the nineteenth century, defenders of southern, agricultural interests decried the nationalizing, pro-commercial impulses of what they saw as an activist Court under the leadership of Chief Justice John Marshall. In the second half of the nineteenth century, abolitionists railed against what they saw as the Taney Court's activist invocation of the Constitution to extend protection to slavery in the territories. From the late nineteenth century through the first third of the twentieth, Populists, Progressives, and finally New Dealers challenged what they saw as the Court's activist view that the Constitution required laissez-faire capitalism. After a very brief post-War quiescence, in 1954 *Brown v. Board of Education*[14] fully launched the period of the liberal Warren Court's "activist" decisions. That period has been winding down since Richard Nixon was elected president in 1968. It therefore could be argued that the current realignment within the Court—in which the conservatives are once again accused of being the activists—is occurring right on cue, more or less at the beginning of the fifth half-century of American constitutional law. On this theory, activism, like the British monarchy, itself persists even as activists succeed one another: judicial activism is dead; long live judicial activism.

Yet this cyclical account omits the extent to which *all* of the current Justices—not just the conservatives who endorse states' rights—still believe in potent judicial power. *All* of the Justices are activists now—in a sense. The liberals on the Court remain committed to the landmark decisions of the Warren and early Burger courts. Surely Justice Stevens's derisive invocation of *Griswold*'s penumbras was not meant to suggest that he would now overrule *Griswold*'s right to contraception.[15] Instead, Justice Stevens's reference is best interpreted as an accusation of hypocrisy—a suggestion that the conservatives only believe that rights have penumbras when it suits them, such as when states', not individuals', rights are at issue.

But charges of hypocrisy, like charges of judicial activism, cut both ways. For example, when the Fourth Circuit Court of Appeals struck down the Violence Against Women Act[16] (a decision affirmed by the Supreme Court in a 5–4 decision in *United States v. Morrison*[17]), Judge Wilkinson's concurrence distinguished judicial activism when the courts act as a "structural referee" among the branches and levels of government from activism in defense of individual rights.[18] It is the liberals, he argued, who are the hypocrites in this debate.

Thus, conservatives routinely condemn judicial activism in the name of individual rights while endorsing it in the name of states' rights. Conversely, liberals condemn judicial activism in the name of states' rights while endorsing it in the name of individual rights.

Is there an alternative? Justices O'Connor and Kennedy have indicated some willingness to protect *both* the states and individuals through what might be termed an all-purpose activism. Thus, although they join with Chief Justice Rehnquist, Justice Scalia, and Justice Thomas in striking down federal laws on state sovereignty grounds,[19] they also join the liberal camp in protecting a woman's right to abortion,[20] and in invalidating egregious denials of equality to gays and lesbians.[21] However, while evenhanded judicial activism such as O'Connor's and Kennedy's may avoid the charge of hypocrisy, this sort of evenhandedness certainly will not satisfy anyone who sincerely believes that judges should generally defer to political actors in hard cases.

Not one of the current Justices takes *that* position. That is not surprising. The constitutional architecture of checks and balances presumes that each institution—the Court no less than the other branches—will seek to maximize its own power at the expense of the others. For example, in *Kimel*, while the nine Justices disagreed vehemently as to the proper result, they apparently all concurred in the majority's statement that the Court, rather than Congress, has the first and last word on the meaning of the Constitution (specifically, in that case, its conception of equality). Thus, despite their disagreement about which brand of activism is good and which bad, the Justices are unanimous in preferring their own power to that of other actors.

Given the trajectory of American constitutional law over the last two centuries, an activist role for the Court now appears all but inevitable. At the same time, because judicial review has always sat somewhat uncomfortably with democratic ideals, periodic accusations that the Court has engaged in unwarranted activism are equally inevitable. We should recognize that such accusations are rarely meant as a genuine critique of judicial power. Instead, they are best understood as a stylized form of constitutional rhetoric. So long as the Supreme Court exercises the power of judicial review, the accusation of activism itself will be largely empty. We should look beneath it, to the substantive arguments it can only mask.

POSTSCRIPT

Since the foregoing first appeared, the charges of judicial activism have continued to fly in both directions. In the 2003 case of *Goodridge v. Department of Public Health*, the Massachusetts Supreme Judicial Court ruled that the state constitution requires the recognition of same-sex marriages.[22] In response to the litigation in Massachusetts and other states, conservatives mobilized to oppose same-sex marriage, including proposing a federal constitutional amendment to ban the practice.[23] When critics charged that such an unprecedented inegalitarian amendment was unseemly and unwarranted, the amendment's proponents, including President Bush, replied that the measure was necessary in response to—you guessed it—judicial activism.[24] (I consider the merits of the proposed amendment in chapter 8.)

Another arresting charge of judicial activism was leveled in March 2005 by House Majority Leader Tom DeLay in response to the refusal of the federal courts to order the reinsertion of Terri Schiavo's feeding tube—on whose sole behalf Congress had enacted a law[25] authorizing federal reconsideration of issues that had been fully litigated in the Florida state courts already. (I discuss that episode in chapter 14.) DeLay denounced the federal judges, many of them conservative Republicans, for their "activism" in *refusing to take any action*.[26] If there had been any lingering doubt on the matter, DeLay's use of the epithet made clear that "judicial activism" had become a synonym for "decisions I dislike."

Still, the most voluble charge of judicial activism in recent years was made by liberals. Their charge was prompted by the Supreme Court's decision effectively terminating the presidential election of 2000, our next topic.

NOTES

1. *See Campaign 2000—A User's Guide*; *Gore Vs. Bush*, L.A. Times, Mar. 19, 2000, at A3.

2. 410 U.S. 113 (1973).

3. 384 U.S. 436 (1966).

4. 370 U.S. 421 (1962).

5. 517 U.S. 620 (1996).

6. 528 U.S. 62 (2000).

7. More recently, in cases involving the public accommodations provision of the Americans with Disabilities Act and the Family and Medical Leave Act, the Court narrowly upheld congressional abrogation of sovereign immunity pursuant to Section 5 of the Fourteenth Amendment. *See* Tennessee v. Lane, 541 U.S. 509 (2004) (upholding provisions of the Americans with Disabilities Act of 1990, Pub. L. No. 101–336, 104 Stat. 327, as applied to the states); Nev. Dept. of Human Res. v. Hibbs, 538 U.S. 721 (2003) (upholding provisions of the Family and Medical Leave Act of 1993, Pub. L. No. 103–3, 107 Stat. 6, as applied to the states).

8. 528 U.S. at 98–99 (Stevens, J., dissenting) (referring to Alden v. Maine, 527 U.S. 706 (1999); Fla. Prepaid Postsecondary Educ. Expense Bd. v. Coll. Sav. Bank, 527 U.S. 627 (1999); Coll. Sav. Bank v. Fla. Prepaid Postsecondary Educ. Expense Bd., 527 U.S. 666 (1999); and Seminole Tribe of Fla. v. Florida, 517 U.S. 44 (1996)).

9. Alden v. Maine, 527 U.S. 706, 763 (1999) (Souter, J., dissenting).

10. Coll. Sav. Bank v. Fla. Prepaid Postsecondary Educ. Expense Bd., 527 U.S. 666, 701 (1999) (Breyer, J., dissenting).

11. 198 U.S. 45 (1905).

12. Fla. Prepaid Postsecondary Educ. Expense Bd. v. Coll. Sav. Bank, 527 U.S. 627, 665 (1999) (Stevens, J., dissenting).

13. 381 U.S. 479, 484 (1965) ("[S]pecific guarantees in the Bill of Rights have penumbras, formed by emanations from those guarantees that help give them life and substance.").

14. 347 U.S. 483 (1954).

15. *Cf., e.g.*, Cruzan v. Dir., Mo. Dep't of Health, 497 U.S. 261, 341–42 (1990) (Stevens, J., dissenting) (citing *Griswold* to support his position in that case).

16. Violence Against Women Act of 1994, Pub. L. No. 103–322, Title IV, 108 Stat. 1902, 1902–55.

17. 529 U.S. 598 (2000).

18. Brzonkala v. Va. Polytechnic Inst. & State Univ., 169 F.3d 820, 895 (4th Cir. 1999) (Wilkinson, J., concurring). For further elaboration, see J. Harvie Wilkinson III, *Our Structural Constitution*, 104 Colum. L. Rev. 1687 (2004).

19. *E.g.*, Printz v. United States, 521 U.S. 898 (1997); *United States v. Lopez*, 514 U.S. 549 (1995).

20. *E.g.*, Planned Parenthood v. Casey, 505 U.S. 833 (1992).

21. *E.g.*, Romer v. Evans, 517 U.S. 620 (1996). Since I originally wrote the column that became this chapter, the trend continued in Lawrence v. Texas, 539 U.S. 558 (2003).

22. 798 N.E.2d 941 (Mass. 2003).

23. H.R.J. Res. 106, 108th Cong. (2004); S.J. Res. 30, 108th Cong. (2004).

24. In his 2005 State of the Union Address to Congress, President Bush declared: "Because marriage is a sacred institution and the foundation of society, it should not be redefined by activist judges. For the good of families, children and society, I support a constitutional amendment to protect the institution of marriage." Transcript, '*Let Us . . . Build a Better World*,' Wash. Post, Feb. 3, 2005, at A14.

25. Act of Mar. 21, 2005, Pub. L. No. 109–3, 119 Stat. 15.

26. *See* Mike Allen, *DeLay Apologizes for Comments; Leader Wouldn't Say Whether He Wants Schiavo Judges Impeached*, Wash. Post, Apr. 14, 2005, at A5.

• 2 •

Is There a Distinction between Law and Politics? Yes, and the *Bush v. Gore* Decision Proves It

December 2000

For roughly the last century, an academic debate has raged over the nature of judicial decision making. The radicals in this debate argue that there is, at bottom, no distinction between law and politics. They have scored important partial victories—for nearly everyone now concedes that, at least in close cases, a judge's philosophy and values play an important role. However, mainstream legal thinkers have, until now, resisted the effort to collapse the categories of law and politics completely.

The widespread perception that the Supreme Court acted politically in *Bush v. Gore*[1] appears to be an important victory for the radical position. If the highest court of the land cannot rise above partisan political divisions, then, many observers may conclude, there really *is* no difference between law and politics; they are one, just as the radicals have always contended.

But that conclusion would be wrong. Ironically, the very fact that the Court's decision in *Bush v. Gore* appears "political"—indeed, more political than any other decision in recent memory—only confirms the existence of the law/politics distinction. If law were just politics, it would be meaningless to criticize a judicial decision as political, and all the Court's decisions would seem equally "political" to observers.

Of course, many issues that are hotly debated in the political arena also become legal issues for resolution by judges—and many of the arguments made in the political forum are also made in the judicial forum. Yet it hardly follows from this overlap that every judicial decision is simply a political one. Judges are bound by legal texts and their own prior precedents to a degree that political actors are not. And crucially, judges have an obligation to explain their results as the product of legal judgment. Thus, law and politics are neither completely distinct nor indistinguishable.

To understand the likely effect of the *Bush v. Gore* decision on future understandings of the law/politics distinction, let us consider a very abbreviated summary of the history of the jurisprudential debate about whether such a distinction exists.

Until roughly the beginning of the twentieth century, the dominant legal philosophy in the United States was formalism. Formalists believed that the application of legal principles embodied in statutes or prior precedents was a largely mechanical enterprise. The decision in any given case, formalists asserted, was a straightforward matter of discerning the meaning of words, aided by canons of construction (interpretive rules, developed over history, by which legal sources are construed) and other neutral tools.

Formalism still has its champions, the most prominent of whom is Justice Antonin Scalia,[2] who is fond of quoting dictionaries in his quest for the "plain meaning" of statutes and constitutional provisions. And it was formalism's vision of the judge as blank slate that Justice Clarence Thomas invoked when he said during his confirmation hearings that upon taking his seat on the bench, he would "strip down like a runner . . . to eliminate ideology."[3]

But despite these well-placed defenders, formalism has been in decline for nearly a hundred years. In the first half of the twentieth century, legal realism emerged to challenge formalism. One familiar formulation of legal realism asserted that what the judge happened to have for breakfast on any given day was as good a determinant of his decision in a particular case as was anything found in the law books. More generally, legal realists argued that legal interpretation is not a neutral, mechanical process but a subjective, human one in which the judge's beliefs, values, and politics come into play.[4]

Today, this claim may seem obvious to the point of banality, but it was not until roughly the middle of the twentieth century that most mainstream legal thinkers accepted the legal realist critique of pure formalism. Accordingly, legal scholars and theorists with widely divergent views now generally acknowledge that constitutional provisions, statutes, and precedents typically leave gaps that must be filled by judges, and that judges with different values and philosophies will fill those gaps differently.

Does that acknowledgment imply, as well, that law is simply politics? That was the next hotly debated theoretical question.

Even as mainstream lawyers, judges, and academics accepted legal realism's critique of formalism, they resisted the claim of some radical legal realists that law is just politics. In the 1950s and 1960s, the legal process school of thought attempted a synthesis of the different, warring philosophies.

According to those in the legal process movement, the fact that the law leaves gaps provides a reason to be careful in the allocation of power among the legislative, executive, and judicial branches.[5] Within that careful allocation, the judge's role is to follow the law as best as he or she can—but the "best" interpretation of the law, the legal process school conceded, may vary somewhat from judge to judge.[6]

Like Bismarck or Clinton, mainstream legal thought defeated the radical vision of the opposition by co-opting its most attractive features. The legal process school rang true with experience, as realism had—for it acknowledged that reasonable judicial minds could differ. But it also held out the hope that judges might operate within some degree of constraint, and within a limited sphere of power.

The debate did not end with the legal process school, however. By the 1970s, the heirs to the radical branch of the legal realist tradition had reformulated their position through the critical legal studies movement (also sometimes referred to by the acronym CLS).

Where legal realism had emphasized the indeterminacy and potential arbitrariness of judicial decision making, critical legal studies focused on politics. The "crits," as they were known, reveled in demonstrating how, throughout American history, judges had resolved ambiguities in the law by rendering decisions that served the interest of the dominant social class—or, at least, the political values held by the particular judges on the bench.[7]

Critical legal studies reached its peak of influence during the 1980s, when several high-profile tenure battles at leading law schools—in which the value of the work of professors who were identified as crits was hotly debated—were taken as microcosmic enactments of the larger war over the nature of law. Law schools that denied tenure to (some) crits on the basis of criteria susceptible to manipulation opened themselves to the accusation that they were no different from courts that invoked formally neutral criteria in the service of a political agenda.

But this tendency for self-absorption prevented CLS from attracting adherents outside the academy. And within the academy, the CLS movement waned because the crits never developed an affirmative program of their own to explain how legal interpretation should be conducted if it really was merely political. As a result, the critical legal studies movement ran out of steam by the late 1980s.

At the same time, though, the CLS movement spawned successor movements like critical race theory and critical feminism, which emphasized the role racial and gender concepts played in the law. In the end, however, these two schools of thought owe more to the civil rights movement and the women's movement, respectively, than they do to critical legal studies.

Indeed, to the extent that critical race theory and critical feminism endorse the idea that rights are meaningful legal concepts that can advance equality, rather than merely the political tools of special interest groups, these schools of thought are in some tension with CLS.[8] Consequently, the crits' most radical claim, that law is simply politics, has remained largely a fringe view.

So matters stood until the Supreme Court decided *Bush v. Gore*. In that decision, the Court's most conservative Justices announced an interpretation of the Equal Protection Clause so broad that if generally applied, it would sweep aside election procedures for nearly every office in a majority of American states. At the same time, the Justices refused to consider the consequences of their sweeping decision for any other circumstances, thereby suggesting that the principle announced would *not* be generally applied, but would be arbitrarily limited to the facts of the Bush–Gore election.

The inconsistencies go on. Most of the conservative Justices' opinions attacked the Florida Supreme Court's interpretation of Florida law, refusing to defer to it. But on the crucial question of whether a recount could proceed beyond December 12, these Justices suddenly, arbitrarily chose to defer to the Florida Supreme Court.

Even worse, the one Florida Supreme Court decision to which the conservative Justices deigned to defer was a decision that court never actually made. According to the anonymously authored 5–4 opinion of the Court, the Florida Supreme Court said that the legislature would prefer meeting the December 12 deadline (for avoiding a challenge to electors in Congress) to obtaining an accurate vote count. Yet the Florida Supreme Court had said no such thing.

The astoundingly unpersuasive reasons given by the Supreme Court for its decision in *Bush v. Gore* have led many observers to conclude that the Justices were (at least subconsciously) voting on the basis of their political views, rather than the legal arguments.[9] And if that is the best account of this most supremely important Supreme Court decision, then one might wonder if perhaps the crits are right after all—there is no distinction between law and politics.

Nonetheless, *Bush v. Gore* feels different from other cases. For one thing, to even seasoned observers, it was surprising. If law were really always just politics, as CLS claims, there would be nothing at all surprising about either of the Court's two decisions—first to stay the manual recount and then to prevent further recounts. Yet many observers quite familiar with the Court's workings (myself included) were stunned by those decisions.

Of course, these subjective reactions do not prove anything. It is possible that, prior to *Bush v. Gore*, we were in a state of denial about the true nature of judicial decision making. Now that we have been shown the light, will we give up our former delusions, or will we, like Plato's cave dwellers, cling to them and mock those who speak the truth?

In this instance, I shall cast my lot with the troglodytes. *Bush v. Gore* not only feels different; it is different. To be sure, we have numerous instances of Justices acting inconsistently from case to case. Most prominently, the Court's conservatives attack judicial activism in the service of reproductive rights, gay rights, and church-state separation while practicing judicial activism in the service of states' rights, color blindness, and associational freedom. And the liberals practice judicial activism in cases involving the first set of issues while attacking it in cases involving the second set.[10]

But it is at least possible to articulate a vision of the Constitution that sanctions greater judicial solicitude for one constellation of values than for another. By contrast, in *Bush v. Gore*, one senses the Justices straining legal logic not in the service of a larger constitutional vision, but in the service of a particular candidate for office.

Many difficult questions of constitutional law have no single obviously correct answer. Should the limits on Congress's power be enforceable by courts, and if so, what are those limits? Do courts have the power to enforce rights not expressly spelled out in the Constitution's text, and if so, what rights? (The right to choose abortion? The right to exclude homosexuals from private associations?) Does affirmative action remedy violations of the Equal Protection Clause, or violate it? In the wake of legal realism, it would be foolish to suggest that anyone could answer such questions without relying in some measure on his or her own somewhat subjective value judgments.

Yet, as I often tell my students as they are studying for exams, the fact that a question has no single right answer does not mean that it has no wrong answers. In denying the crits' claim that law is just politics, mainstream legal thinkers maintain that constitutional provisions, statutes, and precedents rule out certain results, even as they leave open a range of legitimate results. The constitutionality of affirmative action and school vouchers are open questions;[11] the constitutionality of slavery and an official church of the United States are not.

The problem with *Bush v. Gore* is not that the Court made a poor choice among a range of legitimate options. The problem is that the Court appeared to choose a result from completely outside that range. For this reason, the case will likely stand as an exception to the usual form of judicial decision making, rather than an archetypal example of it.

POSTSCRIPT

I stand by what I wrote about *Bush v. Gore* in late 2000, but with the benefit of hindsight and a period to cool off, I should acknowledge an alternate view of the case's implications for the radical legal realist (or CLS) view. Yale law professor Jack Balkin, who is a critic of the decision, suggests that it nonetheless confirms rather than undermines the radical view of law because of a special feature of the case: the haste with which the Court had to decide it. Ordinarily, Balkin contends, courts can disguise their political judgments with legal trappings by concocting post hoc legal justifications. In *Bush v. Gore*, by contrast, there was so little time to do so that the Justices ended up issuing an unpersuasive opinion. Given more time, Balkin's argument goes, they would have done better.[12] In this view, *Bush v. Gore* shows us the Court without, as it were, the legal makeup it painstakingly applies to cover its political blemishes in ordinary cases, but the blemishes are there, if obscured, in all cases.

If Balkin is right, one would expect that by now someone would have come up with a better justification for the result in *Bush v. Gore*, and in fact someone has. My Columbia Law School colleague Henry Monaghan contends that in certain contexts, including review of state court determinations affecting presidential elections, federal courts have long exercised independent rather than deferential judgment about the content of state law, and properly so.[13] Accordingly, Monaghan concludes, the concurring opinion of Chief Justice Rehnquist in *Bush v. Gore* was not—or at least need not have been—inconsistent with more general principles governing state-federal relations.

Monaghan may or may not be right about the proper standard of review in *Bush v. Gore*, but certainly his argument is plausible. An opinion along the lines he suggests would have been subject to criticism, but it could not have fairly been called lawless, as many legal academics described the actual *Bush v. Gore* opinion.

But it does not follow that Balkin is also right that *Bush v. Gore* therefore vindicates the radical legal realist view of law. Principled critics of *Bush v. Gore*—a group of which I like to think I am a member—did not object to the fact that the Court ruled for Bush. We objected to the inadequate legal reasoning used by the Court to support that result. An opinion along the lines suggested by Monaghan would not have been fairly subject to that kind of criticism, showing that we can distinguish between good and bad legal arguments, and that therefore there is a distinction between law and politics.

For Balkin and the crits to succeed, therefore, requires them to show that it is *always* possible for a judge to write a plausible legal opinion justifying a result he favors on political grounds. But there are plenty of such results that are simply ruled out by the law: Judges know that they cannot declare war, that (except in truly extraordinary circumstances) they cannot impose taxes, and that they cannot order funding for a worthy public works project. To be sure, they know these things for reasons that are, as Balkin notes, partly a matter of social convention, but only the most hidebound formalist would contend that social convention is no part of the law itself.

Speaking of hidebound formalists, the next chapter focuses on a division between, on the one hand, Justice Clarence Thomas, a latter-day champion of formalism, and, on the other hand, the rest of the Supreme Court.

NOTES

1. 531 U.S. 98 (2000) (per curiam).

2. *See* Antonin Scalia, *Common-Law Courts in a Civil-Law System: The Role of United States Federal Courts in Interpreting the Constitution and Laws*, *in* A Matter of Interpretation 23–47 (Princeton, N.J.: Princeton University Press, Amy Gutmann ed., 1997). Scalia's formalism, as a method of textual exegesis, is not quite the classical formalism of the nineteenth century, which was principally a tool for common-law decision making. Nonetheless, the family resemblance of these formalisms is sufficient to warrant using the same term.

3. *See* Fred Barbash, *For Committee Democrats, Nominee's Lack of Views Can Be a Target Too*, Wash. Post, Sept. 12, 1991, at A5.

4. *See, e.g.*, Jerome Frank, Law and the Modern Mind 108–21 (Garden City, N.Y.: Anchor Books, 1963) (1930) ("The peculiar traits, disposition, biases and habits of the particular judge will, then, often determine what he decides to be the law.").

5. *See, e.g.*, Henry Hart & Albert Sacks, The Legal Process: Basic Problems in the Making and Application of Law 3–6 (Westbury, N.Y.: Foundation, William N. Eskridge & Phillip P. Frickey eds., 1994) ("[D]ifferent procedures and personnel of different qualifications invariably prove to be appropriate for deciding different kinds of questions. So it is that every modern society differentiates among social questions, accepting one mode of decision for one kind and other modes for others.").

6. *See, e.g.*, *id.* at 143–50.

7. The canonical works of the critical legal studies movement as of 1984 (after which it quickly petered out) are listed in Duncan Kennedy & Karl E. Klare, *A Bibliography of Critical Legal Studies*, 94 Yale L.J. 461, 464–90 (1984).

8. *Compare* Patricia J. Williams, *Alchemical Notes: Reconstructing Ideals from Deconstructed Rights*, 22 Harv. C.R.-C.L. L. Rev. 401, 410 (1987) ("While rights may not be ends in themselves, it remains that rights rhetoric has been and continues to be an effective form of discourse for blacks."), *with* Mark Tushnet, *A Critique of Rights: An Essay on Rights*, 62 Tex. L. Rev. 1363, 1371 (1984) ("If . . . action [is] politically effective, we ought to establish the conditions for its effectiveness, not because those conditions are 'rights' but because politically effective action is important.").

9. *See, e.g.*, Thomas L. Friedman, Op-Ed., *Foreign Affairs; Medal of Honor*, N.Y. Times, Dec. 15, 2000, at A39 ("The shot was fired at the heart of the nation by the five conservative justices of the U.S. Supreme Court, with their politically inspired ruling that installed George W. Bush as president. . . . You don't need an inside source to realize that the five conservative justices were acting as the last in a team of Republican Party elders who helped drag Governor Bush across the finish line."); *see also* Bill Rankin, *Was it Politics? That, Too, Is in Dispute*, Atlanta J. & Const., Dec. 14, 2000, at 2B.

10. *See supra* chapter 1.

11. Since I wrote these words, the Court upheld the constitutionality of some programs of affirmative action in higher education and religious school vouchers. *See* Grutter v. Bollinger, 539 U.S. 306 (2003); Zelman v. Simmons-Harris, 536 U.S. 639 (2002).

12. *See* Jack M. Balkin, Bush v. Gore *and the Boundary Between Law and Politics*, 110 Yale L.J. 1407, 1443–44 (2001).

13. Henry Paul Monaghan, *Supreme Court Review of State-Court Determinations of State Law in Constitutional Cases*, 103 Colum. L. Rev. 1919 (2003).

• 3 •

Clarence Thomas's Challenge to the Rehnquist Court's Vision of Representative Government

March 2001

February 2001 revealed some dramatic divisions within the Supreme Court. On February 21, in *Board of Trustees of the University of Alabama v. Garrett*,[1] a 5–4 "conservative" majority ruled that Congress violated the Eleventh Amendment when it authorized private damages suits for state violations of Title I of the Americans with Disabilities Act. On February 28, in *Legal Services Corp. v. Velazquez*,[2] a different 5–4 "liberal" majority ruled that Congress violated the First Amendment when it forbade lawyers receiving federal dollars to represent indigent clients from challenging the validity of welfare laws.

These two cases provide a reminder that the Court remains sharply divided along ideological lines. Yet such an assessment is too simple. For example, Justice Anthony Kennedy, often described as a conservative, was in the majority in both *Garrett* and *Velazquez*, joining the conservatives in the former and the liberals in the latter. Indeed, on free speech issues, Justice Kennedy is probably the Court's most liberal member.

Meanwhile, two unanimous decisions sandwiched between *Garrett* and *Velazquez* revealed a more subtle cleavage on the Court. In both *Whitman v. American Trucking Ass'ns, Inc.*[3] and *Cook v. Gralike*,[4] Justice Clarence Thomas went along with the Court's rulings but indicated that he did so only because the parties had not pressed what he thought might be winning arguments. Justice Thomas's separate concurrences in these cases raise fundamental questions about the nature of representative government in the United States.

In *American Trucking*, the Supreme Court held that Congress had acted constitutionally when it passed a statute instructing the Environmental Protection Agency to set "ambient air quality standards the attainment and maintenance of which . . . are requisite to protect the public health."[5]

The U.S. Court of Appeals for the D.C. Circuit had held that in the statute, Congress had unconstitutionally delegated some of its legislative power to the EPA. According to the lower court, the statute contained no "intelligible principle" by which the agency could determine how much of each regulated pollutant was too much. As a result, the lower court believed the statute unconstitutionally transformed the EPA into, in effect, a quasi-legislature.

The Supreme Court, however, unanimously disagreed. In an opinion by Justice Antonin Scalia, the Court found that "public health" provided a sufficiently intelligible principle. It was no vaguer, the Court noted, than, for example, statutory delegations authorizing the Attorney General to designate a drug as a controlled substance "to avoid an imminent hazard to the public safety,"[6] or authorizing the Occupational Safety and Health Administration to set worker safety standards that assure that the health of employees will not be impaired.[7] Just as those statutes were valid, the Court concluded, so was the Clean Air Act provision at issue in *American Trucking*.

Justice Thomas agreed with the Court that the "intelligible principle" test was satisfied—and thus voted with the majority. However, he also expressed the belief that this principle permits Congress to pass the buck to administrative agencies in violation of the original understanding of the Constitution. Thus, he stated that if the parties raised the issue in another case, he "would be willing to address the question whether [the Court's] delegation jurisprudence has strayed too far from our Founders' understanding of separation of powers."[8]

Justice Thomas staked out a similar position in *Cook v. Gralike*. That case presented a challenge to a Missouri law.

The Missouri law imposed harsh consequences on candidates for Congress who failed to support a constitutional amendment limiting Senators' and Representatives' terms, or who failed to pledge to abide by term limits. Under the law, such candidates would have such statements as "DISREGARDED VOTERS' INSTRUCTION ON TERM LIMITS" and "DECLINED TO PLEDGE TO SUPPORT TERM LIMITS" printed on the ballot next to their names. Obviously, the law's effect would have been to pressure candidates into supporting a term limits amendment, and abiding by term limits themselves, even absent such an amendment.

The Supreme Court unanimously invalidated the law. The majority opinion by Justice John Paul Stevens, writing on behalf of himself and five other Justices, relied principally on a 1995 precedent, *U.S. Term Limits v. Thornton*,[9] which held that the states do not have the constitutional authority to set term limits for members of Congress. These six Justices saw the Missouri law as an illicit attempt to circumvent that ruling.

Chief Justice Rehnquist and Justice Sandra Day O'Connor concurred in the judgment, reasoning that the Missouri law violated "the First Amendment right of a political candidate, once lawfully on the ballot, to have his name appear unaccompanied by pejorative language required by the State."[10]

And then there was Justice Thomas—who presumably did not agree with the First Amendment argument, since he did not join the Rehnquist/O'Connor concurrence, and did not agree with the majority's invocation of *Thornton*, the original term limits decision, either. He wrote separately to say that if Missouri had asked the Court to overrule the term limits decision—from which he and three other Justices dissented at the time—he would be willing to do so. But, as in *American Trucking*, he was unwilling to rule on the basis of an argument that was not pressed.

Taken together, Justice Thomas's intimations in *Cook v. Gralike* and *American Trucking* reflect a striking vision of American government. In his view, state legislatures should be permitted to hold members of Congress on a short tether (by imposing term limits and directing their votes), while members of Congress must take full responsibility for the actions of the national government rather than delegating important decisions (such as how much of a pollutant is too much) to administrative agencies, and thereby ducking accountability.

By contrast, all of the other Justices would allow much less direct control over the national agenda by state legislatures—and even by voters. Members of Congress are, for these Justices, representatives but not delegates. They come to Washington to represent their districts, not simply to carry out instructions from the folks back home.

Moreover, according to the eight Justices, national policy is further removed from direct control of the people or the states because once in Washington, members of Congress may delegate the details of their work to bureaucrats. These Justices see such delegation as inevitable, given the complexity of modern life; it is simply impossible for Congress to fill in all the details of all the statutes it writes.

Two features of this debate merit notice. First, although the Justices defend their contrasting visions as simply rooted in the text, structure, and history of the Constitution, the constitutional provisions at issue are sufficiently open-ended to admit of various interpretations. The Justices thus prefer one vision or another based in part on normative grounds and perhaps should articulate those grounds.

Second, Justice Thomas's isolation from the rest of the Court on these issues shows that he is not—despite the common caricature—Justice Scalia's clone. Indeed, in some respects, his disagreement with the Court's vision of representative democracy is as fundamental as the more familiar 5–4 divisions over states' rights, abortion, affirmative action, and the other hot-button issues that the Court confronts.

POSTSCRIPT

One curiosity lingers. Why was Justice Thomas willing, in both the *American Trucking* and the *Cooke* cases, to apply doctrinal rules that he pretty clearly thinks should be overruled? His answer is clear: because neither party before the Court asked that the relevant doctrine be overturned. Why should that matter? Because in an adversary system, parties should be given the opportunity to contest legal positions adverse to their interests.

By writing as he did in the two cases, Justice Thomas signaled to future parties that he would be receptive to arguments seeking revision of the Court's doctrines governing delegation of power to federal agencies and state imposition of checks on members of Congress. At the same time, by declining to dissent in either case, Justice Thomas also signaled his willingness not to prejudge the issues. He is willing to acknowledge that perhaps the parties that won victories under the doctrines he would like to reconsider could, if given the chance, persuade him that these doctrines should be retained. This open-mindedness is also at odds with the public image of Justice Thomas.

NOTES

1. 531 U.S. 356 (2001) (striking down portions of Title I of the Americans With Disabilities Act of 1990, Pub. L. No. 101–336, §§ 101–108, 104 Stat. 327, 330–37). The Court subsequently upheld congressional waiver of sovereign immunity under Title II of the Americans With Disabilities Act of 1990, Pub. L. No. 101–336, §§ 201–246, 104 Stat. 327, 337–53, at least with respect to "fundamental" rights such as access to the courts. *See* Tennessee v. Lane, 541 U.S. 509 (2004).
2. 531 U.S. 533 (2001).
3. 531 U.S. 457, 486–87 (2001) (Thomas, J., concurring).
4. 531 U.S. 510, 530 (2001) (Thomas, J., concurring in part and concurring in the judgment).
5. 42 U.S.C. § 7409(b)(1) (2001).
6. 21 U.S.C. § 811(h)(1) (2001), *upheld by* Touby v. United States, 500 U.S. 160 (1991).
7. 29 U.S.C. § 655(b)(5) (2001), *upheld by* Indus. Union Dep't., AFL-CIO v. Am. Petroleum Inst., 448 U.S. 607 (1980).
8. 531 U.S. at 487 (Thomas, J., concurring). Since 1936, the Supreme Court has not struck any federal law on the ground that it constituted an impermissible delegation of authority to an administrative agency.
9. 514 U.S. 779 (1995).
10. 531 U.S. at 530–31 (Rehnquist, C.J., concurring).

• 4 •

Does Federal Tort Reform Unduly Infringe State Sovereignty?

April 2003

President George W. Bush is determined to avoid repeating what he regards as his father's fateful failure to spend the political capital earned by a military victory against Saddam Hussein.[1] Thus, we can expect an ambitious domestic agenda from the President and his congressional allies. In the coming months, tort reform may feature prominently.

If only American enterprise were liberated from the fear of crushing liability, tort reform advocates contend, the economy would soon boom again. In this view, huge verdicts line the pockets of greedy lawyers and a few lucky plaintiffs, while harming most consumers.

The facts do not always cooperate with this picture. In early 2003, for example, doctors at the Duke University Medical Center performed a heart-lung transplant using organs from a donor of the wrong blood type, resulting in the death of the seventeen-year-old patient, Jesica Santillan. The widely publicized mishap undoubtedly robbed some of the momentum from pending tort reform legislation, which would limit recoveries in such cases.

However, the public attention span is short, and for every Jesica Santillan, tort reform proponents can conjure up a case like the $3 million verdict against McDonald's for its hot coffee. Surely "conjure" is the right word, because the plaintiff, who suffered third-degree burns requiring a series of painful skin grafts, recovered far less after the judge reevaluated the jury's punitive damages award.[2]

My interest here, however, is not in whether tort reform is a good or bad idea. Instead, I want to consider whether Congress is the proper body to enact rules of tort law, which have traditionally been a matter for the states. Does the Constitution grant Congress the power to pass sweeping tort reform?

A variety of tort reform measures have been proposed in or to Congress. Some would amend procedural requirements for cases in federal courts. For example, the "Class Action Fairness Act," introduced in Congress in March 2003, would, among other things, give defendants the power to transfer any multi-state class action involving more than $2 million from state court to federal court.[3]

Congress clearly has the authority to enact the Class Action Fairness Act. Article III of the Constitution empowers Congress to confer on the federal courts the authority to hear cases between citizens of different states ("diversity" cases), even when state law governs the underlying dispute.

And indeed, at various points in history, Congress has tinkered with the requirements for federal court jurisdiction over diversity cases. Whatever its wisdom, the Class Action Fairness Act would fall within congressional authority to make rules governing procedure in the federal courts.

However, some of the proposals on the table go far beyond establishing the procedures that govern tort suits brought in federal court. They would intrude into state court suits as well, and they would affect the suits' substance, not just procedure.

Consider the proposed Common Sense Medical Malpractice Reform Act of 2003. The bill would cap damages in medical malpractice cases for non-economic injury at $250,000.[4]

How would that work? A simple example is illustrative. Suppose that as a result of a botched appendectomy, an otherwise healthy patient loses the use of his arms and legs. If he establishes that the surgeon acted negligently, the patient could recover the cost of his medical bills; the earnings, if any, he loses as a result of his condition; and the cost of hiring someone to assist him in the tasks he could formerly perform for himself.

However, he could only recover a total of $250,000 to compensate for his pain and suffering and, if he can prove "conscious, flagrant indifference" by clear and convincing evidence, as punishment for the doctor, hospital, or other tortfeasor. Thus, suppose in this case, the jury gave the patient $1 million in pain and suffering damages and $1 million in punitive damages. The judge, after the verdict, would be legally required to reduce the total of these two sums to $250,000.

The Common Sense Medical Malpractice Reform Act, if enacted into law, would apply to all malpractice cases (against doctors and other health care providers) in federal and state court.[5] It would change the substantive medical malpractice law on the books in most states. (Some states already have damages caps, but in those states, the amount of the cap and the type of damages capped would typically be altered from those the state itself had chosen.)

Where does Congress get the power to do that?

Let's answer that question by looking to first principles. The federal government is a government of enumerated powers. If Congress wishes to enact legislation, it must find authority for that legislation in some provision of the Constitution. Article I, Section 8, contains a list of such powers, but by far the most important of these is the power "To regulate commerce . . . among the several states."

If substantive provisions like those proposed in the Common Sense Medical Malpractice Reform Act can be sustained against the inevitable constitutional challenges they will face, it will have to be under the Commerce Clause.

What is the scope of congressional power to regulate interstate commerce? Beginning with early nineteenth-century rulings of the Supreme Court under Chief Justice John Marshall, the Commerce Clause has generally been construed broadly.[6] Interstate commerce, the Marshall Court said, means more than the shipment of goods across state lines; it encompasses regulation of the national economy.

The Supreme Court took a somewhat narrower view of the Commerce Clause from the end of the nineteenth century through the first third of the twentieth century. However, since then, judicial precedents have validated legislation on a great many subjects under the principle that the regulated activities were connected to commerce.

For example, in the 1942 case of *Wickard v. Filburn*,[7] the Supreme Court upheld the application of a production quota to a farmer who grew a small crop of winter wheat for home consumption, to feed to his animals, and possibly to sell. Did his little crop really affect "interstate commerce"?

The Court said yes, reasoning that the statute was valid as to Filburn even if he and his family intended to consume all the excess wheat themselves: The more wheat Filburn grew for home consumption, the less he would purchase on the market, and as a result, there would be less total market demand for wheat. Thus, Filburn's production affected interstate commerce—by subtracting from it.

After the *Filburn* case, it looked like nearly anything Congress conceivably might enact would be validated under the Commerce Clause, for nearly every activity has at least some indirect impact on the market for some goods or services.

However, in 1995, the Rehnquist Court drew a line in the sand. In *United States v. Lopez*,[8] the Court invalidated a federal statute prohibiting the possession of a gun in the vicinity of a schoolyard. Then, in the 2000 case of *United States v. Morrison*,[9] the Court invalidated a provision of the Violence Against Women Act that permitted the victims of gender-motivated violence to sue their attackers in federal court.

In both *Lopez* and *Morrison*, the Supreme Court reaffirmed the principle drawn from *Filburn* that Congress may regulate activities on the ground that they have an effect on interstate commerce; however, the Court seemed to add an analytical requirement. If the statute does not limit itself to activities directly affecting interstate commerce, then the regulated activities must be economic in nature.

Growing wheat—if not pursued simply as a hobby—the Court implied, is economic activity, whereas possessing a gun or engaging in gender-motivated violence is not economic activity.

How do provisions like the proposed Common Sense Medical Malpractice Reform Act's $250,000 cap on non-economic damages fare under the *Lopez* and *Morrison* precedents? That depends on how one describes the regulated activity.

To begin, one might be tempted to define the regulated activity as malpractice lawsuits. If so, the proposed legislation would be clearly constitutional, for a lawsuit seeking money damages is certainly an economic event.

However, the *Morrison* case forecloses this approach. After all, it was possible in that case to define the regulated activity as lawsuits alleging gender-motivated violence. But the Court thought the right level of analysis was the real-world conduct giving rise to the lawsuit, rather than the lawsuit itself.

And that makes considerable sense, for otherwise, any lawsuit on any subject would fall within the scope of the Commerce Clause. The key question as far as the Constitution is concerned is not whether the plaintiff is suing, but what he is suing for.

So, is medical malpractice an economic activity? Not necessarily. A doctor who negligently misdiagnoses (and thus does not prescribe treatment for) SARS (Severe Acute Respiratory Syndrome) can be held liable for malpractice regardless of whether she received money for her medical services.

Granted, most malpractice occurs in a context in which doctors receive compensation. But so what? Many people who possess guns near schoolyards probably do so in connection with some economic activity, such as planned drug dealing, robbery, or extortion; yet that was not enough to sustain the Gun-Free School Zones Act in the *Lopez* case.

Moreover, in *Lopez* the Supreme Court was especially troubled by the fact that the federal government asserted power over "criminal law enforcement [and] education where States historically have been sovereign."[10] Similarly, the substantive law of torts, including medical malpractice, is an area of traditional state sovereignty.

Hence, there is a non-frivolous argument based on current precedent for judicial invalidation of whatever substantive tort reform measures Congress enacts.

Nonetheless, the precedents are best read to permit Congress to regulate medical malpractice. As I read *Lopez*, *Morrison*, and *Filburn* (as reimagined by the two more recent cases), an act will count as economic—and thus will be subject to regulation by Congress—if people usually or typically engage in the act for economic gain. That seems at least as true of the provision of medical services as of wheat cultivation.

To conclude that Congress has the power to regulate some subject matter, however, is not to say that it should regulate. Federalism is often raised as a legal argument to block enforcement of a law passed by Congress; it may also be raised as a prudential, political argument before a bill becomes a law.

Accordingly, if the Bush Administration and the members of Congress who profess to care about state sovereignty mean what they say, they will hesitate before displacing the substantive tort law of all fifty states.

POSTSCRIPT

Confirming my reading of the Commerce Clause precedents, the Supreme Court ruled in June 2005 that the federal drug laws may be applied to the intrastate cultivation of marijuana for personal medical use.[11] The Justices found no substantial constitutional difference between the growing of wheat and the growing of marijuana.

As for Congress, it has exercised scant restraint on prudential or other grounds. With some changes, the Class Action Fairness Act of 2005 was signed into law.[12] Federal legislation governing medical malpractice remains an important goal of the Bush Administration.[13] And, as I have already noted, in what must qualify as the most spectacular betrayal of principles of federalism in recent memory, in March 2005, Congress passed and the President signed a law authorizing a federal court to revisit rulings made by the Florida state courts after years of exhaustive hearings in the case of Terri Schiavo.[14]

A cynic might be tempted to sum up the difference between law and politics thus: Judges facing hard cases sometimes end up making decisions that appear to betray the jurisprudential principles they typically profess; most politicians, by contrast, do not appear to have any principles beyond what they believe best secures partisan advantage. But I am not a cynic and so I won't put the point that crudely.

NOTES

1. *See* Edwin Chen, *Bush Turns His Attention to Ailing Economy; The Administration Plans a Big Push for His Agenda to Try to Prevent the Political Fate that Befell His Father after the Persian Gulf War*, L.A. Times, Apr. 20, 2003, at 26.

2. Liebeck v. McDonald's Restaurants, P.T.S., Inc., No. CV-93-02419, 1995 WL 360309 (N.M. Dist. Ct. Aug. 18, 1994); *see also* Carl T. Bogus, Why Lawsuits Are Good for America 19–20 (2001) (reporting that the trial judge reduced the punitive-damages

award from $2.7 million to $480,000, and that the compensatory-damages award was reduced by 20 percent after the jury found that the plaintiff's injuries were caused, in part, by her contributory negligence).

3. Class Action Fairness Act of 2003, H.R. 1115, 108th Cong. §§ 4–5; Class Action Fairness Act of 2003, S. 274, 108th Cong. §§ 4–5.

4. Common Sense Medical Malpractice Reform Act of 2003, H.R. 321, 108th Cong. § 4.

5. *Id.* § 2.

6. For a famous and early expression of this view, see Gibbons v. Ogden, 22 U.S. (9 Wheat.) 1, 196–97 (1824).

7. 317 U.S. 111 (1942).

8. 514 U.S. 549 (1995) (striking down provisions of the Gun-Free School Zones Act of 1990, Pub. L. No. 101–647, § 1702, 104 Stat. 4789, 4844–45).

9. 529 U.S. 598 (2000) (striking down provisions of the Violence Against Women Act of 1994, Pub. L. No. 103–322, Title IV, 108 Stat. 1902, 1902–55).

10. 514 U.S. at 564.

11. *See* Gonzales v. Raich, 125 S. Ct. 2195 (2005).

12. Pub. L. No. 109–2, 119 Stat. 4. One of the changes in the enacted version is that the minimum amount in controversy for transferring a class action to federal court is $5 million rather than $2 million as originally proposed. 28 U.S.C. § 1332(d)(2) (2005).

13. *See, e.g.*, Help Efficient, Accessible, Low-Cost, Timely Healthcare Act of 2005 (HEALTH Act of 2005), S. 354, 109th Cong.; *see also* Jeffrey H. Birnbaum & John F. Harris, *President's Proposed Remedy to Curb Medical Malpractice Lawsuits Stalls; Senate Deadlocks; Democrats Plan to Use Filibuster*, Wash. Post, Apr. 3, 2005, at A5.

14. Act of Mar. 21, 2005, Pub. L. No. 109–3, 119 Stat. 15.

II

AID AND COMFORT TO THE ENEMY

I am typically identified as a "liberal" constitutional scholar, and I suppose the label generally fits. I support abortion rights, affirmative action, church-state separation, and gay rights, and I'm skeptical of claims (typically made by conservatives) that the Constitution can or should be interpreted to conform to the original understanding of those who framed and ratified it. The liberal label is not perfect, however, because I'm also sympathetic to some arguments for protecting states' rights against the federal government, a position that is usually held by conservatives, at least in the abstract. Moreover, despite my basically solid liberal credentials, I find that I'm as often distressed by arguments made for liberal results as for conservative ones. Why? Because I'm first and foremost a lawyer, and arguments matter to a lawyer. For courts, reason is the coin of the realm, and if a judge can't provide persuasive reasons for her decision, then she either ought to come up with better reasons or, failing that, reach a different decision.

In the chapters in this part, I try to distinguish between good and bad reasons. Sometimes my disagreements with my liberal friends lead me to that most law-professor-like conclusion: right for the wrong reason. But not always. In other chapters in this section, I end up with the conservatives, or simply declaring a pox on both their houses. And of course sometimes it's impossible to tell what the liberal or conservative position is on a question.

• 5 •

The Supreme Court Case that Pits Free Speech against Church-State Separation

February 2001

The Supreme Court case of *Good News Club v. Milford Central School*[1] presents a clash between two venerable First Amendment principles. On the one hand, government may not discriminate against speech on the basis of viewpoint, and a religious viewpoint is no less a viewpoint than any other. On the other hand, government has an obligation to avoid endorsing religion (or non-religion), an obligation that takes on special significance in the case of a public elementary school.

There is no easy answer in the *Good News* case. One principle or the other will have to yield. Nonetheless, the Justices can steer a middle course by interpreting the First Amendment to place the decision of which of the two principles to sacrifice in the hands of elected state and local officials. Whether they choose this course will depend upon whether they can bring themselves to see the case in terms of federalism and decentralization, rather than as just one more battle in the ongoing culture war.

Located in Otsego County, New York, the Milford Central School educates roughly five hundred students from ages five through eighteen in one school building. As mandated by a New York State law,[2] the school permits outside organizations such as the Boy Scouts, Girl Scouts, and 4-H clubs to use its facilities when classes are not in session.

The Good News Club, an Evangelical Christian organization, applied to use a Milford classroom for meetings immediately following the end of classes. The district denied the request on the grounds that the proposed use would be the "equivalent of religious worship," in violation of school policy.

Good News sued and a federal district court granted a preliminary injunction, directing the school to permit Good News to use school facilities. However, the court later vacated that injunction and granted summary judgment to the school, allowing it to deny Good News use of school facilities.[3] That ruling, in favor of the school, was affirmed on appeal.

That might have been the end of things, but in a similar case, another federal appeals court for a different judicial circuit had already ruled in favor of a Good News Club in Missouri, compelling a public school there to allow Good News access.[4] In light of this "circuit split," the U.S. Supreme Court decided to consider the issue these cases both raise, and thus granted review of the New York case.

The New York *Good News* case features some minor jousting over the precise nature of Good News meetings. Good News describes itself as "a private Christian youth organization that develops children's moral values by using Bible stories, games, scripture, and songs in a fun setting," noting further that it is not affiliated with any specific church and that meetings are open to children of all faiths.[5]

The school, in contrast, characterizes these meetings as essentially Sunday school during the week. There is no dispute that Good News meetings feature the singing of religious hymns, prayer, Bible stories, and religious instruction. The question is whether the school may, or even must, exclude the organization.

The school argues that the First Amendment's prohibition on Establishment of Religion requires it to exclude Good News from its facilities. The school points to the landmark 1940s decisions in *Everson v. Board of Education*[6] and *Illinois ex rel. McCollum v. Board of Education,*[7] which invoke Thomas Jefferson's metaphor of a "wall of separation" between church and state.

The *McCollum* case invalidated a program under which religious instruction substituted for secular subjects during the last period of the school day. The Milford Central School argues that this case is scarcely different. Although Good News meets just after regular classes have ended, the school contends that the close proximity in time will signal a message of official endorsement to impressionable elementary-age students.

Citing the 2000 decision in *Santa Fe Independent School District v. Doe,*[8] which invalidated a student-led prayer at high school football games, the school argues that even nominally private religious speech can violate the Establishment Clause if the government plays a substantial role in facilitating that speech.

Good News counters that the football game prayer case is different in one crucial respect. There, the school authorities set up a forum specifically for the purpose of enabling student prayer. In Milford, by contrast, the school opened its facilities up to a wide range of organizations. Under these circumstances, Good News urges, hosting a religious organization along with other, secular organizations, would not implicate the public school authorities in the religious activities.

Moreover, Good News points to a number of recent precedents in which the Supreme Court has said that if the government creates a forum for the expression of various viewpoints, the First Amendment's free speech clause forbids the exclusion of religious speech from that forum.

For example, in the 1995 decision in *Rosenberger v. Rector and Visitors of the University of Virginia*,[9] the University of Virginia was required to fund a Christian student newspaper in light of the fact that it funded secular student newspapers.

Even more directly on point, in the 1993 decision in *Lamb's Chapel v. Center Moriches Union Free School District*,[10] the Supreme Court considered the application of the same New York State law at issue in *Good News*. In *Lamb's Chapel*, a Long Island, New York, school district had denied an Evangelical church's request to show a six-part film series that discussed family issues and child rearing from a Christian perspective. Although the school district was not obligated to open its facilities to use by any outside groups, the Court said that because the district would permit groups addressing family and child rearing from a secular perspective, it could not exclude a group addressing the same subject from a religious one.

In the appellate-level decision in *Good News*, which the Supreme Court granted review, the Second Circuit Court of Appeals distinguished *Rosenberger* and *Lamb's Chapel* by contrasting "the discussion of secular subjects from a religious viewpoint" with "the discussion of religious material through religious instruction and prayer."[11]

The former, the court suggested, cannot be excluded from schools, due to the First Amendment's ban on viewpoint discrimination, while the latter can be excluded from schools pursuant to the government's legitimate authority to restrict a forum it creates to particular uses. In other words, the Court of Appeals distinguished between *viewpoint* and *subject matter*. The Milford Central School now urges the Supreme Court to do the same.[12]

The viewpoint/subject matter distinction has roots in an arcane area of free speech law known as the "limited," or "designated," public forum doctrine.[13]

Suppose that a city government wishes to foster opera by making a city-owned theater available to private groups. The designated public forum doctrine would permit the city to restrict the theater to opera companies—as opposed to vaudeville troupes, rap singers, and wrestling exhibitions. However, the city could not forbid, say, operas critical of the government (as some interpretations of *Tosca* might be, for example).

The basic disagreement in *Good News* is about whether worship can be characterized as a distinct subject matter, in the same way that rap can in the previous example, and thus excluded from a forum limited to other subject matters. The school says worship can, indeed, be so characterized. Good News says it cannot.

Intriguingly, a group of twenty theologians filed an amicus brief in support of Good News, arguing that for many persons of faith, there is no meaningful distinction between "moral instruction from a religious perspective" and "religious instruction." To draw such a distinction, these theologians say, is to assume the separability of religion and morality, but that assumption is itself a highly controversial viewpoint. These are, the amicus brief asserts, "deep theological waters."[14]

Yet one does not need to have been ordained to see that the basic problem is not a matter of religious doctrine, but of legal doctrine. In distinguishing between viewpoint and subject matter, the Court's cases draw a necessary but somewhat unstable line. When the government says a theater can be used for opera but not rap it inevitably favors some viewpoints over others, even if that is not its intent. As Marshall McLuhan famously said, "the medium is the message."[15]

Accordingly, for Good News to prevail, it must show that distinguishing viewpoint from subject matter is more difficult with respect to religious speech than with respect to other kinds of speech. Perhaps such a showing can be made, but it is has not been made in the briefs submitted to the Court.

The briefs of Good News and its amici go to great lengths to show that there are great difficulties inherent in drawing the line with respect to religion. That may be true, but it may also be irrelevant. They do not much address the more directly relevant, comparative question of whether drawing the line with respect to secular subjects (something the Court has always assumed is possible) is any easier.

Public school officials, and other government officials, face a dilemma. If they are too accommodating of religious groups' requests for public facilities and resources, they risk violating the Establishment Clause. Yet if they are insufficiently accommodating, they risk violating the free speech rights of religious groups.

One permissible approach would be for government officials to deny every organization and individual access to public facilities and resources, but such a Solomonic "solution" would satisfy the Constitution at the cost of neglecting more immediate obligations to the community.

A better approach might be for the Supreme Court to loosen the constraints on government by creating some breathing room between its interpretations of the various provisions of the First Amendment. In a case like *Good News*, that would mean a partial victory for each side. The Court could say that the Establishment Clause did not obligate Milford Central School to exclude Good News, but neither did the Free Speech Clause forbid the exclusion: It's up to the school (and other schools across the country) to decide.

Thus, Good News would be excluded from Milford Central but similar organizations would be permitted access to school buildings in districts that strike a somewhat different balance between free speech and church-state separation.

To be sure, extreme cases of clear hostility to, or sponsorship of, religion must be governed by constitutional rules—and should not be relegated to a limbo between free exercise of religion and establishment of it. But perfectly unclear cases like *Good News* could be left to state and local democratic processes. For a Court that cares about federalism—a system of government in which the states can take diverse approach to similar problems—that may be the best way to stay afloat in these deep waters.

POSTSCRIPT

Much to my satisfaction, the Court adopted exactly the "breathing room" approach to free speech and establishment that I proposed. Much to my chagrin, however, it did so in a *later case*, the 2004 decision in *Locke v. Davey*.[16] In an opinion by Chief Justice Rehnquist, the Court held there that the State of Washington did not violate the First Amendment rights of a college student by denying him the ability to use a state-funded scholarship for the study of theology, even though it funded the study of secular subjects. The Chief Justice approvingly invoked the notion that the First Amendment has some "play in the joints" that permits states to choose between anti-establishment on the one hand and freedom of speech and religion on the other.[17] But in the *Good News* case itself, the Court ruled for the club. I'd proclaim "better late than never" were it not for the competing adage that "justice delayed is justice denied."

NOTES

1. 533 U.S. 98 (2001).
2. N.Y. Educ. Law § 414 (McKinney 2000).
3. Good News Club v. Milford Cent. Sch., 21 F. Supp. 2d 147 (N.D.N.Y. 1998), *aff'd* 202 F.3d 502 (2d Cir. 2000).
4. Good News/Good Sports Club v. Sch. Dist., 28 F.3d 1501 (8th Cir. 1994).
5. Brief on the Merits for Petitioners at 7, 9, *Good News Club,* 533 U.S. 98 (2001) (No. 99–2036), 2000 WL 1793046.
6. 330 U.S. 1 (1947).
7. 333 U.S. 203 (1948).
8. 530 U.S. 290 (2000).
9. 515 U.S. 819 (1995).
10. 508 U.S. 384 (1993).
11. Good News Club v. Milford Cent. Sch., 202 F.3d 502, 510 (2d Cir. 2000).

12. The Supreme Court ultimately criticized the Second Circuit Court of Appeals for not citing *Lamb's Chapel* directly in its majority opinion. Good News v. Milford Cent. Sch., 533 U.S. 98, 109 n.3 (2001).

13. Because the Justices concluded that the parties had agreed that Milford created a limited public forum, they proceeded in their analysis under this assumption, applying the more strict standard of scrutiny that results from such a finding. *See id.* at 106.

14. Brief Amicus Curiae for 20 Theologians and Scholars of Religion in Support of Petitioners at 7, *Good News Club,* 533 U.S. 98 (No. 99–2036), 2000 WL 1803627.

15. Marshall McLuhan, Understanding Media 7 (New York: McGraw-Hill, 1964) (coining the phrase "the medium is the message").

16. 540 U.S. 712 (2004).

17. *Id.* at 718 (quoting Walz v. Tax Comm'n of the City of New York, 397 U.S. 664, 669 (1970)).

• 6 •

How Abortion Politics Impedes Clear Thinking on Other Issues Involving Fetuses

May 2003

So long as *Roe v. Wade*[1] remains the law of the land, the culture war over abortion will continue to focus on side issues—such as parental consent laws for minors seeking abortions, grisly methods of late-term abortion, and the extent, and limits, of the free speech rights of anti-abortion protesters.[2]

Currently, pro-life and pro-choice partisans fight these skirmishes as a kind of proxy battle, since *Roe* resolved the ultimate fight over the legality of abortion itself.

No doubt, one's disposition toward the legality of abortion in general plays a substantial role in determining one's position on the related questions. But the side issues are not *only* side issues. They raise important and difficult questions in their own right.

Consider two recent controversial government actions. First, California authorities decided to charge Laci Peterson's husband with homicide in connection with the death of their unborn child.[3] Second, Florida Governor Jeb Bush decided to appoint a legal guardian for a fetus.[4] If you support a right to choose to have an abortion, must you also oppose these actions?

Not necessarily. Both of these governmental acts illustrate that giving legal consideration to the interests of fetuses need not be inconsistent with recognizing a legal right to abortion. Therefore, those who support the abortion right need not feel compelled to oppose any and all government action that recognizes such interests.

We begin with the facts of the Peterson case. On Christmas Eve, 2002, when she was eight months pregnant, Laci Peterson disappeared. Her body was later recovered in San Francisco Bay. Her husband Scott was subsequently charged with her murder and the murder of the fetus. He pleaded not guilty.

The Peterson case is not unique. From time to time, third parties who kill or harm pregnant women in a way that results in the death of a fetus have been charged under general state prohibitions on murder.

For the most part, courts have held that such charges cannot be brought, but not because of *Roe*. Some courts reasoned that the relevant statutes plainly were not intended to include feticide. Other courts have said that it would be unconstitutional to charge someone with murder for killing a fetus where the statute does not expressly cover fetuses because the right to due process requires that citizens be given fair notice of what conduct is, and is not, permitted by the criminal law.[5] The due process requirement, of course, applies to all criminal laws, not just those that might be construed to cover fetuses.

California's situation however, is different. Earlier, a court had found that California's general murder statute did not apply to feticide.[6] In response, the state legislature amended its homicide law so that it now reads as follows: "Murder is the unlawful killing of a human being, or a fetus, with malice aforethought" *unless the fetus died as a result of a legal abortion*.[7]

Because of the exception, there is no direct conflict between California's prohibition on feticide and the right to abortion. Nonetheless, pro-life and pro-choice activists have divided predictably over the issue.

Pro-life politicians and activists have seized on the Peterson case to push for a federal statute defining feticide as murder.[8] Meanwhile, pro-choice politicians and activists worry that defining feticide as murder will lead to the erosion of abortion rights.[9]

That may be a mistake. Many Americans both believe that women should decide for themselves whether to have an abortion, and are rightly horrified by what happened to Laci Peterson and her fetus.

Pro-choice activists who refuse to allow the killing of a pregnant woman to be punished more harshly than the killing of a non-pregnant woman may only alienate this large constituency. It is not wrong to say that Laci Peterson's death, already a tragedy, was an even greater tragedy because she was carrying a fetus, one she intended to bring to term.

Indeed, in my judgment, the pro-choice movement ought actually to *support* strict laws against feticide. The whole point of an abortion right, after all, is that a pregnant woman—not the state or anyone else—decides whether to have an abortion. A woman who plans to give birth, but is attacked by someone who kills her fetus in the process, is violently deprived of the right to choose *not* to have an abortion.

Reproductive rights include the right to have children too. Certainly pro-choice activists would oppose government-mandated sterilization. For similar reasons, they should support punishing feticide. Both take choice away from women—just as anti-abortion laws do.

I don't doubt that nearly all pro-choicers agree with this line of analysis. However, they nonetheless worry that granting fetuses legal protection against third-party killings will undermine *Roe v. Wade*. *Roe* crucially determined that fetuses are not persons for purposes of the Fourteenth Amendment. How can the state define the killing of someone or something that is not legally a person as murder?

There are two satisfactory answers to the worry that supporting anti-feticide laws undermines *Roe*.

First, laws treating feticide as murder do not need to define fetuses as persons. California's law is illustrative. It defines murder as the killing of a human being *or* a fetus.

Second, there is nothing especially troubling about permitting the law to define the word "person" differently for different purposes. Statutes routinely define various words, including "person," so that they will mean exactly what the legislature intends in a particular context. And even general constitutional language can be interpreted differently depending upon the context. Corporations, for example, are "persons" under the Fourteenth Amendment in the sense that their property cannot be taken without fair processes,[10] but not in the sense that they are entitled to vote on equal terms with natural persons.[11]

Roe v. Wade said that states are not obligated to treat fetuses as persons. It also said that in a conflict with the constitutional liberty of a pregnant woman seeking an abortion before the fetus is capable of survival outside the womb, the fetus may not be given the same rights as the woman.

However, that certainly does not mean that there are no circumstances in which fetuses can be given legal protection. Again, it all depends on the context.

Consider another analogy. Cats and dogs are not "persons" under the Fourteenth Amendment. Yet surely there is nothing constitutionally suspect about laws forbidding cruelty to animals, even though they limit the liberty of those who would perpetrate such acts of cruelty. Indeed, there would be no inherent constitutional problem with terming a malicious cat or dog killing "murder"—though imposing too severe a sentence for that act might run afoul of the Eighth Amendment's ban on cruel and unusual punishment.

In sum, so long as respecting the rights and interests of fetuses does not conflict with the right of a woman to decide whether to terminate her pregnancy, there is no necessary contradiction between the abortion right established in *Roe* and feticide laws.

Nevertheless, severe tensions can arise, as a tragic case from Florida illustrates.

A 22-year-old severely retarded woman—known in court papers as "J.D.S."—who has no family or legal guardian, was apparently raped, and is, as of this writing, more than five months pregnant. She is unable to care for herself, much less an infant, and suffers from a seizure disorder and other physical disabilities that could make childbirth dangerous.

Accordingly, the state Department of Children and Families asked a judge to decide whether an abortion would be in her best interest. At that point, Governor Jeb Bush asked that in addition to appointing a legal guardian for J.D.S., the court ought to appoint a guardian for the fetus she carries.

That request directly contravenes a 1989 Florida Supreme Court decision, *In re T.W.*[12] There, the court, in the course of holding that the state's law requiring parental consent for a minor to obtain an abortion violated the Florida constitution, found that it is improper for a trial judge to appoint a guardian for a fetus.

However, the Florida Supreme Court has become more conservative in the ensuing years, and Governor Bush may be hoping that the current court will reconsider the *In re T.W.* ruling. If the court does reconsider, should pro-choice Floridians be concerned? Yes and no.

On the one hand, as with feticide laws, there is no necessary conflict between recognizing an abortion right and appointing a guardian for a fetus. The appointment of a guardian—whether for a minor, the estate of a dead person, a severely retarded person, or a fetus—simply signals that there are interests involved in a case that, absent the appointment of the guardian, would not be represented. It does not mean that those interests will necessarily prevail.

On the other hand, in the *J.D.S.* case, the particular argument the fetal guardian will make does appear inconsistent with the *Roe* framework. Presumably, the guardian will argue that it is in the interest of the fetus to be born. How is the court to evaluate that argument? If the judge decides that an abortion would be in the best interest of J.D.S., can he nonetheless conclude that the abortion should not occur because of the countervailing interest of the fetus? If he can, why shouldn't the interest of a fetus in being born prevail in every case in which a woman seeks an abortion, whether or not she is competent?

So far as the fetus is concerned, the *J.D.S.* case looks like every other abortion case. By contrast with the feticide context, here the interests of the fetus—as represented by a legal guardian—really do clash with the interests of a woman who wants (or who is determined to need) an abortion.

The problem in the *J.D.S.* case, in other words, is not that appointing a guardian for a fetus is invariably inconsistent with legal abortion. The problem is that appointing a fetal guardian with the specific purpose of making an argument that cuts against any and all abortions—as Governor Bush would do—truly does strike at the core issue of abortion's legality.

POSTSCRIPT

In the spring of 2004, Congress passed and President Bush signed a federal law providing that anyone who harms a fetus in the course of committing a federal offense thereby also commits a distinct federal offense—whether or not the perpetrator knew the victim was pregnant.[13] Later that year, a California jury found Scott Peterson guilty of the murder of his wife and unborn son. The court subsequently accepted the jury's recommendation of the death penalty.[14]

As for J.D.S., she gave birth to a baby girl in August 2003. The Florida courts determined that this event did not render the guardianship issue moot, however, because the issue was, in lawyers' jargon, "capable of repetition yet evading review." Accordingly, in January 2004, a Florida appeals court ruled that the appointment of a guardian for the fetus would have been legally improper. The court held that the relevant guardianship statute did not apply to fetuses; the majority opinion also stated that Florida law nowhere recognizes fetuses as persons.[15]

NOTES

1. 410 U.S. 113 (1973).

2. *See, e.g.*, Stenberg v. Carhart, 530 U.S. 914 (2000) (invalidating "partial-birth" abortion ban); Hill v. Colorado, 530 U.S. 703 (2000) (sustaining limits on protest activity within 100 feet of the entrance to any health care facility); Ohio v. Akron Ctr. for Reprod. Health, 497 U.S. 502 (1990) (upholding parental consent requirement for minors seeking abortions).

3. *See* Nick Madigan, *California Man Arrested in Death of Wife*, N.Y. Times, Apr. 19, 2003, at A8.

4. *See* Dana Canedy, *Gov. Jeb Bush to Seek Guardian for Fetus of Rape Victim*, N.Y. Times, May 15, 2003, at A29.

5. *See generally* Alan S. Wasserstrom, Annotation, *Homicide Based on Killing of Unborn Child*, 64 A.L.R.5th 671 (1998).

6. *See* Keeler v. Superior Court, 470 P.2d 617 (Cal. 1970).

7. Cal. Penal Code § 187 (West 1999).

8. *See* Unborn Victims of Violence Act of 2003, S. 146, 108th Cong.

9. *See, e.g.*, *Laci and Connor's Law Puts Abortion Debate into Focus*, Chi. Trib., May 20, 2003, at 36.

10. *See* Covington & Lexington Tpk. Rd. Co. v. Sandford, 164 U.S. 578, 592 (1896).

11. *See* Desenco, Inc. v. City of Akron, 706 N.E.2d 323, 332 (Ohio 1999) (denying appellants' Fourteenth Amendment Equal Protection Clause claim because "[a]ppellants' right to vote is not affected, as they have no right to vote in the first place. Appellants are

corporations. . . . Corporations cannot vote" [internal quotation marks and citation omitted]).

12. 551 So.2d 1186 (Fla. 1989) (per curiam).

13. Unborn Victims of Violence Act of 2004 (alternatively "Laci and Connor's Law"), Pub. L. No. 108–212, 118 Stat. 568.

14. *See* Maria L. LaGanga & Tonya Alanez, *Scott Peterson Gets Death for Murders; His Wife's Family Denounces Him at the Close of a Court Case that Captivated the Nation*, L.A. Times, Mar. 17, 2005, at B1.

15. *In re* Guardianship of J.D.S., 864 So.2d 534 (Fla. Dist. Ct. App. 2004).

• 7 •

Why the Lawsuit Challenging Tennessee's "Choose Life" License Plates Should Fail

November 2003

A new Tennessee law authorizes the state's Department of Safety to issue specialty license plates bearing the phrase "Choose Life" to car owners who opt for the specialty plates.[1] In addition, part of the fee collected from such plates will be earmarked for an anti-abortion organization, New Life Resources, which will use the funds to promote adoption services.

When the new law was just a bill pending in the state legislature, an amendment was proposed to it that would have authorized optional "Pro Choice" specialty plates as well. That amendment was tabled, though. Tennessee drivers may obviously still use bumper stickers to convey pro-choice messages and wholly unrelated messages on their cars.

The American Civil Liberties Union (ACLU) and Planned Parenthood Federation of America (PPFA) sued to block enforcement of the law as it was enacted. They argue that it impermissibly favors one side in an ideologically charged controversy. Indeed, they seek to bar Tennessee's entire specialty plates program on the ground that specialty plates invariably promote some messages at the expense of others.

Although superficially appealing, the plaintiffs' position ultimately threatens programs—such as government promotion of the arts and public health education—that organizations like the ACLU and PPFA themselves value. Accordingly, it should be rejected by the courts.

Nonetheless, the case falls between the cracks of several distinct lines of free speech precedents. Whether the courts uphold or strike down the law will likely depend upon which of several analogies they find most persuasive.

The Tennessee litigation does not represent the first time a court has been asked to consider the free speech implications of ideological messages on license plates. Beginning in 1969, New Hampshire non-commercial license plates were issued bearing the state motto "Live Free or Die." In 1972, the New Hampshire Supreme Court ruled that a state law making it a misdemeanor to obscure the "figures or letters" on a license plate applied to markings that obscured "Live Free or Die."[2]

That ruling was certainly ironic: It meant that in a state that professed devotion to freedom even over life itself, people were not free to decline to affirm "Live Free or Die."

Responding to this irony and the infringement of personal liberty, the United States Supreme Court ruled in the 1977 decision in *Wooley v. Maynard*[3] that the New Hampshire law violated the First Amendment. The freedom to speak, the Court held, includes the freedom not to speak.

Accordingly, in *Wooley v. Maynard*, the Court threw out the conviction of a Jehovah's Witness who had taped over "Live Free or Die" on his license plate.

The holding of *Wooley v. Maynard* is not directly applicable to the Tennessee controversy because the state does not require anyone to display "Choose Life" on his or her license plate. The law simply makes the "Choose Life" plates available as one of numerous options.

Indeed, Tennessee offers drivers a wide range of specialty plates. Like many states, Tennessee has found that it can raise revenue by offering two sorts of license plates: plain plates that cost $21.50, or specialty plates, which typically cost $56.50. Some portion of the extra $35 for a specialty plate goes to an organization involved with the specialty theme, with the remainder going to the state.

For example, an "animal friendly" plate, depicting a goofy cartoon dog and cat hugging each other, benefits the Humane Society. A National Championship plate featuring a University of Tennessee football helmet benefits scholarships at that institution. And whether a Tennessee car owner chooses generic or specialty plates, for an extra $35 she can make it a vanity plate.[4]

Given the diversity of offerings, Tennessee can hardly be said to be requiring drivers to carry the "Choose Life" message when they can as easily select plates with a cat playing the saxophone and the message "ARTS"; a "helping schools" plate with a shiny apple sitting on a stack of books labeled "READING," "WRITING," and "ARITHMETIC"; or a Mothers Against Drunk Driving plate with a red diagonal slash cutting across icons for a cocktail glass and car keys.

The premise of the lawsuit is not that Tennesseans are being forced, "*Wooley*-nilly," to carry the state's pro-life message. Rather, the plaintiffs invoke the line of Supreme Court cases—discussed above in chapter 5—holding that when the state creates a forum for speech, it may not exclude particular messages.

The forum cases draw highly technical distinctions between various kinds of fora: traditional public fora like parks, streets, and sidewalks; designated public fora; and non-public fora. Different doctrinal rules apply in these different settings, but regardless of what kind of forum is at issue, the government is forbidden from engaging in "viewpoint discrimination."[5]

In other words, if the government allows one side of a debate to have its say, it has to give a fair opportunity to people with opposing viewpoints. In a press release about the lawsuit, Hedy Weinberg, executive director of the ACLU of Tennessee, explained that the new law violates this basic principle. She drew the following analogy: "If the state held a town-hall meeting tomorrow to discuss the posting of the Ten Commandments, it couldn't open the floor only to those supporting the religious displays."[6]

Likewise with license plates. By offering "Choose Life" plates but not "Pro Choice" plates, the ACLU/PPFA lawsuit alleges, the state impermissibly slanted the debate.

There is a certain appeal to the plaintiffs' argument. Surely it seems disrespectful to pro-choice Tennesseans for the state legislature to deny them the same opportunity to express their view on this divisive public issue that was given to pro-life Tennesseans. But disrespectful or unwise legislation is not necessarily unconstitutional legislation.

If Tennessee really cannot favor some viewpoints over others in designating specialty license plates, as the plaintiffs argue, then the entire Tennessee specialty license plate program must be unconstitutional. After all, the state offers "Mothers Against Drunk Driving" plates but not "No-Good Uncles For Drunk Driving" plates. It offers plates bearing the phrase "Children First" and picturing a boy and girl holding balloons, but no plates that say "Children Last," "Middle-Aged People First," or "Me First."

Indeed, even the generic $21.50 plates contain an ideological message. Commemorating Tennesseans' long history of providing volunteers for military service in the War of 1812, the Mexican American War, and (according to some accounts) the Civil War, the generic plates include the phrase "Volunteer State." Yet pacifists and those who associate the state's moniker with its past sympathy for the Confederacy may well prefer to have their cars adorned with a contrary message, such as "State With Some People Who Think War, Or At Least The Confederate Side In The Civil War, Is Wrong, Thank You Very Much."

Such Tennesseans cannot express that message on their license plates and cannot even avoid carrying "Volunteer State" on their plates unless they shell out the extra $35 for specialty plates or, following the example of Maynard in *Wooley v. Maynard*, tape over the offending state motto.

To its credit, the ACLU/PPFA lawsuit owns up to the consequences of its argument. The suit seeks not only to bar the "Choose Life" license plates but the entire program of specialty plates. It thus has the virtue of consistency.

Consistency, however, is not enough. The basic problem is that license plates aren't best understood as a forum for the expression of views. They're government-issued official property. And while *Wooley v. Maynard* establishes that the government may not insist that a person carry the state's ideological message, the case stops short of prohibiting the state from facilitating the expression of some rather than other viewpoints. That's why the result in the case was that Mr. Maynard was allowed to tape over "Live Free or Die" on his license plate. If the ACLU/PPFA view were correct, New Hampshire would have been prohibited from putting the state motto on *anybody's* plates.

State provision of specialty plates thus seems closer to government-funded speech than it does to purely private speech. The leading Supreme Court case on this subject is the 1998 decision in *National Endowment for the Arts v. Finley*. There, the Court upheld federal legislation requiring the NEA to consider "general standards of decency and respect for the diverse beliefs and values of the American public" in awarding grants against a challenge by performance artist Karen Finley and others, who charged that the legislation authorized impermissible viewpoint discrimination. After construing the law to leave grant decisions largely to the artistic judgment of the NEA, the Court concluded that any distinctions drawn on the basis of viewpoint were permissible. "The Government has not discriminated on the basis of viewpoint," the Court said; "it has merely chosen to fund one activity to the exclusion of the other."[7]

Government funding of the arts and other activities is not a perfect analogy to state provision of specialty plates. In the former context, the government may legitimately choose to promote its own message, while in the latter, its ostensible aim is to facilitate speech by individuals. Accordingly, it is possible that a court would side with the ACLU/PPFA argument that the Tennessee specialty plate program is unconstitutional.

That would be unfortunate, however. In controversies over the funding of the arts, political conservatives sometimes argue that the only solution is for government to get out of the business of funding art. In the current Tennessee litigation, political liberals are making the same point; they say that the only way for the state to be neutral is to get out of the business of stamping messages on license plates.

The argument is misguided whether pressed by conservatives or liberals. The fact that the state wishes to fund works of art that lift up the human spirit without also funding art that degrades should not be fatal to government funding of the arts. Likewise, the fact that Tennessee produces license plates that urge the public to "Preserve and Protect" Great Smoky Mountains National Park without also producing plates urging the destruction of this natural haven should not count as a violation of the First Amendment.

POSTSCRIPT

The federal district court disagreed with me. Accepting the classification of the "Choose Life" plates as impermissible viewpoint discrimination, it enjoined them. The court declined to rule on the plaintiffs' facial challenge to the entire specialty plates program.[8]

Readers of the last two chapters may be wondering what exactly I meant when I wrote in the introduction to this section of the book that I support abortion rights. That was something of an oversimplification, so let me explain my views a little more carefully. (This ought to ensure that I'm never nominated to serve in any federal office that requires Senate confirmation.) I think that abortion is usually immoral after the point in pregnancy when a fetus has subjective experiences such as pain. I nonetheless think that abortion should generally be legal for three principal reasons: first, because I recognize the fallibility of my own moral judgment on this matter and the fact that few women who decide to obtain an abortion do so without serious moral reflection; second, because laws prohibiting abortion tend to make it unsafe for the thousands of women who obtain illegal back-alley abortions; and third, because the burden of laws prohibiting abortion falls almost entirely on women as a class.

As for the *constitutional* question—which is, after all, the only question as to which I can claim any special expertise—I am profoundly ambivalent about whether *Roe v. Wade* was rightly or wrongly decided as an original matter. I will say that whether or not *Roe* was mistaken, it was certainly a hard case: Having established in earlier decisions that there is a prima facie constitutional right to make fundamental decisions about child-rearing and childbearing, the Supreme Court's difficult task in *Roe* was to decide whether the government's interest in unborn life outweighed that prima facie right. That judgment called for truly Solomonic wisdom, and it is accordingly not surprising that the Justices' decision has drawn its fair share of criticism over the years.

NOTES

1. *See* Tenn. Code Ann. § 55–4-306 (2004).

2. State v. Hoskin, 295 A.2d 454 (N.H. 1972) (upholding N.H. Rev. Stat. Ann. § 262:27-c (Supp. 1975)).

3. 430 U.S. 705 (1977).

4. Specialty plates can be viewed on the Internet at http://tennessee.gov/safety/plates.html.

5. *See generally* Ark. Educ. Television Comm'n v. Forbes, 523 U.S. 666 (1998).

6. Press Release, ACLU, ACLU and Planned Parenthood Ask Tennessee Court to Block Anti-Abortion License Plate (Nov. 6, 2003), *at* http://www.aclu.org/FreeSpeech/FreeSpeech.cfm?ID=14342&c=42.

7. Nat'l Endowment for the Arts v. Finley, 524 U.S. 569, 588 (1998) (quoting Rust v. Sullivan, 500 U.S. 173, 193 (1991)) (upholding 20 U.S.C. § 954(d)(1) (1995)).

8. *See* ACLU of Tenn. v. Bredesen, 354 F. Supp. 2d 770, 773–74 (M.D. Tenn. 2004). In addition to the *Bredesen* court, the Fourth Circuit has held that specialty license programs similar to the one I have described are impermissible government regulations of private speech. *See* Planned Parenthood of S.C., Inc. v. Rose, 361 F.3d 786 (4th Cir. 2004); Sons of Confederate Veterans, Inc. v. Comm'r of the Va. Dep't of Motor Vehicles, 288 F.3d 610 (4th Cir. 2002). However, individual judges of the Fourth Circuit have advanced the reasoning that I have presented here, arguing that the license plates programs are constitutionally permissible regulations of government speech. *See, e.g.*, Planned Parenthood of S.C., Inc. v. Rose, 373 F.3d 580, 587 (4th Cir. 2004) (Shedd, J., dissenting from the denial of rehearing en banc, joined by Williams, J.); Sons of Confederate Veterans, Inc. v. Va. Dep't of Motor Vehicles, 305 F.3d 241, 250 (4th Cir. 2002) (Niemeyer, J., dissenting from the denial of rehearing en banc); *id.* at 251 (Gregory, J., dissenting from the denial of rehearing en banc).

• 8 •

Three Bad Reasons—and One Very Good Reason—to Oppose a Constitutional Amendment Barring Same-Sex Marriage

February 2004

Recently, the Massachusetts Supreme Judicial Court affirmed that the state constitution requires the recognition of same-sex marriage—and not just civil unions.[1] Among opponents of same-sex marriage, the ruling has revived interest in a proposed federal constitutional amendment that would define marriage throughout the country as "the union of a man and a woman."[2] The amendment has been pending in Congress since May 2003, but now it may move to the front burner of American politics.

Presidents do not have a formal voice in the adoption of constitutional amendments, which become effective upon passage by a two-thirds vote in each house of Congress and ratification by three-fourths of the state legislatures. Nonetheless, support for, or opposition to, the proposed amendment could well become an issue in the 2004 presidential election.

Senator John Kerry, the Democratic presidential frontrunner, hales from Massachusetts, and though he opposes same-sex marriage while favoring legal recognition for civil unions,[3] that distinction may be difficult to explain to the sort of swing voters who pay only intermittent attention to politics, yet can play the crucial role in a close election. And President Bush, who appears determined not to neglect his socially conservative base, may view same-sex marriage as the sort of wedge issue that enables him to attract even those voters whose economic interests might be better served by policies favored by Democrats.[4]

Politics aside, is the proposed amendment a good idea or a bad one? My own unequivocal answer is that a constitutional ban on same-sex marriage would be horrific. Marriage is a basic civil right, which, if offered to straight couples, cannot be denied to gay or lesbian couples without branding the latter as second-class citizens.

Yet some opponents of the same-sex marriage ban have gone further, arguing that the constitutional amendment would be a bad idea even if one thought that the institution of marriage should be reserved for heterosexual couples.

In support of this view, they invoke three notions: states' rights; the idea that constitutional amendments can legitimately expand, but not contract, individual rights; and a general hostility to constitutional amendment.

None of these three arguments survives close analysis. Opponents of the same-sex marriage ban would do better to focus on its real flaw: it is morally repugnant.

As of this writing, no state officially recognizes same-sex marriage. In response to a judicial ruling by the Vermont Supreme Court, that state permits same-sex couples to enter into civil unions that provide the same legal benefits as marriage.[5] A number of other states and some municipalities have similar laws.[6] But as the Massachusetts Supreme Judicial Court ruled, this status is not quite the equivalent of marriage; even if states grant same-sex couples the economic and other benefits of marriage, denying the formal status of marriage is a gratuitous insult.

Under the Massachusetts court's rulings, that state will soon have to begin granting full marriage rights to same-sex couples. Efforts are underway to amend the Massachusetts constitution and thereby reverse the state high court's ruling. However, under the state constitutional procedures, any amendment would not take effect for several years. Thus, at least in the short run, there is no question that one state—Massachusetts—will grant marriage licenses to same-sex couples.

Opponents of same-sex marriage fear that Massachusetts will become a haven for gay and lesbian couples from around the country to tie the knot, much as Nevada (with its permissive standards) has long been a magnet for straight couples seeking "quickie" marriages or divorces. Are these fears realistic?

The answer is unclear. Article IV of the Federal Constitution requires that each state grant "full faith and credit" to "the public acts, records, and judicial proceedings" of its sister states.[7] Ordinarily, that includes marriage certificates, but a murky judge-made exception to the full-faith-and-credit requirement permits states to deny recognition to out-of-state marriages on public policy grounds.[8] States whose public policy condemns same-sex marriage might be able to invoke this exception to deny recognition to Massachusetts weddings.

Moreover, a federal statute, the Defense of Marriage Act, or "DOMA," specifically authorizes states to deny recognition to same-sex marriages of sister states.[9] But the statute may not be constitutional.[10] The Federal Constitution empowers Congress to prescribe the "manner" in which states accord full faith and credit; yet, it does not appear to give Congress the authority to regulate the substance of full faith and credit. Establishing rules of evidence for proof that a marriage was performed would clearly fall within congressional power; establishing rules about who can marry whom would not.

Accordingly, *if* no judge-made public policy exception permits states to deny recognition to same-sex marriages performed in other states, and *if* DOMA is unconstitutional (as I believe it is), then, once the Massachusetts ruling goes into effect, every state in the country could be required to recognize Massachusetts same-sex marriages.

The proposed constitutional amendment would change that, however. It would make clear that no state would have to grant recognition to same-sex marriages.

Indeed, the proposed amendment would go considerably further than DOMA. It would affirmatively *prohibit* states from recognizing same-sex marriages even if they wanted to for purely internal purposes.

Under the proposed amendment, then, Massachusetts could not recognize even its very own same-sex marriages—or, say, those performed in Ontario or the Netherlands, where they are legal.

The proposed amendment would thus define marriage throughout the United States, at every level: national, state, and local.

Now let us turn to the supposedly neutral arguments against the proposed same-sex marriage ban. Some opponents of the proposed constitutional amendment argue that it would inappropriately intrude into the domain of the states. Marriage, they say, has traditionally been governed by state law, and so if Massachusetts or some other state decides (whether legislatively or by judicial interpretation of the state constitution) to recognize same-sex marriages, people in other states have no business interfering with that decision.

The states' rights argument is both disingenuous and wrong. It's disingenuous because the opponents of the proposed constitutional amendment also typically argue that DOMA is unconstitutional in limiting the full faith and credit due to same-sex marriages. In other words, proponents of same-sex marriage think that if any state recognizes same-sex marriages, then all states must do so as well.

That may well be a sound interpretation of the Full Faith and Credit Clause, but it's hardly consistent with the claim that the question whether to recognize same-sex marriage should properly be left to each individual state.

Moreover, it's wrong to suggest that the federal Constitution does, or should, leave the definition of marriage entirely to the states. Virginia used to prohibit marriages between blacks and whites, but in the 1967 case of *Loving v. Virginia*,[11] the Supreme Court—quite correctly—held that the prohibition violated the Fourteenth Amendment's Equal Protection Clause. And, had the Court decided *Loving* the other way, it would have been entirely appropriate for the people to have amended the Constitution to require states to recognize interracial marriage.

Is there a difference, however, between the proposed constitutional amendment mandating opposite-sex marriage only, and my hypothetical amendment requiring state recognition of interracial marriage?

One argument now being advanced against the proposed constitutional amendment suggests that there is an important distinction between *expanding* constitutional rights by banning a form of discrimination—as in my hypothetical example—and *restricting* rights by requiring a form of discrimination—as the actual proposed amendment barring same-sex marriage would do. Opponents argue that such an amendment would be the first such retrenchment in the history of the American Constitution.

There is a genuine distinction between the hypothetical and actual proposed constitutional amendments, but not the one being touted. Some prior constitutional amendments have in fact shrunken rights, and appropriately so. Before the Civil War, many state constitutions were interpreted to recognize slaveowners' legal right to property in other human beings. The Thirteenth Amendment, in abolishing slavery, eliminated what had previously been an economically valuable (though morally odious) right.

Likewise, in the late nineteenth and early twentieth centuries, state and federal courts often treated laws regulating relations between capital and labor as illicit "class legislation" that impermissibly discriminated against the wealthy. In the 1930s, President Franklin D. Roosevelt and his allies were prepared to propose a constitutional amendment that—from the perspective of a great many people—would have authorized discrimination against rich people.

That amendment was rendered unnecessary when the Supreme Court, in the so-called "switch in time that saved nine," essentially abandoned the project of reading the Constitution to protect the rich.[12] But it's fair to view modern constitutional doctrine as accomplishing through the courts what Roosevelt sought to accomplish by constitutional amendment.

Of course, I do not mean to say that there is no difference between, on the one hand, depriving people of slaves and requiring employers to pay their workers a decent wage, and on the other hand, denying same-sex couples the marriage status afforded to opposite-sex couples. There is an enormous moral distinction. But the distinction is not between expanding rights and contracting rights: it's between adjusting the allocation of rights for a good cause, and adjusting them for a bad one.

Yet another morally neutral argument offered against the proposed amendment barring same-sex marriage says that whatever one thinks about same-sex marriage, it's not the sort of issue that warrants a constitutional amendment. Americans, the argument goes, suffer from what constitutional scholar Kathleen

Sullivan once called "amendmentitis," a desire to amend the Constitution at the drop of a hat.[13]

Sullivan is doubtless correct that some matters are not fit subjects for constitutionalization. Tax rates, for example, should be subject to frequent adjustment depending upon economic conditions as judged by Congress, rather than fixed by a constitutional amendment.

But as Sullivan herself has observed, our Constitution has been amended with remarkable infrequency. In the last two hundred years, there have been only seventeen amendments.

To be sure, thousands of amendments have been proposed. But because the Constitution requires that amendments obtain super-majorities in both houses of Congress, and an even larger super-majority of state legislatures, nearly all of these proposals have been defeated.

In light of this history, it seems fair to say that we don't need a working presumption that tinkering with the Constitution is a bad idea to protect us from amendmentitis. The evidence indicates that the arduous amendment procedure set forth in Article V provides us with robust immunity against any ill effects of that disease. If a proposed amendment is ill advised or not truly important, it will be unlikely to secure the votes necessary for its adoption.

That brings us to the real and obvious objection to the proposed constitutional ban on same-sex marriage: it's a terrible idea.

For one thing, the proposal now pending before Congress would bar not only same-sex marriage itself, but also any of "the legal incidents" of marriage. That means that states and cities could not even provide for civil unions or domestic partnership arrangements that fall short of marriage. So it is not just Massachusetts' pioneering recognition of same-sex marriage itself that is under threat. Other states' alternative solutions would also be rejected.

More broadly, there is simply no good reason why the government should confer official recognition and financial benefits on straight couples, while refusing the same to gay and lesbian couples.

Many people, of course, object to same-sex marriage on religious grounds, and it is accordingly their right to practice a religion that does not recognize same-sex marriage. But the legal institution of marriage is distinct from the religious one. No church, synagogue, or mosque will be forced by the government to recognize or perform same-sex marriages. Even in Massachusetts, the mandate affects county clerks, not country priests.

Nor does the fact that heterosexual marriage plays an important role in providing a stable environment for child-rearing distinguish it from same-sex marriage. The law has never denied the right to marry to infertile heterosexual couples, or to heterosexual couples that do not wish to raise children. And conversely, increasing numbers of gay and lesbian couples choose to have and raise children.

In the end, the argument against same-sex marriage comes down to the claim that it is somehow a threat to traditional marriage: Thus Congress enacted the *Defense* of Marriage Act, to defend the institution of marriage against an ostensible attack from same-sex marriage.

Apparently, people who oppose same-sex marriage think that loving, committed relationships among gays and lesbians are so different in kind from loving, committed relationships among heterosexuals, that dignifying the former with the term "marriage" makes a mockery of heterosexual marriage.[14]

I understand that a majority of Americans feel this way, but that doesn't make it so. Gays and lesbians asking for the right to marry, far from undermining the traditional institution of marriage, pay it homage.

The struggle for a right to same-sex marriage requires for its success that the millions of people of good will, who nonetheless oppose that right, be made to understand that what they regard as a matter of principle is ultimately a prejudice. But to persuade such people will require that the real issue—the moral issue of equality—be tackled head on. Arguments rooted in states' rights, and the supposed sanctity of the existing constitutional text, just won't cut it.

POSTSCRIPT

To be clear, I do not think that it is never appropriate to buttress moral arguments with institutional ones. One could, for example, oppose national legislation imposing stiff penalties for marijuana possession both on the grounds that such a law would be substantively bad as a matter of policy and that the issue ought to be left for the states. My point is simply that weak or insincere institutional arguments tend to be unhelpful. Indeed, they may even be harmful, as they tend to suggest that one does not have confidence in the strength of one's substantive views.

At least that's how these questions look to an academic. Politicians, who undoubtedly know more than I do about how the public will react to various official positions, tend to embrace institutional arguments that permit them to straddle both sides of any divisive controversy. Nonetheless, that's not an excuse for the rest of us, who do not have to stand for election, to make or be taken in by bad arguments. And as I explain in the next chapter, that's even true when the bad arguments are made by courts reaching results we like on policy grounds.

NOTES

1. *In re* Opinions of the Justices to the Senate, 802 N.E.2d 565 (Mass. 2004).

2. H.R.J. Res. 56, 108th Cong. (2003) (proposing the addition of a new article to the Constitution that reads: "Marriage in the United States shall consist only of the union of a man and a woman. Neither this Constitution or the constitution of any State, nor state or federal law, shall be construed to require that marital status or the legal incidents thereof be conferred upon unmarried couples or groups"); S.J. Res. 26, 108th Cong. (2003) (same).

3. *See* Susan Milligan, *Kerry Says GOP May Target Him on 'Wedge Issue'; Gives His OK to Civil Unions, Not Marriage*, Boston Globe, Feb. 6, 2004, at A24.

4. As noted in chapter 1, in his 2005 State of the Union Address to Congress, President Bush declared: "Because marriage is a sacred institution and the foundation of society, it should not be redefined by activist judges For the good of families, children and society, I support a constitutional amendment to protect the institution of marriage." Transcript, '*Let Us . . . Build a Better World*,' Wash. Post, Feb. 3, 2005, at A14.

5. *See* Vt. Stat. Ann. tit. 18, §§ 5160–169 (2000); Baker v. State, 744 A.2d 864 (Vt. 1999).

6. *E.g.*, Cal. Fam. Code §§ 297–99.6 (West 2004); N.J. Stat. Ann. §§ 26:8A-1 to -12 (West Supp. 2005).

7. U.S. Const. art. IV, § 1.

8. *Cf.* Nevada v. Hall, 440 U.S. 410 (1979).

9. 1 U.S.C. § 7 (2004); 28 U.S.C. § 1738C (2004).

10. One court has ruled DOMA to be valid. *See* Wilson v. Ake, 354 F. Supp. 2d 1298, 1303–04 (M.D. Fla. 2005).

11. 388 U.S. 1 (1967).

12. *See, e.g.,* NLRB v. Jones & Laughlin Steel Corp., 301 U.S. 1 (1937); W. Coast Hotel Co. v. Parrish, 300 U.S. 379 (1937).

13. Kathleen M. Sullivan, *Constitutional Amendmentitis*, Am. Prospect, Fall 1995, at 20.

14. *See, e.g.*, 150 Cong. Rec. H7898, 7900 (2004) (statement of Rep. Feeney) ("[I]n establishing same-sex marriage, what the Massachusetts court did is to belittle the traditional definition of marriage and all of the States that actually believe that.").

• 9 •

A Federal Appeals Court Rules that Universities Can Bar Military Recruiters without Losing Federal Grant Money: A Welcome Result Based on Flawed Reasoning

December 2004

As this book goes to press, the Supreme Court is slated to decide the constitutionality of a federal statute withholding grant money from universities that deny military recruiters access to students on the same terms as other prospective employers. The appeals court decision in the case, *Forum for Academic and Institutional Rights ("FAIR") v. Rumsfeld*,[1] invalidated the statute. The court found a violation of the universities' First Amendment rights.

At issue is a law that cuts off nearly all of an educational institution's federal funding if even one unit of that institution applies its general anti-discrimination policy to military recruiters. Law schools had refused to allow military recruiters on campus because of the military's "don't ask, don't tell" policy—which discriminates on the basis of sexual orientation. The Department of Defense then invoked the law to threaten the universities affiliated with these law schools with the loss of millions of dollars of federal funding.

The statute is truly odious, threatening both equal opportunity in the military and the institutional autonomy of universities. Yet, as I shall explain, the logic of the court's opinion striking it down is flawed.

In the end, the way to combat the discriminatory exclusion of a large class of patriotic Americans from service in the armed forces is to simply recognize "don't ask, don't tell" for what it is: invidious discrimination.

For many years, the U.S. armed forces have excluded homosexual service members. When President Clinton attempted to end the exclusion through executive action early in his first term, a political backlash resulted in Congress's codifying the policy in a federal statute.[2]

The current policy is sometimes called "don't ask, don't tell" because the military does not proactively investigate the sexual orientation of service members without some reason to suspect homosexuality ("don't ask"), and the statute forbids service members from declaring that they are homosexual ("don't tell").

However, "don't ask, don't tell" is a misnomer insofar as it suggests that the military is indifferent to sexual orientation. That is not so. On average, nearly a thousand service members per year have been discharged for their sexual orientation under "don't ask, don't tell."[3]

The policy has been challenged in the courts, although the issue has not yet reached the U.S. Supreme Court. Lower courts have upheld "don't ask, don't tell," typically citing the deference due the political branches in military matters.[4]

Meanwhile, over the last decade and a half, municipalities, states, and other institutions have been expanding their anti-discrimination policies beyond traditionally suspect grounds such as race, religion, national origin, and sex, to include other categories such as veteran status, physical disability, age, and sexual orientation. Thus, in 1990, the Association of American Law Schools (AALS) required that member schools not discriminate or tolerate discrimination based on sexual orientation.[5]

Pursuant to the AALS policy, no major law school in the United States can engage in sexual orientation discrimination. Moreover, and also pursuant to the AALS policy, American law schools cannot permit prospective employers to recruit on campus unless they certify that they do not discriminate on the basis of sexual orientation (or the other AALS-forbidden grounds of "race, color, religion, national origin, sex, handicap or disability").

Under the AALS policy, therefore, American law schools cannot allow military recruiters seeking law graduates for the Judge Advocate General's (JAG) Corps to recruit on campus, because in light of "don't ask, don't tell," the armed forces cannot honestly certify that they do not discriminate on the basis of sexual orientation. On the contrary, they openly so discriminate, and, indeed, are required to do so as a matter of federal law.

Despite the AALS policy, for years many American law schools nonetheless accommodated the military and their graduates seeking careers in the military by arranging space for recruiters and students to meet off campus. The litigation that led to the pending Supreme Court case arose when that compromise proved unacceptable to the Defense Department.

Irked by what it regarded as second-class treatment of the military, in 1994 Congress enacted legislation withholding federal grant money from educational institutions that denied military recruiters full access to students. Dubbed the "Solomon Amendment" for its principal sponsor, Congressman Gerald Solomon, the provision has been modified a number of times.

In its 2005 form, the Solomon Amendment withholds all funds otherwise appropriated through the federal Departments of Defense, Labor, Health and

Human Services, and Education, as well as under the Related Agencies Appropriations Act, from any educational institution that "prohibits or in effect prevents" military recruiters from having access to students at any sub-element of the institution.[6]

Thus, for example, suppose Columbia University's law school (where I teach), denies access to military recruiters. Doctors in Columbia's College of Physicians and Surgeons therefore become ineligible for money disbursed by the federal Department of Health and Human Services. Likewise, professors conducting research in the Columbia physics department are ineligible for most federal grants. It does not matter whether the unit of the university where the funds would otherwise be spent supports the law school's non-discrimination policy.

Furthermore, an educational institution will be treated as "prohibiting" or "preventing" access to military recruiters if it denies to these recruiters access that is equal in scope and quality with the access provided to other employers. Thus, the former compromise policy of many law schools—facilitating off-campus interviewing by JAG Corps recruiters—is no longer allowed.

Given the breadth and severity of the Solomon Amendment and the manner in which it has been implemented, every university has succumbed to the pressure. Under protest, all American law schools—despite the sexual orientation portion of their non-discrimination policies—do allow military recruiters on campus.

A number of these schools, however, sued the Secretary of Defense, seeking to have the Solomon Amendment declared unconstitutional. The appeals court decision was a clear victory for the schools. Technically, it only authorizes a *preliminary* injunction. But as a practical matter, that ruling, if not reversed by the Supreme Court, will end the case.

In constitutional law, nearly everything depends on what lawyers call the "level of scrutiny" that applies to a challenged law or policy. A law that infringes a constitutional right must be subject to exacting scrutiny—essentially, a requirement that the government come forward with very strong evidence that the law is necessary to further some very important policy objective.

In the *FAIR* case, the appeals court said that the Solomon Amendment and its implementing procedures infringed the First Amendment rights of universities. It reasoned, therefore, that the government had to show how its underlying policy satisfied exacting (or "strict") scrutiny.

The appeals court conceded that military readiness is a very important interest. But crucially, it also thought it clear that on-campus interviewing was not essential to the recruitment of talented JAG Corps attorneys.

Why not? The court cited loan repayment incentives and targeted advertising as alternative means by which the military could recruit. And the court even suggested that the ill will generated by the Solomon Amendment itself impeded JAG Corps (and other military) recruiting. (The court might also have noted that the government could better achieve its objective simply by abandoning "don't ask, don't tell," which prevents the recruitment of talented and patriotic gays and lesbians into all branches and divisions of the armed forces.)

Accordingly, the appeals court concluded that the Solomon Amendment is not necessary—or in lawyerspeak, not "narrowly tailored"—to achieve its objective. That conclusion is eminently reasonable. However, it is not at all clear that the Solomon Amendment should have been subject to exacting judicial scrutiny in the first place.

The court applied strict scrutiny because it thought the Solomon Amendment infringed First Amendment rights. But did it? The court's argument proceeded in two steps. Both steps are necessary to the court's decision to apply strict scrutiny to the Solomon Amendment; yet both steps are flawed.

The appeals court first reasoned that educational institutions are "expressive associations" that cannot be forced to bear a government message contrary to their own views. It did so based almost entirely on an analogy to the Supreme Court's 2000 decision in *Boy Scouts of America v. Dale.*[7] But in the end, that analogy is unconvincing.

In *Dale*, the Supreme Court ruled that the Boy Scouts—which, as a matter of national policy, disapprove of homosexuality—could not be required to retain an openly gay scout master. Having a gay man as a role model and spokesman for the organization, the Court reasoned, would undermine the ability of the Scouts as a whole to profess their anti-homosexual message.

Dale was and is a difficult case, mostly because it seems to provide a loophole through which organizations can evade national, state, and local anti-discrimination law. And for that reason, courts should be reluctant to expand *Dale*. Yet the appeals court decision in *FAIR* expanded *Dale* dramatically.

To be sure, *Dale* can apply in the university context. Suppose, for example, that a federal law mandated that universities hire for their biology departments otherwise qualified professors who espouse "intelligent design"—a theory of the origins of life that is almost universally regarded by professional biologists as unscientific. Such a law would violate the First Amendment, as interpreted in *Dale*. If it were forced to accept among its members someone it regards as engaged in theology rather than science, the department's message about what constitutes science would be undermined—in just the way that the Boy Scouts' message was undermined in *Dale*.

But there's no "forced acceptance" argument—and hence no genuine analogy to *Dale*—in the Solomon Amendment context. The military recruiters are not teaching at the law schools—let alone, say, teaching anti-discrimination law there. Instead, they are visiting campus to offer jobs to law students. Such annual visits hardly undermine the laudable message of the law schools, in part because no reasonable person would think that military recruiters on campus speak for a law school or university in the way that a scout master speaks for the Boy Scouts or a biology professor speaks for a biology department.

Moreover, the recruiters' visits occur in a context that is far removed from the academic mission of universities. It is probably just a historical accident that universities have job placement offices, rather than outsourcing the task to employment agencies or allowing their students to fend for themselves.

In sum, by extending the rationale of *Dale* beyond membership to peripheral activities of an organization, the appeals court broadened that case's potentially mischievous loophole in anti-discrimination law.

The appeals court's second step on the road to applying strict scrutiny was also problematic. The government argued that the Solomon Amendment did not require universities to grant access to military recruiters; it merely refused to subsidize those universities that denied such access.

The court rejected this argument under the rubric of what is known as the "unconstitutional conditions" doctrine. At bottom, that doctrine states that, as the appeals court put it (quoting an earlier Supreme Court decision), "the Government may not propose a penalty to produce a result which it could not command directly."[8]

This way of seeing things has intuitive appeal, and indeed, unconditional-conditions arguments sometimes make sense: Clearly, the government could not enact a law denying the home mortgage interest deduction to anyone who publicly expressed a view critical of the President—for that would be perilously close to simply silencing First Amendment–protected dissent.

But other unconstitutional-conditions arguments are plainly untenable, as we saw in our discussion of Tennessee's specialty license plate program.[9] Suppose the government hires an advertising agency to run a public education program urging people to "vote for the candidate of their choice." Surely the government is under no obligation to spend equal sums funding a competing agency's advertising campaign urging people to "skip the long lines at the polls and go to the movies" on Election Day.

Is the "unconstitutional conditions" argument in *FAIR* a winner or a loser? The question is a tough one—but the appeals court in *FAIR* ducked it. In a footnote, it simply announced that the Solomon Amendment "does not create a spending program; it merely imposes a penalty—the loss of general funds."[10] Therefore, the court reasoned, the Amendment does not fall under the "pick your own advertising message" rule—the rule that the government need not fund a message with which it disagrees.

To be sure, the appeals court found some support for the distinction between spending programs and pure penalties in Supreme Court cases. But the distinction nonetheless makes little sense.

Suppose, for example, that the government wishes not to fund organizations that engage in what the public regards as an odious practice—the employment of child labor overseas, say, or involuntary euthanasia of the severely disabled. And suppose government officials plausibly conclude that withholding subsidies for the particular activity insufficiently distances public policy from the odious practice; it wants, instead, to cut off funds to the whole organization.

Shouldn't the government sometimes be permitted to cut off funding with an axe rather than a scalpel? Money, after all, is fungible. When government funds go to an organization's innocuous programs, the organization has that much more money to spend on the odious practices.

When should government be permitted to condition all funding to an organization based on the activities of just one part of that organization? That is a difficult question.

But the problem with the court's logic is this: It makes no sense for the answer to turn on whether the condition—no child labor, or no involuntary euthanasia, for example—appears in an across-the-board law versus in the particular funding measures themselves.

Yet the appeals court relied on that meaningless distinction to find that the Solomon Amendment is a penalty (and thus constitutionally unacceptable), rather than the withholding of funds (and thus constitutionally acceptable).

None of this is to say that the bottom-line decision in *FAIR* is wrong. For one thing, it may be possible to construe the access given by law schools to military recruiters as complying with the letter of the Solomon Amendment. More obviously, the result reached by the appeals court could be justified by the argument that the underlying exclusion of gays and lesbians from the armed forces is unconstitutional.

As I noted above, the lower courts have tended to reject this claim. But most of the relevant cases predate the Supreme Court's more recent suggestions that discrimination on the basis of sexual orientation is constitutionally problematic.[11] Were a direct Equal Protection challenge to "don't ask, don't tell" to reach the Supreme Court now, it is far from clear that the Justices would reject it.

In the meantime, the weaknesses in the appeals court's opinion invalidating the Solomon Amendment—and the fact that the Supreme Court will therefore likely uphold the Amendment against this First Amendment challenge—should not blind us to the real evil at work here: invidious discrimination against Americans who seek an equal opportunity to serve their country.

POSTSCRIPT

Pending the Supreme Court's decision, one further point deserves mention. The desire of law schools and other educational institutions to exclude military recruiters is sometimes portrayed as unpatriotic. Especially during wartime, critics charge, military recruiters should be shown respect. It is important to understand, however, that the schools express no hostility to the military as such. They are attempting to apply a general rule that denies campus access to any prospective employer that discriminates on the basis of sexual orientation—law firms no less than the Defense Department. The Solomon Amendment, therefore, is not an effort to punish schools that discriminate against the military. On the contrary, it is an effort to force the schools to give the military a special exemption from their anti-discrimination policies.

NOTES

1. 390 F.3d 219 (3d Cir. 2004) (invalidating 10 U.S.C. § 983 (2004)), *cert. granted*, 125 S. Ct. 1977 (2005).
2. 10 U.S.C. § 654 (2004).
3. Government Accountability Office, GAO-05–299, Military Personnel: Financial Costs and Loss of Critical Skills Due to DOD's Homosexual Conduct Policy Cannot Be Completely Estimated 4 (2005) ("The military services separated 9,488 members pursuant to the homosexual conduct policy statute from fiscal year 1994 through fiscal year 2003.").
4. *See, e.g.,* Richenberg v. Perry, 97 F.3d 256, 261 (8th Cir. 1996); Thomasson v. Perry, 80 F.3d 915, 925 (4th Cir. 1996) (en banc).
5. *See Forum for Academic and Institutional Rights*, 390 F.3d at 224–25.
6. 10 U.S.C. § 983(b) (2005).
7. 530 U.S. 640 (2000).
8. *Forum for Academic and Institutional Rights*, 390 F.3d at 229. The quoted language is from Speiser v. Randall, 357 U.S. 513, 526 (1958), which held that a state may not condition a tax exemption on a loyalty oath.
9. *See supra* chapter 7.
10. *Forum for Academic and Institutional Rights*, 390 F.3d at 229 n.9.
11. *See* Lawrence v. Texas, 539 U.S. 558 (2003); Romer v. Evans, 517 U.S. 620 (1996).

• 10 •

Justice Scalia's Persuasive but Elitist Response to the Duck Hunting Controversy

March 2004

In response to a request that he recuse himself from the case of *Cheney v. United States District Court*, Justice Scalia issued a memorandum[1] explaining his reasons for denying the recusal motion. Despite having gone duck hunting in a group that included Vice President Cheney, Justice Scalia said, he could impartially adjudicate the issues of statutory interpretation and separation of powers that the case raises.

The heart of Justice Scalia's argument is both simple and persuasive. Nobody "who thought [Scalia] could decide this case impartially despite [his] friendship with the Vice President would reasonably believe that [he] cannot decide it impartially because [he] went hunting with that friend and accepted an invitation to fly there with him on a Government plane."[2]

That's exactly right, and under the law, it fully justifies Justice Scalia's refusal to recuse himself. Yet Justice Scalia's memorandum is nonetheless troubling because of the uncomfortable truth it reveals—that the capital of the world's most powerful nation is run by, and arguably for, an elite establishment.

The *Cheney* case arises out of the 2001 advisory committee on energy policy that Vice President Cheney headed. According to the complaint in the suit, that committee included energy industry executives, thus requiring disclosure of documents produced by the committee pursuant to the Federal Advisory Committee Act. Vice President Cheney argued in response that, among other things, such disclosure would amount to an unconstitutional interference with the functioning of the executive branch.

The Sierra Club is one of the parties seeking disclosure of the energy policy committee materials. It argued that Justice Scalia had created at least the appearance of impropriety by going on the duck-hunting trip with Vice President Cheney after the Court accepted review of the case. Per the Court's custom, Justice Scalia himself decided the recusal motion.

A federal statute provides that a Justice "shall disqualify himself in any proceeding in which his impartiality might reasonably be questioned."[3]

The Sierra Club argued that because numerous mainstream—and thus not unreasonable—newspaper editorials have called for Justice Scalia to recuse himself, his impartiality has reasonably been called into question.

Not so, said Justice Scalia, in refusing to recuse himself. Many of the newspaper editorials simply had the facts wrong, Justice Scalia claimed, and the relevant legal test turns on what a well-informed observer might reasonably conclude, not what an uninformed observer might think.

Contrary to some press accounts, Justice Scalia explained, he was never alone with Vice President Cheney for any substantial period, they did not discuss the case, and he did not derive any financial benefit from flying one-way on the Vice President's plane (because he had to purchase a round-trip ticket anyway).

The questions about Scalia's impartiality were also unreasonable, the Justice said, because they were poorly informed with respect to the law.

Under the law, he explained, friendship is appropriately a basis for recusal where the friend's personal interest—such as his liberty or property—is at stake. But where, as in the energy policy committee case, the question concerns the official actions of a friend, no recusal is necessary.

In support of his point, Justice Scalia cited numerous historical precedents of Justices socializing with Presidents and other executive officials with business before the Court. And he pointed out that were the rule otherwise—that is, were friendship or specific social contacts arising out of a friendship sufficient to require recusal in a case involving the friend in his official capacity—the Court would be overrun with recusal motions, and would have difficulty conducting much of its most important business with a full complement of Justices.

Recognizing the distinction between official and personal capacity cases, the Sierra Club had argued that Vice President Cheney's personal reputation is on the line in the pending litigation because, should he lose, he will be branded a lawbreaker who has corruptly turned the nation's welfare over to private profiteers.

But Justice Scalia thought that this sort of political damage would not substantially differentiate Cheney from any other losing litigant in an official capacity case. "[P]olitical consequences," Scalia wrote, "are not my concern."[4]

For the millions of Americans who still feel that Justice Scalia and the Court acted out of a concern for political consequences in *Bush v. Gore*,[5] that line is no doubt hard to swallow. But Justice Scalia is right that if that's the objection—if people think that Scalia and other Justices decide cases in a way that is calculated to advance the political careers of their friends—then the duck-hunting trip was a disingenuous basis for the recusal motion.

Suppose that Justice Scalia and his friend Vice President Cheney had also been accompanied on their duck-hunting trip by Justice Scalia's friend Justice Ruth Bader Ginsburg. (If you have difficulty imagining Justice Ginsburg hunting ducks, imagine the threesome at the opera instead.) Would anyone think that her impartiality would be called into question because of social interaction with the Vice President? Would the Sierra Club have sought her recusal?

Of course not. And why not? Because Justice Ginsburg is, as a matter of judicial philosophy, less prone to accept claims of executive power than Justice Scalia.[6]

The real objection, as everyone who understands what's going on here knows, is not that Justice Scalia went duck hunting with Vice President Cheney. The objection isn't that they're friends, either. The real objection is that Justice Scalia and Vice President Cheney share an approach to executive power that the plaintiffs dislike.

I dislike that approach as well. I also think that killing animals for sport (or food, for that matter) is wrong. But I don't see how either of those substantive views I hold counts as a basis for recusing Justice Scalia.

Thus, Justice Scalia was right not to recuse himself, and he has persuasively explained the grounds for his decision. Nonetheless, there is something objectionable about the tone, if not the substance, of his memorandum.

The not-so-subtle subtext of the opinion goes something like this: "We Supreme Court Justices are part of the ruling elite and we're entitled to live like it. How dare you commoners question our integrity!"

Indeed, these sentiments are not just in the subtext. Without a hint of apology, Justice Scalia writes that "[m]any Justices have reached this Court precisely because they were friends of the incumbent President or other senior officials."[7] Having friends in high places is, in other words, a qualification for the job, the Justice suggests—and it would be hypocritical to pretend otherwise.

To be clear, I believe that Justice Scalia made the right call and I do not mean to single him out among his colleagues. The elitism I detect in his memorandum could have emanated from any of the Justices. Even Justice Thomas, who grew up poor, is by this point part of the Washington establishment.

The problem the Sierra Club thought it saw in Justice Scalia's hunting trip was that he was too closely connected to the Bush Administration. Ultimately, that's exactly backwards.

The real problem with the Court is not its connection to the other powerful elites that run the country. The problem is the collective disconnection of all of these elites, taken together, from the masses of ordinary citizens. That's something to ponder at a time when the presidential election offers voters a choice between two Skull and Bones men.

POSTSCRIPT

The actual decision in the underlying case that gave rise to the duck-hunting controversy was something of an anti-climax. In June 2004, Justice Kennedy wrote an opinion for the Court that—pardon the expression—ducked the main issues and remanded to the appeals court for consideration of the separation-of-powers questions raised by Vice President Cheney.[8] That court then unanimously sided with Cheney on the merits.[9] In the Supreme Court decision itself, Justice Scalia joined a separate opinion by Justice Thomas that was more favorable to the Vice President than the position taken by any other Justice. Does that show that Justice Scalia acted improperly by failing to recuse himself? Hardly. After all, Justice Thomas wasn't on the duck-hunting trip. The votes of both Justices Scalia and Thomas are readily explained by their longstanding jurisprudential views.

NOTES

1. Cheney v. U. S. Dist. Court, 541 U.S. 913 (2004) (mem.) (Scalia, J.).
2. 541 U.S. at 928–29.
3. 28 U.S.C. § 455 (2000).
4. 541 U.S. at 920.
5. 531 U.S. 98 (2000) (per curiam).
6. *Compare, e.g.,* Clinton v. City of New York, 524 U.S. 417, 436–49 (1998) (Ginsburg, J., joining in the opinion of the Court) (holding the Line Item Veto Act, Pub. L. No. 104–130, 110 Stat. 1200 (1996), unconstitutional), *with id.* at 463–69 (Scalia, J., concurring in part and dissenting in part) (finding the President's authority under the Line Item Veto Act constitutional as applied to the facts of the case).
7. Cheney v. U.S. Dist. Court, 541 U.S. at 916.
8. Cheney v. U.S. Dist. Court, 542 U.S. 367 (2004).
9. *In re* Cheney, 406 F.3d 723 (D.C. Cir. 2005) (en banc).

• *11* •

Can a State Make It a Crime to Refuse to Identify Yourself to the Police? In a Narrow Ruling, the Supreme Court Says Yes

June 2004

In *Hiibel v. Sixth Judicial District Court,*[1] the U.S. Supreme Court upheld the conviction of Larry Dudley Hiibel, who had violated a Nevada statute that requires persons temporarily detained on "reasonable suspicion" of criminal activity to identify themselves to a police officer.

Hiibel—who claimed he had done nothing wrong and was simply the victim of mistaken identity—believed he had no obligation to tell the officer his name. But the Court found that neither Hiibel's Fourth Amendment right against unreasonable searches and seizures, nor his Fifth Amendment right against self-incrimination, was violated.

In so doing, the Court took some liberties in construing its own past precedents, prompting four Justices to dissent. But despite its technical deficiencies, the *Hiibel* decision does not threaten civil liberties.

Nor does it, as some commentators have suggested, pave the way for a system of compulsory national identification cards. Moreover, even if it did, such a system would not necessarily be unwise or unconstitutional.

Let's begin with the constitutional text. The Fourth Amendment prohibits "unreasonable searches and seizures," and authorizes search and arrest warrants only upon a showing of "probable cause" that a crime has been committed. This language has been construed by the Supreme Court to require that in most circumstances, the police must obtain a warrant for a search or an arrest.

But there are exceptions to the warrant requirement, including for "exigent circumstances": Where an emergency prevents the police from obtaining a warrant from a neutral magistrate, they may perform a warrantless search or arrest—if the facts known to them establish probable cause to believe that a crime has been committed.

In addition, there is an exception to the "probable cause" requirement for a warrantless search or arrest. In the 1968 case of *Terry v. Ohio*,[2] the Court held that police could "stop and frisk" a suspect on "reasonable suspicion" that he had already committed, or was about to commit, a crime. Such a pat-down search, of course, would be warrantless.

It has been generally understood that the "reasonable suspicion" standard is qualitatively and quantitatively lower than the "probable cause" standard that applies to full searches and arrests. Why was a lesser standard appropriate? The Court reasoned that because a stop and frisk subjects the suspect to a lesser forfeiture of his liberty, it could be justified by a lesser burden of proof—hence, the "reasonable suspicion" standard.

Later, in 1979, the Court refused to go further, and establish a standard even lower than "reasonable suspicion." In *Brown v. Texas*,[3] it held that absent reasonable suspicion of criminality, the police may not simply stop people on the street and ask for their names.

The issue in *Hiibel* was whether someone who had been lawfully subject to a *Terry* stop—that is, someone as to whom the police *did* have reasonable suspicion—can also be required to provide his name to the police officer who stopped him.

The Justices answered yes. But they divided 5–4 on the issue.

All nine Justices agreed that a person who is not behaving in a way that gives rise to an articulable suspicion of criminality may not be required to state his name or show identification. All nine Justices also agreed that under the Court's prior precedents, the police could *ask* a person who has been subject to a *Terry* stop for his name.

The only disagreement that split the Justices—and the specific issue the case addressed—was whether the person could be prosecuted for failing to answer that question.

Drawing upon the Supreme Court's prior precedents, the dissenting Justices—led by Justice Breyer—noted that the Court had previously stated that a person detained for a *Terry* stop "is not obliged to respond" to a police request that he identify himself.[4]

These dissenters acknowledged that the Court's prior statements were "technically dicta." ("Dicta" is a lawyer's term for non-binding asides that are included in a judicial opinion in the course of resolving other issues.) However, the dissenters opined that such "strong dicta" were by now part of the law.[5]

The dissenters also thought that the suspect's right to decline to provide his name was part of the original justification for permitting *Terry* stops on less than probable cause. The idea behind the lower "reasonable suspicion" standard, they pointed out, was that a *Terry* stop was a relatively minimal incursion on liberty. But a requirement that the suspect give his name—and the reality that he would be prosecuted if he did not—is an additional intrusion.

A fourth dissenter, Justice Stevens, thought that requiring a *Terry* detainee to answer questions violated his Fifth Amendment right against self-incrimination. Citing cases such as *Miranda v. Arizona*,[6] Justice Stevens insisted that the Court's own precedents recognized that the right against self-incrimination is not just a trial right.

If the right applies at the police station, as the *Miranda* decision says it does, Justice Stevens explained, surely it applies at a *Terry* stop as well. And if it applies at a *Terry* stop, then the subject has a right not to give his name; after all, giving one's name to a police officer investigating a possible crime puts one at risk of prosecution. It is thus compelled self-incrimination.

How did the majority respond to the dissenters? Speaking for the Court, Justice Kennedy pointed out that prior dicta were only dicta, after all. He noted that the Court had never formally decided the question at issue: whether a suspect must respond to a police officer's request that he identify himself.

Turning to that question, Justice Kennedy said that in many cases, knowing the identity of a *Terry* detainee would be of great value to the police in evaluating the situation. Consider Hiibel's case itself. There, the police had received a call describing an assault. Knowing the suspect's identity would enable them to know whether to make a full arrest, or to release Hiibel and continue to look for someone else. According to the majority, the same factors that make it reasonable for the police to ask a *Terry* detainee his identity make it reasonable to require that he answer.

Interestingly, Justice Kennedy's response to Justice Breyer's Fourth Amendment objections made his argument somewhat more vulnerable to the Fifth Amendment objections posed by Justice Stevens. Suppose one agrees with Justice Kennedy that the requirement that a suspect identify himself is indeed justified on the ground that his identity is relevant to determining whether he has engaged in criminal conduct. On that assumption, the requirement to identify oneself (or be prosecuted) appears to be a requirement that the suspect not just identify himself but in the process incriminate himself—in violation of the Fifth Amendment right against self-incrimination.

Justice Kennedy and the majority nonetheless attempted to thread the needle between the Fourth and Fifth Amendments—contending that compulsory identification fell in the territory between the two, and thus violated neither. They argued that a suspect's identity could be sufficiently relevant to make the requirement that he reveal it "reasonable" within the meaning of the Fourth Amendment, but could still not be so very relevant as to make it "incriminating" within the meaning of the Fifth Amendment.

The majority acknowledged that there might be rare cases where the mere statement of a person's name—in connection with other information known to the police—was so incriminating as to privilege a *Terry* detainee in refusing to identify himself. But the majority thought that in the typical case, and in Hiibel's case, there was no basis for Fifth Amendment protection.

Civil libertarians may worry that in the wake of *Hiibel*, the government will require all persons to carry formal identification papers with them or risk arrest. However, as noted above, the *Hiibel* majority took care not to disturb precedents like *Brown v. Texas*. Accordingly, it is clear that even after *Hiibel*, the Supreme Court will protect the right to remain anonymous of persons who are not suspected of any criminal wrongdoing.

To be sure, the reasonable suspicion standard is not as protective as the probable cause standard. But it is hardly toothless. On any given day, the overwhelming majority of the population takes no action that gives rise to reasonable suspicion for the police to stop and frisk.

Moreover, the fear that the *Terry* stop power will be converted into a police power to identify people seems backwards. A stop and frisk—in which the police physically accost and pat down a person—is more intrusive than a request for identification.

So if, as some commentators have claimed,[7] the reasonable suspicion standard is toothless, then since 1968 it has been causing more serious privacy invasions than anything authorized by the *Hiibel* decision.

Nonetheless, civil libertarians have good cause to see *Hiibel* as one step down a road—albeit a long road—toward allowing the government to require all persons to carry official identification, including a national identification card. And such a requirement would undoubtedly sacrifice privacy.

The ability to proceed about their daily business anonymously gives people a sense of privacy. To invert the old *Cheers* song, many of us want to go to a place where *nobody* knows our name.

But the sacrifice of privacy that a system of national identification cards would entail may well be justified if it provides greater security. Already, we as a society routinely produce identification to enter government buildings, sports arenas, and private office buildings.

Why is the requirement of producing identification before entering these venues tolerated? Presumably *not* because the edifices deserve special protection. Rather, those responsible for our security understand that terrorists target places in which large numbers of people congregate.

But as shown by bombings of a discotheque and private residences in Bali and Riyadh, respectively, terrorists will attack "soft targets" when more obvious targets are hardened.[8] And that means that if we want to protect not just buildings but people, we will want the police and FBI to be able to identify possible terrorists wherever they are.

In other words, given the nature of the threat, the reasonableness of identification requirements in selected public venues entails the reasonableness of identification requirements in general.

The real constitutional problem with a system of national identification cards is not that they sacrifice privacy for security. The Fourth Amendment sensibly makes the legality of a search or seizure turn on whether it is reasonable, and few would deny that a reasonableness standard must balance costs and benefits.

Likewise, although the Fifth Amendment's prohibition on compelled self-incrimination appears to speak in absolute terms, as with any constitutional provision, there is sufficient wiggle room in the doctrine to allow an interpretation that would permit a generally applicable requirement that people carry identification.

The real problem with a system of national identification cards is the potential for abuse. Government officials armed with detailed information about individuals' movements could use that information for private gain, personal vendettas, and mere prurient interest.

Indeed, as biometric identification systems advance, law enforcement officials will be able to obtain this information *without* any sort of national identification card and, given longstanding interpretations of the Fourth and Fifth Amendments, *without* constitutional constraint.

Thus, whether or not we move toward a system of national identification cards, and quite apart from any implications of the *Hiibel* decision, we need to find institutional mechanisms to ensure that the government does not abuse information about individuals' movements.

Strong statutory prohibitions backed by judicial review would comprise one such mechanism, so long as we can trust the courts to stand up to executive overreaching. Supreme Court decisions in cases arising out of the war on terror and other military conflicts will be a good test of that proposition.

POSTSCRIPT

As I discuss below in chapters 21 and 22, the courts have been somewhat willing to stand against the Bush Administration's boldest assertions of power to curtail civil liberties. That fact suggests that judges will do their duty if charged with enforcing laws limiting the ability of government officials to curtail other civil liberties, by, for example, abusing information about the movements of law-abiding citizens. But post hoc sanctions by a court are of limited utility at best. What is most needed in the event that we authorize law enforcement to gather identifying information about law-abiding citizens are internal checks that prevent abuses from occurring in the first place. And we are only likely to get those if politicians perceive that the public cares about threats to privacy. Accordingly, let me do my tiny bit by saying that what I have written about national identity cards should be taken as endorsing them only on the condition that they are accompanied by a regime of effective monitoring for abuse.

NOTES

1. 542 U.S. 177 (2004) (upholding Nev. Rev. Stat. § 171.123 (2003)).
2. 392 U.S. 1 (1968).
3. 443 U.S. 47, 52–53 (1979).
4. *Hiibel*, 542 U.S. at 198 (Breyer, J., dissenting) (quoting Berkemer v. McCarty, 468 U.S. 420, 439 (1984)).
5. *Id.*
6. 384 U.S. 436 (1966).
7. *See, e.g.*, Danielle Sucher, *Must Americans Carry Identification, or Else Risk Arrest?* Findlaw, Nov. 12, 2003, http://writ.news.findlaw.com/student/20031112_sucher.html.
8. *See* Raymond Bonner & Don Van Natta Jr., *Regional Terrorist Groups Pose Growing Threat, Experts Warn*, N.Y. Times, Feb. 8, 2004, at A1.

• 12 •

Why Swift Boat Veterans for Truth and Other 527 Organizations Can't Be Silenced

September 2004

When asked whether he supports the attacks on John Kerry's Vietnam War record by Swift Boat Veterans for Truth, President Bush has repeatedly dodged the question.

To his credit, the President has said that Kerry admirably served his country. But Bush has not specifically condemned the Swift Boat advertisements, which falsely claim that Kerry lied about the events that led to his combat medals.

Instead, the President has called for an end to all political ads by so-called 527 organizations, which are not subject to the restrictions on campaign finance that apply to campaigns and the major parties.[1] His position would eliminate ads by the Swift Boat Veterans for Truth, which is a 527, but would also shut down wholly truthful ads by every other such organization as well.

Then, Bush upped the ante. Calling the "shadowy" 527s "bad for the system," he enlisted campaign finance hero John McCain's support for new legislation.[2] Their proposed law would forbid 527s from raising and spending money outside of the federal restrictions.[3]

It's true that, as Bush and McCain claim, 527s do circumvent the spirit—if not the letter—of existing campaign finance limits. Yet new legislation is unlikely to cure the problem. That's because the "problem" is that the people who contribute to 527s are thereby exercising their First Amendment rights to engage in political speech.

What is a 527 organization? Section 527 of the Internal Revenue Code sets forth the very limited circumstances under which a political organization may be required to pay federal tax.[4] The key to a 527, however, is not the tax rules that apply to it, but the campaign finance laws that do not apply to it.

To be more precise, the campaign finance laws don't apply to one particular kind of 527. Political Action Committees (or PACs) and some other political entities are 527s, but they are subject to campaign finance restrictions. In contrast, there are non-PAC 527s like Swift Boat Veterans for Truth and America Coming Together (a pro-Democratic group), which, as of the 2004 presidential election cycle, are not subject to such restrictions.

Under the current interpretation of the laws governing federal elections, a political organization can raise and spend unlimited sums of money if it fits two criteria: First, it must raise money only from individuals (as opposed to raising so-called soft money from corporations and unions). Second, it cannot coordinate its activities with the candidates or parties.

Thus, while an individual billionaire can give no more than $2,000 to Bush or Kerry, he can give millions to Swift Boat Veterans or America Coming Together. And unlike an organization that receives soft money funding from unions or corporations, a 527 is free to run as many political advertisements as it wants, as close to the election as it wants, as long as it doesn't coordinate its activities with the official campaigns.

President Bush's opposition to 527 spending, it turns out, is not simply altruistic. Republicans traditionally enjoy a fundraising edge over Democrats. But pro-Kerry (or at least anti-Bush) 527s have had greater fundraising success than pro-Bush 527s in the 2004 electoral cycle—thus cutting into the Republicans' overall dollar advantage.

In March 2004, the Bush-Cheney campaign filed a complaint with the Federal Election Commission (or FEC). The campaign charged that various pro-Kerry 527s were violating federal campaign finance laws. It alleged, among other things, that the supposed non-PAC 527s are in fact PACs subject to campaign finance restrictions—because their primary purpose is to support or oppose a particular candidate.

Meanwhile, both campaigns have complained that 527s supporting the other candidate have been violating the rules—by accepting soft money, and by coordinating their activities with the candidates and parties.

Will the FEC take action clarifying the status of 527s? That is extremely unlikely, at least until after the 2004 presidential election. For that reason, the Bush-Cheney campaign has dropped its action before the FEC and taken its case to court.

The prospects of the litigation are uncertain. But whatever the outcome,[5] making 527s subject to campaign finance laws will not, in the end, do much to address the underlying issue that the lawsuits, FEC actions, and proposed legislation have raised.

In its 2003 decision in *McConnell v. FEC*,[6] the Supreme Court upheld most of the Bipartisan Campaign Reform Act (or BCRA).[7] The majority opinion, jointly written by Justices Stevens and O'Connor, explained why: According to the Court, the law serves a compelling interest in avoiding the appearance and reality of corruption that can arise when candidates are beholden to large donors, and this interest is sufficient to justify the Act's free speech restrictions.

Interestingly, however, even as the majority Justices upheld BCRA, they concluded their opinion with the frank admission that they did not expect BCRA to be fully effective: "Money, like water, will always find an outlet."[8]

Here's why BCRA is at best a partial solution to the influence of money on politics. Suppose a person with cash to spend really wants to support a candidate. Then she will donate to that candidate's campaign. If she is limited in how much money she can give to the campaign, she will give to the candidate's party. If she is limited in how much she can give to a party, she will give to an independent organization that shares her goals, like a 527. And if all 527s are brought within the campaign finance system, she will become more creative still, perhaps fronting large sums of money to would-be Michael Moores interested in making films with a political message she supports.

Does that mean that laws like BCRA are wholly ineffective? Not necessarily. One effect of successive rounds of legislation and court rulings has been to move money further upstream from the candidates. That is probably the right thing to do if one is concerned about the appearance of corruption.

If they are large enough, direct campaign contributions to candidates do look suspiciously like bribes. In contrast, truly independent expenditures create less suspicion of a quid pro quo. Candidates whose campaigns receive a boost by action at several removes from large donors are less susceptible to requests for favors than candidates who receive cash directly.

Yet corruption in the sense of bribery is not, or should not be, the law's only concern in this area. There is also the matter of truth and accountability, and pushing money upstream from the candidates works *against* these values.

For example, one of the provisions of BCRA requires that a federal candidate appear in his television advertisement and state that he approved it.[9] The "stand-by-your-ad" provision was designed to promote positive campaigning by making candidates take the heat for their negative or unfair ads. But of course, this provision, while applicable to candidates, does not apply to independent ads by 527s.

That explains, to some extent, the actions of one non-PAC 527 organization—Swift Boat Veterans for Truth. They presumably felt free to sling mud at Senator Kerry without worrying that it would splash back on President Bush, because they thought they could plausibly claim to be independent of the President's campaign.

Suppose that our campaign finance laws permitted the people now contributing to groups like Swift Boat Veterans to give more money to the campaigns. They probably would redirect their funds to the candidates, who would then have an incentive to spend the money on more responsible ads—or, at least, if the candidates chose to spend their money on irresponsible ads, they could be held accountable for that choice.

Faced with these perverse consequences, one may be tempted to follow the course outlined by President Bush: make the non-PAC 527s comply with the same federal fundraising and spending rules as other political organizations.

But the individuals who give money to non-PAC 527s are exercising their constitutional rights. Taken together, the right to freedom of speech and the right of political association entail a right of individuals to band together and pool their resources to support a common message.

To be sure, *McConnell* and other Supreme Court decisions recognize that this right can be restricted to avoid corruption. At some point, however, the anti-corruption rationale runs out, and the constitutional rights of the speaker take over.

Plausible arguments can be made that 527s are engaged in campaign speech, and that they are thus subject to regulation under existing law—or, at least, that our laws could be amended to make 527s subject to regulation without doing violence to the First Amendment. But if the Supreme Court is right, the effect of doing so would simply be to push the money still further upstream.

Is that what we want? Recall the tradeoff: As the speakers have to be more and more distant from the candidates, in order to escape campaign finance regulation, the candidates become less and less accountable for that speech. In other words, the effect of closing the 527 "loophole" could be to spur the creation of even less responsible speakers next time around.

There is, however, an alternative response to irresponsible advertisements by groups like Swift Boat Veterans for Truth, one that is true to our First Amendment heritage: more speech. As Justice Brandeis memorably stated in his concurrence in the 1927 case of *Whitney v. California*, "the fitting remedy for evil counsels is good ones."[10]

So what action should be taken by Kerry supporters upset by the falsehoods presented by Swiftboat Veterans for Truth, or by Bush supporters distressed by the conspiracy theories fostered by *Fahrenheit 9/11*? Don't run to the FEC or the courts. Instead, rally your own 527s. As both Bush and Kerry like to say, bring it on.

POSTSCRIPT

The debate over campaign finance regulation is a nice example of how labels like "conservative" and "liberal" oversimplify complex policy and legal positions. Supporters of campaign finance regulation include both prominent Democrats like Senator Russ Feingold and Representative Marty Meehan as well as prominent Republicans like Senator John McCain and Representative Christopher Shays. The most outspoken politician opposing campaign finance regulation is Republican Senator Mitch McConnell, but traditionally Democratic groups, such as labor unions, have also opposed campaign finance limits that they view as interfering with their constitutional rights.[11]

Accordingly, when this chapter first appeared as a column, I was not sure what to expect by way of reaction. As it turned out, I was deluged with critical mail. But much to my surprise, the critics did not object to my analysis of the campaign finance issues. Instead, nearly all of my critical mail came from Kerry haters who were outraged at my offhand statement that the representations in the Swift Boat Veterans advertisements were false.[12] Sometimes you can't win.

NOTES

1. *See* Jim Rutenberg & Kate Zernike, *Bush Says He Will Back McCain on Ad Crackdown*, N.Y. Times, Aug. 27, 2004, at A17.

2. *See* The President's News Conference in Crawford, Texas, 40 Weekly Comp. Pres. Doc. 1671 (Aug. 23, 2004); Tim Jones & John McCormick, *Attack Ads by 527s Spark Bitter Debate*, Chi. Trib., Aug. 27, 2004, at C1.

3. Within a month of the date that this chapter was originally published as a column, Senator McCain and others introduced the 527 Reform Act of 2004, S. 2828, 108th Cong. The bill was reintroduced with changes in 2005, 527 Reform Act of 2005, S. 271, 109th Cong., and as of summer 2005, the bill had undergone further modifications and was on the Senate Legislative Calendar. *See* 527 Reform Act of 2005, S. 1053, 109th Cong.

4. 26 U.S.C. § 527 (2004).

5. On September 15, 2004, the D.C. District Court denied the Bush–Cheney '04 campaign's motion for a preliminary injunction that would have forced the FEC to rule on the campaign's two prior administrative complaints within thirty days, or, in the event that the FEC failed to meet the deadline, granted a federal cause of action to the campaign. Bush–Cheney '04, Inc. v. FEC, No. CV 04–1501 (D.D.C. Sept. 15, 2004), *available at* http://www.brookings.edu/dybdocroot/gs/cf/20040915_argument.pdf. Information on that case, as well as information on a separate suit that the campaign brought against the FEC, is available at the FEC's website: http://www.fec.gov/law/litigation.shtml.

6. 540 U.S. 93 (2003).

7. The BCRA can be found at Pub. L. No. 107–155, 116 Stat. 81 (2002) (codified primarily in scattered sections of 2 and 47 U.S.C. (2005)).

8. *McConnell*, 540 U.S. at 224.

9. *See* 47 U.S.C. § 315(b)(2)(C) (2004).

10. 274 U.S. 357, 375 (1927) (Brandeis, J., concurring).

11. *Compare* Brief for Intervenor-Defendants Sen. John McCain, Sen. Russell Feingold, Rep. Christopher Shays, Rep. Martin Meehan, Sen. Olympia Snowe, and Sen. James Jeffords at 8, McConnell v. FEC, 540 U.S. 93 (2003) (No. 02–1674) 2003 WL 21999280 ("BCRA responded to the collapse of the [previous federal campaign contribution] regime in a considered and measured way. The law should be sustained in its entirety.") *with* Reply Brief of AFL-CIO Appellants/Cross-Appellees, *McConnell*, 540 U.S. 93 (No. 02–1674) (arguing that BRCA is unconstitutional for various reasons), 2003 WL 22002434. *See also* Shays v. FEC, 337 F. Supp. 2d 28 (D.D.C. 2004) (finding in part for Representatives Shays and Meehan in their suit against the FEC).

12. I based my statement on the definitive account of Kerry's service in Vietnam: Douglas Brinkley, Tour of Duty: John Kerry and the Vietnam War (New York: William Morrow, 2004). Brinkley's account details the events that earned Kerry his first Purple Heart, *id.* at 147–48, his second Purple Heart, *id.* at 287, his third Purple Heart, *id.* at 303–18, and both his Silver Star, *id.* at 289–95, and Bronze Star, *id.* at 303–18.

• 13 •

Does the Constitution Permit the Blue States to Secede? With Permission, Perhaps; Unilaterally, No

November 2004

Still smarting from the results of the 2004 presidential and congressional elections, a number of Democrats and liberal pundits have opined that the "blue states" ought to secede from the Union. The electoral map looks amenable to the plan. By joining with culturally sympathetic Canada, the blue states of the East Coast, the West Coast, and the upper Midwest could create a contiguous land mass, with only the islands of the blue state of Hawaii left at a distance.

Talk of secession is not meant to be taken literally. Instead, those who raise the subject wish to underscore the degree to which cultural and political divisions track geographic ones. Appearances can be deceptive, however. Blue states contain many Republicans, just as red states contain many Democrats.[1] Even the rhetorical point of contemporary secessionists is thus subject to question.

But the legality of secession nonetheless warrants serious consideration. Understanding why it is not a realistic option will help us understand the sense in which the United States is—for all its divisions—a Union.

As I explain below, it is settled law that the Constitution does not permit unilateral secession: A state or group of states cannot simply leave the Union over the objections of the national government. However, the arguments that led to this settled understanding are hardly unassailable, and the Constitution is probably best read as permitting the mutually agreed upon departure of one or more states.

Almost immediately upon entering the Union, with the ratification of the Constitution in 1789, states began threatening to secede. In 1790, the House of Representatives received a petition from a group of Pennsylvania abolitionists that included Benjamin Franklin. In response, members of the Georgia and South Carolina congressional delegations intimated that if Congress attempted to manumit slaves, their states would leave the Union.

The threat was taken seriously. Congress denied the Pennsylvanians the relief they sought, an immediate abolition of the slave trade. Moreover, in response to the petition, a House resolution was passed affirming that Congress lacked any power to abolish slavery.

Secessionist sentiment in the early American republic was not confined to Southern defenders of slavery. In 1804, members of the declining Federalist Party in New England and New York plotted secession from a country ruled by the Republican Thomas Jefferson. And again in 1815, at the Hartford Convention, New England Federalists considered (though they ultimately rejected) secession as a means of promoting the sectional interests that they thought President James Madison's prosecution of the War of 1812 was harming.

For the rest of the pre–Civil War period, Southerners such as John Calhoun typically made arguments for secession whenever it appeared that national action to limit slavery was under contemplation.

The U.S. Constitution does not expressly recognize or deny a right of secession. Accordingly, the argument for a right of unilateral secession begins (and pretty much ends) with a claim about the very nature of the Constitution.

That document, by the terms of its Article VII, only obtained legal force through ratification by nine states, and then only in the states so ratifying it. Because the Constitution derived its initial force from the voluntary act of consent by the sovereign states, secessionists argued, a state could voluntarily and unilaterally withdraw its consent from the Union.

In this view, the Constitution is a kind of multilateral treaty, which derives its legal effect from the consent of the sovereign parties to it. Just as sovereign nations can withdraw from a treaty, so too can the sovereign states withdraw from the Union.

Most of the arguments against a right of unilateral secession can be found in President Abraham Lincoln's First Inaugural Address of March 1861. But as University of Texas Law Professor Sanford Levinson observes in a recent article in the *Tulsa Law Review*, Lincoln's case against a unilateral right of secession is hardly airtight.[2]

First, Lincoln asserted that the fundamental law in every national government rejects the idea of its own termination. And indeed, as of 1861, no national constitutions *expressly* provided for their own dissolution. But this argument does not respond to the secessionists' claim that the U.S. Constitution's Article VII *impliedly* provided for the possibility of dissolution.

Second, Lincoln denied that the Union was a mere voluntary association—and claimed that even if it were, ordinary principles of contract law would bar unilateral secession. Lincoln noted that while one party can *breach* a contract, the consent of all parties is required to *rescind* a contract. But secessionists analogized the Constitution to a treaty, not a contract—on the ground that each state was more like a sovereign nation than a human being. And while the modern international law of treaties also prohibits unilateral rescision except on terms spelled out in the treaty itself, arguably the notion of sovereignty to which eighteenth-century secessionists appealed would have permitted unilateral rescission of a treaty.

Third, Lincoln claimed that the Union was older than the Constitution. In his view, it dated as far back as the Articles of Association of 1774, when the signatory parties were all colonies of England. Lincoln's claim, however, does not respond to the secessionist argument rooted in Article VII; in the secessionists' view, the Constitution implicitly affirmed a right to secede from the Union, regardless of the pre-Constitution character of the Union.

Moreover, experience in the very early days of the Constitution belies Lincoln's assertion. Nationalists frequently claim that the states were never sovereign: As colonies, they were under British dominion, and they declared and won their independence as the *United* States. Thus, the nationalists opine, there was no time during which any of the states exercised full sovereignty. Yet, as Professor Levinson has noted, that is not entirely true: North Carolina and Rhode Island, which did not ratify the Constitution until after President Washington was inaugurated, were treated by the new national government as essentially foreign sovereigns until they formally accepted the Constitution. That treatment, Levinson argues, and I tend to agree, indicates that *all* the states were in an important sense sovereign when they entered into the Constitution.

Fourth and finally, Lincoln denied that the Constitution was silent with respect to secession. The immediate predecessor to the Constitution, the Articles of Confederation, purported to establish a "perpetual Union." By seeking to create what the Preamble calls "a more perfect Union"—in an echo of the Articles' language—the Constitution, Lincoln said, simply strengthened the already indissoluble bonds between the states.

But the Constitution itself was established in violation of the terms of the Articles—which required unanimous consent of the states for any amendment. Moreover, how do we know that the "perfection" of the Union required stronger, rather than weaker bonds? To infer this point from the fact that, on the whole, the Constitution created a stronger national government than existed under the Articles, is to acknowledge that the real work in this argument is not being done by the language of the Preamble.

Perhaps the best argument for Lincoln's view is one that he did not make expressly, but that can fairly be inferred from his general approach: Whatever the status of the states when they entered the Union, they perpetually gave up important attributes of sovereignty in doing so. Among these was—and is—any right of unilateral secession.

In this view, it is significant that Article VII sets out the provision for original ratification, and that Article IV empowers Congress to admit new states, but that no provision of the Constitution authorizes a state to leave the Union. The juxtaposition of what the Constitution says about states entering the Union with what it does not say about them leaving, indicates that the door to the Union swings in but not out.

But this inference is only that, an inference, and there was considerable uncertainty about the legality of unilateral secession in the first seven decades following the Constitution's adoption. That uncertainty was put to rest not by the superior strength of the anti-secessionist argument, but by Lee's surrender to Grant at Appomattox.

The military resolution of the secession question was then given legal force by the U.S. Supreme Court in the 1868 case of *Texas v. White*. The Court ruled there that even Texas—an independent republic before it joined the Union in 1845—had no right to secede. "The Constitution," the Court said, "in all its provisions, looks to an indestructible Union, composed of indestructible States."[3]

In this regard, *Texas v. White* is settled law. It stands for the proposition that the Constitution prohibits unilateral secession. What does *Texas v. White* have to say about secession by mutual agreement?

If the Union is truly indestructible, then states cannot secede, even if the national government is willing to let them go. Can that be right? Are the states trapped in a permanent marriage that even an amicable divorce cannot end?

There is reason to think that the Supreme Court's "indestructible" formulation in *Texas v. White* was hyperbole. After all, Article IV makes clear that the *states* are not indestructible. Congress can, with the approval of the state in question, shatter a state into fragments.[4] That is how Massachusetts divided into what we now call Maine and Massachusetts in 1820.

So if the states are not really indestructible, as the Court in *Texas v. White* claimed, perhaps the Union isn't indestructible either.

And indeed, the Supreme Court in *Texas v. White* recognized that secession by mutual agreement stands on a different footing from unilateral secession. After finding against a state's right of unilateral secession, the Court acknowledged an exception for secession "through revolution, or through consent of the States."[5]

Let us put aside the possibility of revolution, for a revolution is the repudiation of the existing legal regime. Presumably, any change at all could be authorized by a successful revolution—in the sense that after the revolution the legal rules that existed under the prior constitution would have no further independent force. What about the reference to "consent of the States?"

Despite their rhetoric about the permanence and indestructibility of the Union, both Lincoln in his First Inaugural, and the Supreme Court in *Texas v.*

White, strongly implied that it would be possible for one or more states to leave the Union with the consent of the Union as a whole.

By what legal mechanism would such secession through mutual agreement be accomplished? The most obvious answer is a statute enacted by Congress. Just as Congress can approve the admission of new states, the argument would go, so it can let old states leave.

Yet lodging the power to approve secession in Congress presents at least two difficulties.

The first difficulty is a matter of arithmetic. Suppose that Congress simultaneously received secession petitions from all the blue states, and that the congressional delegations of these states all supported these petitions. Suppose further that a minority of the congressional representatives of the red states also supported the petitions. (Their reaction: "Good riddance.") Adding the votes of representatives from the blue states to the votes of representatives from the minority of red states would yield a pro-secession majority in the *existing* Congress.

But notice what happens if Congress permits secession under these circumstances: Secession will have been allowed even though a majority of the representatives of one of the resulting pieces—the remaining red state rump United States—opposed it. That hardly seems consistent with the notion of secession by *mutual* agreement.

One might thus conclude that Congress can only approve a secession petition if the controlling bill obtains a majority of the votes of representatives of non-seceding states in both houses of Congress.

But while that solution makes some theoretical sense, it is also, from a constitutional perspective, arbitrary. Why this particular mechanism rather than some other mechanism—such as a national referendum, or a two-thirds (or three-quarters or three-fifths) vote in the existing Congress?

Once we acknowledge the ad hoc character of any mechanism by which Congress would approve secession petitions, we must confront a deeper conceptual problem: Congress only has the powers enumerated in the Constitution. Yet as we saw in our discussion of unilateral secession, despite granting Congress the power to admit new states, the Constitution says nothing about secession. And under the Tenth Amendment, silence in such matters means there is no federal power: Powers not enumerated "are reserved to the states respectively, or to the people."

How might the states respectively, or the people, act collectively to approve the secession of one or more states? The Constitution sets forth no mechanism to answer this question either, although the process of constitutional amendment would pretty clearly suffice.

Although the Constitution sets forth a number of mechanisms for its own amendment, the same procedure has almost always been used: proposal of amendments by a two-thirds vote in each house of Congress, followed by ratification by three-fourths of the state legislatures.[6] This formula seems well designed to ensure that any secession petition has the backing of the nation as a whole.

Recent Canadian experience is instructive on this last point. In 1998, in the *Reference re Secession of Quebec*,[7] the Supreme Court of Canada held that neither the Constitution of Canada, nor international law, gives Quebec a right to secede unilaterally. Nevertheless, the Court also said that if a secession referendum were to be adopted by the people of Quebec, the national government of Canada would incur a duty to enter into good-faith negotiations toward a secession agreement that would then be adopted by constitutional amendment.

But the notion that secession by mutual agreement in the United States requires a constitutional amendment itself creates conceptual difficulty. A plain reading of the U.S. Constitution makes clear that secession can be approved by amendment: The text of Article V purports to make only two provisions of the rest of the Constitution unamendable, and the absence of authority to approve secession is not one of these unamendable features. So if the Supreme Court in *Texas v. White* thought that secession could only be approved by constitutional amendment, why did the Justices distinguish between unilateral secession and secession by mutual agreement?

In so doing, the Court must have meant to imply that *under the existing Constitution*, there is some mechanism for secession by mutual agreement. A constitutional amendment, once adopted, could authorize unilateral secession as well as secession by mutual agreement. It only made sense for the *White* Court to distinguish between unilateral secession and secession by mutual agreement on the assumption that the Constitution we have already permits the latter—albeit through a wholly unspecified mechanism.

With respect to the possibility of secession by mutual agreement, we are left in much the same position that Americans in the first seven decades of the Union occupied with respect to unilateral secession: We must struggle to interpret the sounds of the Constitution's silence.

That conclusion in turn suggests that no court will likely answer the question—except perhaps in the way that the Supreme Court in *Texas v. White* gave its retroactive approval to the verdict of the Civil War battlefield.

Fortunately, the prospect of a twenty-first-century civil war that, like the Civil War of the nineteenth century, results in the deaths of over half a million Americans, still seems unthinkable. That should serve as a useful reminder that, whatever the real differences between Americans in blue states and red states are today, they are nothing like the differences that just a few generations ago divided citizens of the blue states and the gray states.

POSTSCRIPT

Not only does time heal all wounds; it also permits sober reflection on legal issues that were once inextricably intertwined with political ones that are no longer salient. Thus, I can write today that the original Constitution might plausibly have been understood to permit secession without fear that in doing so I encourage bona fide secessionists whose cause (whether they admitted this to themselves or not) was bound up with the preservation of slavery. Thankfully, that issue has passed into history.

It is more difficult to maintain some historical perspective on today's politically salient issues. Consider, for instance, that since the Republican Party gained control of both the Senate and the White House in 2002, Republicans have criticized the Democratic minority in the Senate for its use and threatened use of the filibuster against judicial nominees they deem too far to the right of the legal mainstream.[8] Yet just a few years earlier, when President Clinton was nominating judges to a Senate narrowly controlled by Democrats, the parties' respective positions were precisely the opposite.[9] There are undoubtedly good arguments for and against the filibuster, but surely they don't turn on whether it's deployed by Democrats or Republicans.

In a famous 1959 law review article, my late Columbia Law School colleague Herbert Wechsler argued that whatever practices prevail in the political realm, judges should only rely upon arguments that do not depend on the identity of the party that they happen to help in a particular case.[10] The article drew considerable criticism, mostly because Wechsler opined, at its end, that although he personally disapproved of racial segregation, he had not yet been persuaded that the Supreme Court's 1954 decision invalidating segregation was correct as a matter of constitutional law. But putting that issue aside, Wechsler's larger point should not have been controversial. For surely it is fair to demand of our judges that, at a minimum, they consistently apply the legal principles that they invoke to justify the decisions they reach. Principles can have exceptions, to be sure, but these too must be rooted in principle. An exception for Republicans, or Democrats, or white people, or some other arbitrarily chosen group, won't cut it.

NOTES

1. *See generally* Morris P. Fiorina et al., Culture War? The Myth of a Polarized America (New York: Longman, 2004).

2. Sanford Levinson, *"Perpetual Union," "Free Love," and Secession: On The Limits to "The Consent of The Governed,"* 39 Tulsa L. Rev. 457, 481 (New York: Pearson Education, 2d

ed., 2004) ("So, what is my own conclusion with regard to Lincoln's argument against secession? It is the classic 'Scotch verdict,' i.e., 'not proven.'").

3. 74 U.S. 700, 725 (1869).

4. "[N]o new State shall be formed or erected within the Jurisdiction of any other State; nor any State be formed by the Junction of two or more States, or Parts of States, without the Consent of the Legislatures of the States concerned as well as of the Congress." U.S. Const. art. IV, § 3, cl. 1.

5. *White*, 74 U.S. at 726.

6. The alternative mechanism for proposing amendments, a national convention, has never been used, and the alternative method for ratifying them, state conventions, has been used only once—to ratify the Twenty-First Amendment, which repealed Prohibition.

7. [1998] 2 S.C.R. 217.

8. A May 2005 compromise among moderates of both parties for the time being averted a showdown over the filibuster. *See* Carl Hulse, *Bipartisan Group in Senate Averts Judge Showdown*, N.Y. Times, May 24, 2005, at A1. As this book goes to press it remains unknown what will happen should Democrats—or, in a future Senate, Republicans—attempt to filibuster a judicial nominee.

9. For example, Republican Senate Majority Leader Bill Frist, who led the charge against the Democrats filibustering in 2005, voted against cloture during the filibuster of Richard Paez, a Clinton nominee to the Ninth Circuit Court of Appeals. *See* Dana Milbank, *The Killer Instinct*, Wash. Post, May 19, 2005, at A14. In 1995, some current Democratic Senators, including Barbara Boxer, Joseph Lieberman, Russ Feingold, Edward Kennedy, and John Kerry, supported a proposed rule change more extensive than the one suggested by Republicans in 2005. Not limited to judicial nominees, the 1995 rule change would have effectively ended the filibuster. *See* 141 Cong. Rec. S430 (1995); Craig Gilbert, *GOP Says Democrats Have Flip-Flopped on Filibuster; Feingold Voted to Curb it 10 Years Ago; Now He Says it's Essential*, Milwaukee J. Sentinel, Apr. 24, 2005, at A1.

10. Herbert Wechsler, *Toward Neutral Principles of Constitutional Law*, 73 Harv. L. Rev. 1, 12 (1959).

• 14 •

How the *Schiavo* Federal Court Case Might Have Been Won

March 2005

The Terri Schiavo case made headlines with its swift and unsuccessful journey through the federal courts. The string of court defeats might have left the impression that the case was doomed from the outset. Yet the litigation's failure may owe more to a poor tactical choice by the lawyers advising the Schindlers—Terri's parents—than to the case's underlying merits.

The original Schindler complaint included a variety of federal constitutional and statutory claims. Each of them was weak at best, as was quickly reflected in Federal District Judge James Whittemore's ruling that the Schindlers had failed to establish a likelihood of success on the merits of any of them.[1]

Moreover, the claims set forth in the Schindlers' original complaint failed to take advantage of the procedural opportunities that Congress presented them in the special bill it passed on their behalf, commonly known as Terri's Law.[2] Each of the claims in the original complaint permitted the district court to decide the merits without receiving new evidence. Thus, Judge Whittemore refused to issue an order restoring the feeding tube pending the outcome of a trial he thought unnecessary. And neither the Eleventh Circuit Court of Appeals nor the U.S. Supreme Court was willing to intervene.[3]

After their first unsuccessful trip all the way up the federal judicial ladder ended on March 24, 2005, the Schindlers returned to the federal district court the next day. The amended complaint they then filed contained one potentially meritorious claim, but by that time the courts had probably concluded that there was nothing to their case. Accordingly, Judge Whittemore and the Eleventh Circuit Court of Appeals made short work of their five new claims.[4]

Had the Schindlers put their best foot forward in the initial complaint and motion for a preliminary injunction, however, they might well have fared better.

What was the potentially successful claim that appears to have been tacked onto the end of the amended complaint as a mere afterthought? It asserted, fittingly enough, that disconnecting Terri Schiavo from her feeding tube violated a constitutional right to life protected by the Fourteenth Amendment. That claim was stronger than the others and should have positioned the Schindlers to make good use of Terri's Law. It had the added virtue of encapsulating what the case was really about, at least from their perspective. But presented as it was at the eleventh hour, the right-to-life claim came across as too little, too late.

To see how the Schindlers might have won, it is first worth examining why they lost—by looking at the weaknesses of each of the claims in their original complaint.

First, the Schindlers contended that the state court trial judge who had ordered the removal of Terri's feeding tube had denied her federal constitutional right to an impartial decision maker. Rather than acting as a judge, they argued, Florida Circuit Judge George Greer had become her health care surrogate.

But Florida law expressly authorizes a trial judge to resolve disputes between a spouse designated as health care proxy and other family members, where they arise.[5] Judge Greer was simply acting as a judge, looking at evidence to decide a factual matter: whether Terri's husband or her parents were right about what she would have wanted.

Second, the Schindlers claimed that Judge Greer violated constitutional due process by failing to appoint a *guardian ad litem* or a lawyer for Terri. But due process simply requires representation—and Terri had that in abundance. Michael Schiavo's lawyers made the arguments tending to show that she was in a persistent vegetative state and would want the feeding tube out, while the Schindlers' lawyers made the arguments tending to show that she had some cognitive function and would want the feeding tube to remain in. That is exactly how the adversary system is supposed to work, and additional lawyers would not have raised additional points.

Third, the Schindlers claimed that Judge Greer violated due process in that he never personally visited Terri. But there is no federal constitutional right to have a judge make a fact-finding field trip: Courts routinely hear evidence in their courtrooms. Here, the court took testimony from five physicians who had personally examined Terri.

Fourth, the Schindlers alleged that Florida law violates the Fourteenth Amendment's Equal Protection Clause by discriminating against incapacitated persons such as their daughter. How so? In general, Florida law permits judges to serve as proxy decision makers for their own family members but not for others; yet Florida permits judges to play this role (in certain circumstances) when a party before the court is incapacitated.

Under the relevant Supreme Court precedents, including the 2001 decision in *Board of Trustees of the University of Alabama v. Garrett*,[6] distinctions on the basis of physical or mental disability are only subject to the most minimal judicial scrutiny; if they are barely "rational," that is enough. And of course it's rational to distinguish for this limited purpose between people who are too incapacitated to express their wishes and people who are not.

Fifth, the Schindlers argued that Terri's First Amendment right to the free exercise of religion had been infringed. But under the 1990 Supreme Court precedent of *Employment Division v. Smith*,[7] the government does not infringe on the constitutional right to free exercise of religion when it applies a general law to someone whose religion would otherwise require a different outcome. And here, the Florida law for determining when a feeding tube may be removed was generally applicable.

Sixth, the Schindlers invoked the Religious Land Use and Institutionalized Persons Act[8] (RLUIPA), which mandates a more generous standard for judging free exercise claims by persons whom the government has confined to an institution. For them, a condition is legally impermissible if it imposes a "substantial burden" on religious exercise, even if the burden arises out of a general law or policy—unless the burden serves a compelling interest.

Judge Whittemore thought this claim had little likelihood of success because the statute's language only applies to conditions imposed by "government." As I discuss below in connection with the "right-to-life" claim, that reasoning is questionable. Nonetheless, Judge Whittemore appears to have been correct in his bottom line conclusion that the RLUIPA claim had little likelihood of success on the merits. In addition to requiring government action, RLUIPA requires that the person on whose behalf the claim is being asserted be in a *state-run* institution, and The Hospice of the Florida Suncoast, Inc., where Terri was institutionalized, probably does not count.

Terri's Law gave the Schindlers a remarkable—and in some ways, unprecedented—opportunity. Congress empowered them to litigate anew any issues relating to their daughter's condition. Violations of Terri's rights were to be determined without regard to any prior rulings by the state courts: de novo, in lawyer's jargon.

Yet for the most part, the Schindlers and their lawyers squandered their opportunity by initially presenting claims that alleged that the state courts themselves had denied Terri her procedural rights. The only way for the federal courts to evaluate those claims was to look at what happened in state court—that is, to *evaluate* rather than *ignore* what occurred in state court. Not surprisingly, the federal courts were reluctant to say that anything that happened in state court was so irregular as to constitute a denial of due process.

To be sure, the religious freedom claims were capable of fresh evaluation but they had a different problem: They were subject to dismissal as legally insufficient without the necessity of a factual determination.

In sum, what the Schindlers needed—but what they failed to include in their original complaint—was some plausible allegation that would have required the district court to take evidence anew on two critical questions: (1) Was their daughter in a persistent vegetative state? (2) What would her wishes be, given her condition?

Only after they lost in the district court, in the three-judge panel of the Eleventh Circuit, in the en banc Eleventh Circuit court, and in the U.S. Supreme Court, did the Schindlers' lawyers discover the claim on which they should have staked their case in the first place. They asserted, finally, that their daughter has a federal constitutional right not to have her life extinguished by the state-ordered withdrawal of her feeding tube, absent evidence that she would have wished that result. Even then, they only included this potential winner after asserting four more fairly weak claims.

What is the basis for a federal constitutional right to life? Although there is no direct judicial authority for such a right, there is good indirect authority. In particular, in the 1990 Supreme Court case of *Cruzan v. Missouri Department of Health*,[9] five Justices clearly stated their view that a person has a right not to be involuntarily connected to a feeding tube, and that the state must respect that right in the case of an incapacitated person by abiding by his or her previously expressed wishes. The *Cruzan* case permitted states to require clear and convincing evidence of a desire to be disconnected, but where such evidence is present, the ruling implied, the patient's wishes are paramount.

It stands to reason that if there is a right to have a feeding tube disconnected, there is also a right *not* to have such a tube disconnected—at least where the evidence shows that a patient would wish to remain connected. After all, most constitutional rights include their opposites: The right to speak includes a right not to speak;[10] the right to have an abortion includes a right not to have an abortion; and so on.

To be sure, constitutional rights are also generally rights *against* state interference rather than rights *to* government assistance. *Cruzan* was rooted in the common law right to refuse medical treatment, and there is no corresponding right to receive medical treatment from the government.[11]

But that distinction should have counted for little here, because the Schindlers were not asking for any affirmative assistance from the state. They were willing to provide care for their daughter. They just didn't want the state to prohibit them from doing so. In that sense, their constitutional right-to-life claim, like the claim in *Cruzan*, was also a claim *against* state interference.

Accordingly, Judge Whittemore appears to have been mistaken in his second ruling.[12] He found that the right-to-life claim failed to allege "state action," a requirement that a plaintiff show that it is the government, not just a private party, which is the cause of injury. The Eleventh Circuit affirmed that result based on the same argument.[13]

Yet, both Judge Whittemore and the Eleventh Circuit failed to come to grips with the fact that Judge Greer issued an order instructing Michael Schiavo to remove Terri's feeding tube, even specifying the exact date and time when he should do so. The state court did not merely stand idly by while permitting Michael to take such action; the court affirmatively mandated the disconnection. That ought to have counted as state action by a state actor—Judge Greer—who was a named defendant in the federal court lawsuit.

Had the Schindlers gotten over the state action hurdle, they would have had to contend with the response that the state had good reason to order Terri's feeding tube removed—namely the evidence that this is what she would have wanted. Yet the federal court could not have reached that conclusion without conducting a new trial of its own. Terri's Law required de novo determination of such matters.

The federal court, then, could have directed that the feeding tube be reinserted so that this new trial could take place. (Remember, under Terri's Law, prior state court determinations could not be cited to show that the Schindlers were unlikely to succeed at trial. So the "likelihood of success on the merits" component of the preliminary injunction showing necessity to reinsert the tube would have been easier for the Schindlers to satisfy.)

There remains the question of whether the federal statute was constitutional. The answer is not entirely clear.

The most obviously objectionable aspect of Terri's Law was that it established a rule of law for just one person—Terri Schiavo. Although that made it a bizarre and, in my view, an unjustifiable, exercise of congressional power, this is not a constitutional flaw. There is a long history of so-called "private bills." As long as such bills do not impose criminal penalties, they do not run afoul of the Constitution.[14]

What about the fact that Terri's Law required the federal courts to disregard prior determinations by state courts? That too is objectionable on policy grounds but probably not on constitutional grounds. In habeas corpus cases, for many years, the federal district courts engaged in de novo review of federal legal questions that had previously been determined by state courts.[15] The Supreme Court and Congress subsequently cut back on the scope of habeas review, but there is no reason to believe they were *constitutionally required* to do so.

Granted, Terri's Law goes further than the old interpretation of the habeas statute in authorizing federal courts to give de novo reconsideration to questions of fact rather than just to questions of law, and in seeming to authorize even de novo reconsideration of questions of *state* law. (For reasons unknown, the Schindlers did not raise any claims under state law, even though there would have been jurisdiction to raise such claims once they were in federal court with federal claims.)

But while Terri's Law may be criticized as unwise, de novo review is probably constitutionally valid. Congress will sometimes have good reason to want to make a federal forum available for de novo litigation of suspect state court factual findings. For example, during Reconstruction and subsequent periods of racial conflict, Congress could have thought that state courts would not give African American litigants a fair hearing.

I would argue that Congress would have had the power to authorize de novo federal court proceedings in those circumstances—to replace racist state court fact determinations with fairer federal court ones. If so, then the question whether the Schiavo case presents comparable circumstances is simply a policy question, not a constitutional one.

Perhaps Terri's Law ran afoul of the constitutional doctrine forbidding Congress from changing the outcome in a litigated case in which there has been a final judgment. Yet it didn't quite do that either; Terri's Law afforded a new forum, but it did not require a particular substantive outcome. (We know, of course, that Congress was hoping that the federal courts would rule for the Schindlers.[16] But the very fact that they did not shows that the law did not mandate any particular outcome.)

Finally, Terri's Law could be seen as a violation of *Cruzan* itself. Five Justices in that case said that when there is clear and convincing evidence that a patient wishes to have a feeding tube disconnected, the government cannot insist that the tube remain in place. Yet in some sense, that is exactly what Terri's Law attempted to do. It authorized federal courts to hold extensive proceedings—and to prolong Terri's attachment to the feeding tube during those proceedings—even after her constitutional right to be disconnected had been established by clear and convincing evidence in the Florida courts.

Whether that or another constitutional attack on Terri's Law would have succeeded will likely remain forever unknown, for as I write these words in the early hours of March 26, 2005, the Schindlers appear to have run out of options in the federal courts. They may yet obtain relief in the state courts or elsewhere, but the federal courts that once seemed their best hope have turned a deaf ear to their claims.

To be sure, even if the Schindlers had brought their right-to-life claim at the outset, they might well have lost. Judge Whittemore and the Eleventh Circuit could have issued exactly the same legal rulings that they actually did, and even if the Schindlers managed to win on the law, at the end of the day, the federal courts might well have agreed with the state courts on the facts.

Yet given the weaknesses in the claims the Schindlers did bring in their original complaint, one is left to wonder why they didn't assert the one claim that had a better chance of success. One possibility is simply the rush of events. The Schindlers' lawyers were undoubtedly drafting their complaint even as the legislation in Congress was changing by the minute.

Haste may indeed explain the Schindlers' initial failure to raise the right-to-life claim, but there is another intriguing, though highly speculative, possible explanation: Perhaps their lawyers were blinded by ideology. A federal "right to life" based on *Cruzan* falls within the general doctrine of "substantive due process," under which the Supreme Court has invalidated state laws prohibiting contraception, abortion, and sodomy. That doctrine is anathema to religious conservatives, who scorn it as judicial activism run amok. It is the doctrine that underwrote *Roe v. Wade*.[17]

It is possible that in drafting their original complaint, the Schindlers' lawyers could not bring themselves to rely on cases that the pro-life movement abhors, and that they did so, in their second federal complaint, only when their desperation would color the courts' perception of the issue.

If this explanation is accurate, it would be ironic indeed, for it would mean that the Schindlers' and their lawyers' intellectual consistency precluded them from using to their advantage a gift bestowed by a Congress with no such qualms—a Congress that in enacting Terri's Law was willing to cast aside the spirit, if not the letter, of principles it often professes to hold dear: principles of federalism, separation of powers, and the rule of law.

POSTSCRIPT

Despite repeated pleas by the Schindlers, the courts did not intervene further and nearly two weeks after her feeding tube was removed, and fifteen years after she lost consciousness, Terri Schiavo finally died. An autopsy later confirmed that she had indeed suffered severe and irreversible brain damage consistent with the conclusion that she was in a persistent vegetative state.[18] In the swirl of political and legal questions, it is easy to lose sight of the fact that this case—like so many others that become the center of national controversy—was, at bottom, a human tragedy.

NOTES

1. Schiavo *ex rel.* Schindler v. Schiavo, 357 F. Supp. 2d 1378, 1384–88 (M.D. Fla. 2005).
2. Pub. L. No. 109–3, 119 Stat. 15 (2005).
3. *See* Schiavo *ex rel.* Schindler v. Schiavo, 125 S. Ct. 1692 (2005) (denying the application for stay of enforcement of judgment); Schiavo *ex rel.* Schindler v. Schiavo,

403 F.3d 1223 (11th Cir. 2005) (per curiam) (affirming the denial of the petition for injunctive relief), *reh'g denied*, 403 F.3d 1261 (11th Cir. 2005) (en banc).

4. Schiavo *ex rel.* Schindler v. Schiavo, 358 F. Supp. 2d 1161 (M.D. Fla. 2005), *aff'd*, 403 F.3d 1289 (11th Cir. 2005) (per curiam).

5. *See* Fla. Stat. § 765.105 (2005); *see also* Fla. Stat. §§ 765.101–765.404 (2005).

6. 531 U.S. 356, 366–68 (2001).

7. 494 U.S. 872, 878–82 (1990).

8. *See* 42 U.S.C. § 2000cc-1 (2000).

9. 497 U.S. 261 (1990).

10. *See* Wooley v. Maynard, 430 U.S. 705 (1977) (discussed *supra* in chapter 7).

11. *See* Rust v. Sullivan, 500 U.S. 173, 201–03 (1991); Deshaney v. Winnebago County Dep't of Soc. Servs., 489 U.S. 189, 196 (1989).

12. Schiavo, 358 F. Supp. 2d at 1164–65, 1167–68 (2005).

13. Schiavo *ex rel.* Schindler v. Schiavo, 403 F.3d 1289, 1293 n.2 (11th Cir. 2005).

14. An individual bill imposing criminal sanction would violate the Bill of Attainder Clause. U.S. Const. art. I, § 9, cl. 3. But the Supreme Court has not applied the principle outside the criminal context. *See generally* Nixon v. Adm'r of Gen. Servs., 433 U.S. 425, 468–84 (1977).

15. *See, e.g.,* Schiro v. Farley, 510 U.S. 222, 232 (1994) ("Ordinarily on habeas review, we presume the correctness of state court findings of fact. See 28 U.S.C. § 2254(d). The preclusive effect of the jury's verdict, however, is a question of federal law which we must review de novo.") (citations omitted).

16. *See, e.g.,* 151 Cong. Rec. H1731 (2005) (statement of Rep. Hastert) ("Over the last few days, Members of both parties and chambers have worked tirelessly to reach this agreement. We hope that these efforts will help give Terri Schiavo new hope and a new chance at life.").

17. 410 U.S. 113 (1973).

18. *See* Abby Goodnough, *Schiavo Autopsy Says Brain, Withered, Was Untreatable*, N.Y. Times, June 16, 2005, at A1.

III

IN DEFENSE OF LIBERAL JUDGING

As I observed in the introduction to part II, I'm not embarrassed to admit that I generally hold liberal political views. And although I would distinguish my political views from my legal views, I regard myself as a legal liberal as well.

What exactly does that mean? The commitments of legal liberalism are principally methodological. Legal liberals generally doubt the claims by formalists that the law is determinate, although we don't take these doubts nearly as far as the most radical legal realists. Legal liberals also reject the prescription of legal conservatives and others who say that where the text of a constitutional provision or law is unclear, judges should aim simply to discover its original meaning. Instead, legal liberals tend to look to the general policy of the provision in question, having special regard to how circumstances may have changed since its adoption. And perhaps most importantly, legal liberals believe that as between two otherwise equally plausible interpretations of an ambiguous legal provision, the more humane interpretation ought to be preferred. The chapters in this section provide examples of these commitments.

• 15 •

Washington Yankees in King Arthur's Court: The Supreme Court Journeys to Eighteenth-Century England to Define the Rights of Twenty-First-Century Americans

May 2001

Many Americans were no doubt surprised to learn that the Fourth Amendment's prohibition against "unreasonable searches and seizures" does not prevent the police from arresting them and taking them to jail for committing misdemeanors such as not wearing a seatbelt—even where the maximum statutory penalty is a $50 fine.

Almost as disturbing as the result in *Atwater v. City of Lago Vista*,[1] however, is the reasoning process the majority used to arrive at it. The crucial factor in the majority opinion was the determination that *eighteenth-century* English and American statutes and precedents generally permitted peace officers to make warrantless arrests for misdemeanors. Consequently, the Court reasoned, twenty-first-century Americans have no constitutional protection against such arrests.

The case is practically a primer on the pitfalls of the originalist approach to constitutional interpretation. Remarkably, the author of this primer is someone who has been a foe of originalism: Justice David Souter.

In 1997, Gail Atwater was driving her pickup truck with her two small children in the front seat. None of the three were wearing seatbelts, a misdemeanor under Texas law. Rather than issuing Atwater a citation, however, Lago Vista police officer Bart Turek arrested her and took her to jail.

The experience disturbed Atwater and traumatized her children. She ultimately pled guilty to the seatbelt offense and paid the maximum fine of $50. She then sued the police department for violating her Fourth Amendment rights.

The Fourth Amendment, which the Supreme Court has long held applicable to the states via the Fourteenth Amendment, begins: "The right of the people to be secure in their persons, houses, papers, and effects, against unreasonable searches and seizures, shall not be violated."

An arrest, all agree, is a "seizure" of the "person." So the question in Atwater's case was solely whether her arrest by Turek was "unreasonable."

Atwater argued that the arrest was indeed unreasonable, because the underlying offense is not punishable by imprisonment and involves no breach of the peace. Four Justices agreed with her, and thus would have ruled that her arrest violated the Fourth Amendment, but a majority disagreed.

The majority opinion authored by Justice Souter (and joined by Chief Justice Rehnquist and Justices Scalia, Kennedy, and Thomas) acknowledged that "Atwater's claim to live free of pointless indignity and confinement clearly outweighs anything the City can raise against it specific to her case."[2] In other words, the majority recognized that Atwater's liberty and dignity had been unjustly invaded. Nevertheless, the Justices declined to fashion a *general* constitutional rule barring arrest for minor offenses.

Why not fashion such a rule? The Court provided a number of practical reasons, but the heart of the opinion turned on the original understanding of the Fourth Amendment. That understanding, in turn, according to the Court, can be derived from the common law and statutes in force in England and America just prior to and at the time of the adoption of the Bill of Rights in 1791.

As we have seen, the view that the Constitution should be interpreted to reflect the original understanding of its framers and ratifiers is known as originalism. While the term is often invoked—sometimes to praise, and sometimes to vilify—its precise meaning is not often made clear.

Virtually all judges and constitutional scholars agree that the original understanding is at least one relevant factor in constitutional interpretation. If nothing else, it provides useful context and a starting point for seeing how the meaning of a provision has developed over time.

But people who call themselves originalists give original understanding a more prominent place. For them, the original understanding is either always dispositive, or creates a strong presumption that can only be overcome by very powerful arguments.

The majority opinion in *Atwater* adopts the strong presumption approach. In an important footnote, Justice Souter's majority opinion takes issue with the claim, made by Justice Sandra Day O'Connor in dissent, that history is just "one of the tools" relevant to a Fourth Amendment case. According to the majority opinion, there is a "heavy burden" on any litigant urging a departure from the original understanding.[3]

These are strong claims, especially coming from Justice Souter, who is not easily classified as an originalist. In the 1997 right-to-die case of *Washington v. Glucksberg*, for example, Justice Souter wrote a separate opinion endorsing the view of the late Justice Harlan.[4] There, he approvingly quoted Justice Harlan's famous statement that the process of elaborating constitutional rights involves finding the appropriate balance between liberty and order, "having regard to what history teaches are the traditions from which [the balance struck by society] developed as well as the traditions from which it broke. That tradition is a living thing."[5]

Souter's invocation of the "living" Constitution in *Glucksberg* is anathema to self-styled originalists like Chief Justice Rehnquist and Justice Scalia, each of whom has criticized this idea. Why then did Justice Souter author an originalist opinion in *Atwater*?

One possibility is that he did so to attract the votes of the Chief Justice and Justice Scalia, as well as Justices Kennedy and Thomas. Perhaps thinking that *Atwater* should lose even if the Fourth Amendment is understood as a living thing, Justice Souter might have been willing to add arguments in which he did not fully believe in order to forge a compromise.

Another possibility is that Justice Souter was simply responding to Atwater's own claims. She argued in her brief that the original understanding actually supported her position.

Thus, it is possible that the *Atwater* case does not imply Justice Souter's conversion to originalism. But the express language of the opinion certainly suggests such a conversion. If true, that is terribly unfortunate, for *Atwater* itself illustrates a number of the difficulties that plague originalism.

Proponents of originalism contend that it constrains judges. They point out that many of the issues addressed by the Constitution arouse contentious debate. And they argue that if unelected judges are to invoke the Constitution to displace the policies of politically accountable actors, they should at least do so on the basis of more than their own subjective values.

Originalists believe that a judge who interprets a constitutional provision in accordance with the original understanding avoids the danger of subjectivity. Such a judge relies not on his or her own views, they claim, but rather on the views of those who enacted that provision. The inquiry is objective, not subjective.

Arguments like these offer originalism as a solution to what Alexander Bickel called the "countermajoritarian difficulty" in constitutional interpretation.[6] The difficulty, which has troubled judges and constitutional scholars for generations, is that even though we live in a democracy, our constitutional system includes a distinctly unmajoritarian aspect: a life-tenured federal judiciary that can invalidate statutes and other actions of elected officials.

Yet originalism frequently fails at its own game of suppressing subjectivity and individual judicial discretion. *Atwater* itself is a good example. As Justice Souter frankly admitted, the historical evidence about the permissibility of arresting minor offenders is ambiguous. Many prominent legal historians writing in the nineteenth and twentieth centuries took the view that traditional common law principles barred such arrests, as did no less an eighteenth-century authority than Sir William Blackstone.

Justice Souter recognized that opinion was divided, but he nonetheless concluded that the weight of authority supported the police. Others may draw different conclusions. Even if the materials used to arrive at such conclusions are objective, the fact they lead to different results in the hands of different judges renders any decision itself subjective in the literal sense—dependent on the identity of the judge, the subject, who makes the decision.

The larger point that originalism overlooks is that many of the issues addressed by the Constitution were contentious even when the Constitution was adopted. The revolutionary era was a time of great social, political, and intellectual tumult during which there were strong disagreements about the nature of government and rights. The ratification votes in some states were exceedingly close, with Federalists and Anti-Federalists often expressing radically different views of what the Constitution's text meant.

Searching for a consensus of meaning in the eighteenth century will often prove more rather than less difficult than searching for a contemporary consensus, because judges must rely on an imperfect historical record of a tumultuous world that is long gone.

Professional historians differ sharply in interpreting the very same evidence. It is no wonder that judges, who typically lack professional training in history, do too.

Furthermore, even when judges can confidently reconstruct the past, interpretive puzzles abound. The world inhabited by the framers and ratifiers of the Constitution and Bill of Rights was profoundly different from our own. In Fourth Amendment cases, this fact is particularly salient because so much of contemporary police work would have been impossible in the eighteenth century, as two cases from the October 2000 Supreme Court term illustrate.

In *Ferguson v. City of Charleston*,[7] the Court ruled that, absent consent, warrantless drug testing of hospital patients for law-enforcement purposes violates the Fourth Amendment. Unsurprisingly, none of the Justices in either the majority or the dissent addressed the question of whether such drug testing was generally considered permissible in the eighteenth century. Such an inquiry would, of course, have been fruitless, as modern drug-testing techniques were unavailable then.

Kyllo v. United States posed the question whether using a thermal imaging device to detect heat emerging from a home constitutes a "search" within the meaning of the Fourth Amendment.[8] What did eighteenth-century English and American cases have to say about thermal imaging? The very question is preposterous.

Indeed, *Atwater* itself presents a case of profoundly changed circumstances. Automobiles did not exist in the eighteenth century. One might be tempted to look to analogies, such as the horse and buggy, but the horse and buggy played a different role in eighteenth-century America from the role played in modern America by the automobile, to put it mildly.

Moreover, organized police forces as we now know them did not come into existence until well into the nineteenth century. During the revolutionary era, law enforcement was a largely volunteer undertaking. Granting the police the power to arrest people for minor offenses may work a much more profound invasion of personal security in the modern world than it would have in the days when suspected criminals were apprehended by the hue and cry and the *posse comitatus*—that is, the volunteer police.

To be sure, it is not obvious which way the changed circumstances cut in this case. Automobiles can travel at greater rates of speed than horses, and accordingly one might think that the safety interest in law enforcement is greater now than in the eighteenth century. So too, one might think that an organized police force subject to supervision by elected officials poses less of a threat of arbitrary power than a volunteer force.

But the important point is that drawing analogies and distinctions is not simply a matter of reading the historical record. The process involves subtle value judgments of precisely the sort that originalism is supposed to, but does not in fact, eliminate.

Furthermore, even when the evidence of the original understanding is clear, and even when it is simple to locate an appropriate analogy, originalism may still yield bad answers because values change.

For example, the people who wrote and ratified the Equal Protection Clause of the Fourteenth Amendment in 1868 thought it was consistent with separate spheres for men and women. In the nineteenth century, and well into the twentieth, women were denied the most basic rights and opportunities because their proper role was understood to be that of wife and mother. Yet the modern Supreme Court has quite correctly held that, given modern understandings, official sex discrimination is presumptively unconstitutional.

Here, too, the *Atwater* case is instructive. The very eighteenth-century statutes that Justice Souter cites as evidence of the broad arrest power could not withstand scrutiny under modern vagueness doctrine. These eighteenth-century statutes authorize the arrest of "vagrants," "vagabonds," and "night-walkers," among others.[9] Yet just two years before the *Atwater* decision, in *City of Chicago v. Morales*,[10] a majority of the Court (including Justice Souter), invalidated a Chicago prohibition against "gang loitering" on the ground that it vested too much discretion in the police to decide who is illegally loitering, and who is simply innocently standing around.

Police discretion to arrest a citizen for the most minor misdemeanor is liable to be abused. That fact puts everyone's liberty in jeopardy. But expanding the scope of arrest authority is likely to have its greatest impact on those most likely to be singled out for mistreatment by the police. As the dissent in *Atwater* pointed out, the majority's decision will therefore exacerbate the problem of racial profiling.

Would the framers and ratifiers of the Fourth Amendment have worried about racial profiling? That seems unlikely. Many of them owned slaves. However, that should hardly count as a reason to write the prejudices of a bygone age into our constitutional doctrine.

It is true that in a few instances, the framers chose constitutional language that would appear to lock in their own understanding. The Seventh Amendment, for example, states that the right to a civil jury trial "shall be preserved."

Accordingly, the Supreme Court has interpreted the civil jury trial right as co-extensive with the jury trial right in the eighteenth century—inferring that the Constitution sought to "preserve" the right just as it was then. In light of changes in civil procedure, that interpretive enterprise is quite tricky, but at least it appears faithful to the constitutional text.[11]

For the most part, however, the Constitution does not ask us to preserve the past, but simply to make our own best judgment. The Fourth Amendment's prohibition on "unreasonable searches and seizures" invites us to figure out for ourselves what searches and seizures are unreasonable, not to ask what people long gone would have thought about problems they never envisioned.

We are enormously lucky that our forebears wrote most of the Constitution in language that did not lock in their own view of the world. Originalism would rob us of one of the Constitution's great virtues: its adaptability.

Because originalism tends to favor past views over present ones, it is "conservative" in the literal sense of the word. However, it does not necessarily lead to politically conservative results.

For example, in the 1995 case of *Wilson v. Arkansas*, the Court unanimously held that police must generally "knock and announce" before executing a search warrant at a home.[12] This conclusion was based on an evaluation of the common law of the eighteenth century.

The fact that originalism can be used to produce liberal as well as conservative results does not, however, justify the leading role the Court gave to historical arguments in *Wilson* or in *Atwater*. Any sincere method of constitutional interpretation can produce a variety of results. But a method such as originalism that places so much weight on the past is likely to miss many of the most important aspects of contemporary problems.

Originalism is a seductive philosophy because it offers judges the possibility of resolving difficult cases without making difficult choices. Ultimately, however, originalism does not deliver on its own promises, and the promises it makes are often not worth keeping. In the words of the late Justice William Brennan, originalism "is arrogance cloaked as humility."[13]

POSTSCRIPT

One of the most high-profile opinions authored by John Roberts during his brief tenure as a circuit court judge was *Hedgepeth v. Washington Metropolitan Area Transit Authority*. In that case, the court confronted a Fourth Amendment claim even more disturbing than the one in *Atwater* itself: A twelve-year-old girl was arrested, searched, handcuffed, and taken into police custody for three hours for the offense of eating a single French fry in violation of a rule prohibiting eating in Washington Metrorail stations. She argued, among other things, that the arrest and search were unreasonable within the meaning of the Fourth Amendment, but the court, citing *Atwater*, found otherwise. Notably, then-Judge Roberts did not merely state that he was bound by *Atwater*; he denominated the practice of unearthing the 1789 understanding, "the usual first step of any analysis of whether particular government action violates the Fourth Amendment."[14] Whether the *Hedgepeth* case portends a thoroughgoing originalism by Chief Justice Roberts remains to be seen.

More broadly, notwithstanding originalism's evident flaws, it might be defended on the ground that it alone provides a plausible account of constitutional legitimacy. Accordingly, originalists sometimes pose the following sorts of questions for non-originalists like myself: "If you don't think that we are bound by the original understanding of the Constitution, why do you think we are bound by the Constitution itself? If the thoughts of the framers and ratifiers don't bind us, why do their words?" These are excellent questions, because they force us to ask ourselves why we think that laws enacted by generations long dead have any hold over us.

The originalist has a simple answer. Law derives its binding force from the authoritative acts of the sovereign, and in a democracy such as our own, the people are sovereign. Hence, we are bound by enactments of the people, including the Constitution, until and unless the people change those enactments. And, the originalist adds, to connect the law with its source of legitimacy, judges must interpret the people's past enactments in accordance with what they thought those enactments meant.

Yet this line of reasoning ignores the embarrassing fact that most of our Constitution was adopted by an electorate that was not anything like democratic by modern standards. African American males were formally denied the vote in most states until 1870 (and long after that in practice), while women did not obtain the constitutional right to vote until 1920. So the Constitution's claim to legitimacy cannot rest on a past democratic pedigree.

We might think that the Constitution is nonetheless legitimate because it is *now* subject to change by democratic means. If We the People today don't like what it says, we can amend it.

But of course, the super-majority requirements for amending the Constitution mean that our collective failure to amend any given provision or doctrine cannot be taken as reliable evidence that We the People currently accept that provision or doctrine.

In the end, the best we can do in answering the originalist's question is to acknowledge that the Constitution's legitimacy rests on no single foundational principle. The originalist is right to point to past acts of consent—however imperfectly democratic—as providing some basis for the Constitution's current force as law. So too the possibility of change, however difficult, connects the Constitution we have to popular sovereignty today. But to these sources we must add at least two others.

First, all things considered, the Constitution is a pretty good charter of government. The Constitution, in other words, deserves to be treated as legitimate because it is basically good and just. Not by any means perfect, mind you, but good enough so that we can take the absence of revolutionary sentiment in our nation as evidence of tacit consent.

Second, the Constitution attains some of its legitimacy from the fact that it is not simply the work of long-dead generations. Rather, when we speak of "the Constitution," we usually invoke not just the text of the document, but the authoritative gloss that the courts have given it over the years. That authoritative gloss includes many *non-originalist* decisions that we deem fundamental to who we are as a people—like those invalidating racial apartheid and the formal subordination of women. Accordingly, part of the answer we can give to the originalist's question as to why we are bound by the Constitution is this: "because our courts have been wise enough to interpret it in light of current conditions and values, thus connecting it to the contemporary popular sovereign." In other words, upon close inspection, the originalist's challenge ends up undermining originalism itself.

NOTES

1. 532 U.S. 318 (2001).
2. *Id.* at 347.
3. *Id.* at 345 n.14.
4. 521 U.S. 702, 752–89 (1997) (Souter, J., concurring).
5. *Id.* at 765 (quoting Poe v. Ullman, 367 U.S. 497, 542 (1961) (Harlan, J., dissenting)).
6. Alexander M. Bickel, The Least Dangerous Branch: The Supreme Court at the Bar of Politics 16–17 (Indianapolis: Bobbs-Merrill, 1962) ("[W]hen the Supreme Court declares unconstitutional a legislative act or the action of an elected executive,

it thwarts the will of representatives of the actual people of the here and now; it exercises control, not [on] behalf of the prevailing majority, but against it.").

7. 532 U.S. 67 (2001).

8. 533 U.S. 27 (2001). The Court ultimately ruled that the use of such imaging *does* constitute a search, for which a warrant supported by probable cause is ordinarily required. *Id.* at 40.

9. *See* Atwater v. City of Lago Vista, 532 U.S. 318, 337–38 (2001).

10. 527 U.S. 41 (1999).

11. *See, e.g.,* Granfinanciera, S.A. v. Nordberg, 492 U.S. 33, 40–49 (1989).

12. 514 U.S. 927, 929 (1995).

13. William J. Brennan Jr., The Constitution of the United States: Contemporary Ratification, Address to Georgetown University Text and Teaching Symposium (October 12, 1985), *in* 19 U.C. Davis L. Rev 2, 4 (1985).

14. 386 F.3d 1148, 1159 (D.C. Cir. 2004).

• 16 •

How a Recent, Unanimous Supreme Court Public Housing Decision "Exiles Compassion from the Province of Judging"

April 2002

In 1988, at the height of the crack cocaine epidemic, Congress enacted a statute barring tenants involved in illegal drug activity from public housing. In *Department of Housing and Urban Development ("HUD") v. Rucker*,[1] a unanimous Supreme Court gave the statute a truly draconian reading.

The Court interpreted the statute to authorize the eviction of even those public housing tenants who did everything within their power to prevent their relatives and guests from bringing drugs into their homes. This interpretation is defensible—the statute can indeed be read to reach tenants such as these—but it is hardly inevitable. A more compassionate and fair interpretation was also possible. Sadly, however, the Court did not opt for it.

It is not surprising that a majority of the Rehnquist Court would be unmoved by the pleas of public housing residents. What is more alarming about *Rucker* is its unanimity: Not a single Justice gave voice to the concerns of the poor. Nor did a single Justice recognize the deep, plain unfairness in evicting an innocent tenant who has shown that he or she has done everything possible to ensure that drug use does not take place in his or her apartment.

The relevant statutory language states that a "public housing agency shall utilize leases which . . . provide that . . . drug-related criminal activity on or off such premises, engaged in by a public housing tenant, any member of the tenant's household, or any guest or other person under the tenant's control, shall be cause for termination of tenancy."[2]

To give effect to this provision, HUD adopted a policy authorizing eviction even when the "tenant did not know, could not foresee, or could not control behavior by other occupants of the unit."[3] If, for example, a caregiver for an elderly or disabled occupant of public housing uses cocaine without the occupant's knowledge, the housing authority can evict the occupant.

That example is not made up. It is what happened to Herman Walker, one of the plaintiffs in the *Rucker* case—and a 75-year-old disabled public housing tenant whom the Oakland Housing Authority sought to evict from his home under these very circumstances.

The Oakland Housing Authority also sought to evict 63-year-old Barbara Hill from her home of 30 years because her grandson possessed marijuana in the apartment complex's parking lot. The Housing Authority did not claim that Walker or Hill had in any way facilitated, condoned, or even had reason to know about the drug activity.

The plaintiffs in *Rucker* argued that the statute itself (unlike the HUD policy) is silent on the question of the degree of culpability of a public housing tenant that is necessary to trigger eviction. The statute's language, quoted above, appears to support this argument.

Must the tenant know of the illegal drug activity? If not, must he or she at least have acted recklessly or negligently with respect to the risk of illegal drug activity? As the plaintiffs noted, these questions cannot be answered based on the statute itself, for the statute does not specify a mental state.

Thus, the plaintiffs argued, HUD was unjustified in assuming, when it adopted its formal policy, that Congress intended evictions to result even for completely innocent tenants—those who "did not know, could not foresee, or could not control" the drug activity for which they were to be evicted.

The federal district court agreed with the plaintiffs' contentions. As a result, it enjoined the Oakland Housing Authority from evicting tenants "for drug-related criminal activity that does not occur within the tenant's apartment unit when the tenant did not know of and had no reason to know of" it.[4]

A three-judge panel of the Court of Appeals for the Ninth Circuit then reversed the district court's ruling.[5] However, a larger panel of that court subsequently reinstated the district court's injunction.[6]

That larger panel, called an en banc court, relied on two additional arguments. First, the court emphasized that the statute refers to a "person under the tenant's control." Accordingly, when the person engaged in the illegal drug activity is completely beyond the control of the tenant, the tenant should not be held accountable.

Second, the en banc court thought that permitting the HUD policy to stand would potentially violate the constitutional rights of public housing tenants. A lease is property, and for the government to take away that property without any showing of wrongful conduct by the tenant is—in the words of both the Fifth and Fourteenth Amendments—to "deprive any person of . . . property without due process of law."

The Supreme Court rejected each of these arguments in turn—holding that the statute sweeps in even blameless tenants, and suggesting that in doing so, the statute is perfectly constitutional.

First, the Justices said that the statute is not truly silent with respect to mental state. Rather, by not specifying a mental state, the Court reasoned, the statute makes clear that it requires none. The statute thus permits eviction *regardless of the tenant's mental state*—in other words, no matter how unknowing, unwilling, or otherwise blameless the tenant may have been with respect to the illegal drug use of third parties.

Second, with respect to the "under the tenant's control" language, the Supreme Court said that these words only applied to the preceding phrase "other person," and only required that the tenant have admitted the "other person" to the apartment. As noted above, the statute refers to a "guest or other person under the tenant's control." Accordingly, the Court thought that a "person under the tenant's control" simply meant a person who, like a guest, had been permitted onto the premises by the tenant.

Thus, according to the Court, a person was "under the tenant's control," for purposes of the statute, simply in that he was on the premises. He did not also have to be "under the tenant's control" in the sense that the tenant could reasonably have stopped him from using drugs in the apartment. The result is that a grandmother can be said to have her grandson's friends "under [her] control" if he let them in while she was out—and can lose her apartment if they use drugs there, even if she tries but fails to stop them.

Third, the Court rejected the due process objection—the argument that the statute should be construed to include a blameless tenant exception so as to avoid rendering it unconstitutional. Courts may, under established principles of constitutional interpretation, interpret a statute narrowly—here, so as not to reach innocent tenants—to preserve its constitutionality, on the theory that Congress would not have sought to enact an unconstitutional statute.

But the Court said that the principle of narrow construction only applies where a statute is unclear. Because the Justices thought the statute unambiguously rejected an innocent tenant defense, the narrow construction principle did not come into play. Any claim that the statute operated to deny due process in a particular case, the Court said, could only be raised in the state court eviction proceeding. Not content to put the issue aside, however, the Court strongly hinted that it thought the due process objection without merit.

Finally, the Court explained that HUD had a sound reason to reject an innocent tenant defense: By holding tenants strictly accountable for illegal drug activity in their dwellings, the HUD policy gives tenants a very strong incentive to do whatever it takes to prevent their relatives and guests from engaging in such activity.

Although technically defensible as a matter of statutory interpretation, the Court's decision in *Rucker* was hardly dictated by the statute. Both the district court and the en banc appellate court certainly thought otherwise. And had the Court taken the due process argument more seriously, it could have chosen a reading of the statute that not only would have been more compassionate, but would have avoided future constitutional challenges.

Moreover, the Supreme Court's policy argument misses the point. No matter what their incentives, tenants are not in a position to control unforeseeable conduct by third parties—except in the wholly unrealistic sense that everything is, at some level, foreseeable.

In an influential 1964 article in the *Yale Law Journal*, Charles Reich spoke of "the new property."[7] Reich argued that the Constitution, which was adopted in substantial measure as a means of preserving the property rights of slave-owners, was becoming a vehicle for protecting the interests of ordinary people, poor as well as rich.

In its 1970 decision in *Goldberg v. Kelly*, a majority of the Court cited Reich's article en route to ruling that welfare recipients have a right to a hearing before they have their benefits taken from them.[8] The benefits, as the Court saw it, are no less the "property" of a poor person than a mansion is the property of a rich person. Neither can be taken away without due process of law—meaning notice and a hearing.

As the 1970s progressed, Reich's hope that the Court would interpret the Constitution to provide special protection for the rights and interests of the downtrodden was repeatedly dashed. Still, as recently as the late 1980s, there was at least a two-sided debate on the Supreme Court about the question.

Consider, for example, the 1989 case of *DeShaney v. Winnebago County Social Services Department*,[9] which, like *Rucker* and *Goldberg*, called upon the Court to interpret what "due process of law" means for those who are disadvantaged. In *DeShaney*, the Court held that a state child welfare agency could not be held constitutionally accountable for what amounted to criminal recklessness in failing to prevent the gross abuse of an infant. But Justices William Brennan, Thurgood Marshall, and Harry Blackmun all dissented passionately.

Taking issue with the majority's claim that its result was required by precedent, Justice Blackmun argued that the due process clause was much more open-ended than the Court acknowledged. Faced with such ambiguity in the relevant legal text, he said, "compassion need not be exiled from the province of judging."[10]

Justices Brennan, Marshall, and Blackmun have all passed away. And though it is fashionable to speak about conservatives and liberals on the Supreme Court, *Rucker* reveals that this is a highly contextualized categorization. Judged by the standards of the previous generation, there are no strongly committed liberals on the current Court.

No doubt that fact reflects both major political parties' turn to the right. Justices Brennan and Blackmun were both appointed by Republican Presidents. By contrast, in nominating John Roberts and Samuel Alito to the

Supreme Court, the current President Bush appears to have made good on his promise to strengthen the Court's conservative bloc,[11] while President Clinton—the only Democrat to appoint any Supreme Court Justices since President Johnson put Thurgood Marshall on the Court—named two moderates. Thus, we are unlikely to see Justices like Marshall, Brennan, or Blackmun any time soon.

Even if one thinks, as I do, that the last generation's liberal Justices sometimes under-appreciated the social costs of the rights they recognized, surely there is value in having a Court that includes their perspective. Our current Court is, in this respect, the poorer for its unanimity.

POSTSCRIPT

From a certain perspective, the *Rucker* decision is compassionate—for the potential innocent victims of drug-related violence. As it happens, residents of public housing tend to support strict enforcement of anti-drug leases, (albeit over substantial dissent).[12] Presumably the tenants themselves know better than do judges how to balance the risk that they might unwittingly shelter a drug user and thus be subject to eviction, against the risk that one of their neighbors might knowingly or unknowingly permit the housing complex to become a haven for drug dealers. Thus, the Justices might have said that as between innocent victims of the law, and innocent victims of drug violence, they would accept the value judgment of the tenants themselves. A decision based on such a principle of respect for local community values might or might not have been justifiable, but it would not have been subject to the charge that it lacked compassion. Unfortunately, however, the Court did not make this argument, relying instead on an antiseptic analysis of the statutory language.

NOTES

1. 535 U.S. 125 (2002).
2. 42 U.S.C. § 1437d(l)(6) (2000).
3. 56 Fed. Reg. 51,560, 51,567 (Oct. 11, 1991).
4. Rucker v. Davis, No. C 98–00781, 1998 WL 345403, at *13 (N.D. Cal. June 19, 1998).
5. Rucker v. Davis, 203 F.3d 627 (9th Cir. 2000).
6. Rucker v. Davis, 237 F.3d 1113 (9th Cir. 2001) (en banc).
7. *See generally* Charles A. Reich, *Individual Rights and Social Welfare: The Emerging Legal Issues*, 74 Yale L.J. 1245 (1965).

8. 397 U.S. 254, 262 n.8 (1970).

9. 489 U.S. 189 (1989).

10. *Id.* at 213 (Blackmun, J., dissenting).

11. Remarks at a Fundraiser for Senatorial Candidate Saxby Chambliss in Atlanta, 38 Weekly Comp. Pres. Doc. 530 (Mar. 27, 2002).

12. *See* Adam P. Hellegers, Comment, *Reforming HUD's "One-Strike" Public Housing Evictions Through Tenant Participation*, 90 J. Crim. L. & Criminology 323, 324–25 & nn.8–11 (1999).

• 17 •

Could Justice Scalia's Affirmative Action Dissent Become a Self-Fulfilling Prophecy?

November 2003

In a November 2003 order, the United States Supreme Court declined review of a federal appellate ruling upholding Denver's affirmative action program for minority-owned and female-owned construction firms.[1] Because the Supreme Court turns down vastly many more cases than it accepts for review, it does not ordinarily give any reasons for its decision. Following that practice, the Court did not explain its decision in the Denver case.

Yet Justice Scalia, joined by Chief Justice Rehnquist, was so incensed by the Court's action that he took the unusual step of publishing a dissent from the denial of review. In the dissent, he accused his colleagues of undermining the principle of color blindness that the Court has found in the Fourteenth Amendment's Equal Protection Clause.

Ironically, however, if the Denver case undermines the color blindness principle, that may be more the result of Justice Scalia's loud protestations than any decision of the Court's majority. Supreme Court denials of petitions for review set no precedent, but official pronouncements of two Supreme Court Justices—including the Chief Justice—tend to get noticed by the lower courts and the practicing bar.

Nor is this the first time that Justice Scalia has undermined positions he supports by painting a majority decision from which he dissented in extreme terms. In June 2003, for example, in *Lawrence v. Texas*, the Court invalidated a Texas law that barred same-sex sodomy, and Justice Scalia dissented.[2] In that dissent, Scalia opined that the Court's ruling logically entailed state recognition of same-sex marriage. Later that same year, the Massachusetts Supreme Judicial Court took him at his word.[3]

Make no mistake: Because I often find myself disagreeing with the substantive positions Justice Scalia takes, I'm delighted when he suggests that rulings of the majority have consequences that he rues and I welcome.

The question nonetheless remains—and it is a question perhaps better answered by a psychoanalyst than by a constitutional law professor—why on earth Justice Scalia writes what he regards as parade-of-horribles dissents that risk becoming self-fulfilling prophecies.

Let's begin with the Denver case. Since the late 1970s, the federal government and the City of Denver have been concerned about the fact that relatively few minority-owned business enterprises and female-owned business enterprises are awarded contracts for construction projects in the city. Accordingly, the city has enacted and repeatedly amended an ordinance that sets percentage goals and imposes other requirements for contractors and subcontractors on public projects.[4]

In 1992, Concrete Works of Colorado, Inc., which is neither minority owned nor female owned, sued the City of Denver. It argued that by awarding preferences on the basis of race and sex, Denver had violated the Equal Protection Clause. Over the course of the next eleven years, the case yo-yoed back and forth between the trial and appeals courts, while the city repeatedly revised its contracting requirements.

Then, in 2003, the appeals court ruled that Denver's affirmative action program was constitutional, because it was justified by historical and ongoing official discrimination, as well as by the city's desire not to act as a passive conduit for private discrimination.

The appeals court based that decision on the historical, statistical, and anecdotal evidence contained in over three thousand pages of trial testimony, and over ten thousand pages of the appellate appendix. The court invoked the leading Supreme Court precedent dealing with local affirmative action programs in the construction trade: the 1989 ruling in *City of Richmond v. J.A. Croson Co.*[5]

Croson established the principle of color blindness, under which state and local affirmative action programs are judged by the demanding "strict scrutiny" test. This is the same test that the courts apply to instances of official discrimination that burden traditionally disadvantaged groups. Thus, under *Croson*, blatantly racist or sexist programs face the same scrutiny as affirmative action programs.

The petition for Supreme Court review argued that the federal appellate court—the U.S. Court of Appeals for the Tenth Circuit—had misapplied *Croson*. In his dissent from the denial of review in the Denver case, Justice Scalia agreed. He opined that the court of appeals had paid mere lip service to the *Croson* precedent, departing from its spirit and letter.

Among other defects he saw in the appellate court's reasoning, Scalia thought that the court improperly placed the burden of proof on *Concrete Works* to *disprove* that the affirmative action program was justified. He said that, properly understood, *Croson* imposes upon the *City of Denver* the burden of *proving* that the program was justified.

Significantly, Justice Scalia added that his colleagues' willingness to let the appellate court's decision stand could be taken as an endorsement of that court's approach. "Coming on the heels of our decision last Term in" the Michigan affirmative action case, he said, "the Court's decision to let this plain disregard of *Croson* stand invites speculation that that case has effectively been overruled."[6]

Yet if Justice Scalia had not published a dissent from denial of review in the Denver case, no informed Court watcher would have interpreted the Justices' action as having any substantive significance at all. The Court frequently denies review for reasons having nothing to do with the merits—such as a complex procedural posture that may make it difficult to render a clear decision.

Thus, it is Scalia's vocal dissent—rather than the Court's silent denial of review—that invites speculation about the Court's commitment to *Croson.*

Justice Scalia shot himself in the foot in a similar fashion in his dissent in *Lawrence v. Texas.* There, a six-Justice majority of the Court held that a Texas law prohibiting same-sex sodomy violated the constitutional rights of homosexual persons. In dissent, Justice Scalia complained that the majority's ruling called into question "State laws against bigamy, same-sex marriage, adult incest, prostitution, masturbation, adultery, fornication, bestiality, and obscenity."[7]

To my knowledge, lawsuits challenging state prohibitions on adult incest, masturbation, and bestiality have not yet been filed. But in *Goodridge v. Department of Public Health*, the highest court of Massachusetts did strike down a ban on same-sex marriage.

Although the Massachusetts decision was based on the state rather than the federal Constitution, the court cited the *Lawrence* decision as relevant authority eleven separate times. It could not have been lost on the Massachusetts Supreme Judicial Court that no less an authority than Justice Scalia believed that *Lawrence* was directly on point.

Thus we return to our puzzle: Why does Justice Scalia repeatedly characterize decisions from which he dissents in ways that will likely give ammunition to those with whom he disagrees, enabling them to extend what he regards as improper precedents even further?

One possibility is tactical. Justice Scalia may think that if he doesn't point out the logical consequences of his colleagues' decisions, somebody else will. Our nation faces no shortage of creative lawyers who know how to read a Supreme Court opinion for all it's worth. Perhaps Justice Scalia reasons that he does his own causes no harm by skewering his colleagues with what he regards as the plainly undesirable consequences of their decisions.

But such tactics—if that is what they are—seem ill advised. There is a world of difference between a lawyer arguing that a precedent entails some result and a Supreme Court Justice doing so. In the latter case—especially if the majority does not specifically respond to the dissenting Justice's parade of supposed horribles—it is a plausible inference that the majority accepts those results as consequences of the principle it has announced (and may not even find them so horrible after all).

Ultimately, Justice Scalia's pointed dissents in the Texas sodomy case and the Denver affirmative action case seem more the product of ill temper than of careful tactics. But this hypothesis only deepens the puzzle, for Justice Scalia is not a man of ill temper. He is charming, witty, and often downright jovial.

At the risk of venturing into psychological speculation, I would offer the following very tentative hypothesis: Justice Scalia views his colleagues' approach to some issues—such as abortion, affirmative action, and gay rights—as not merely *different* from his own, but as fundamentally *illegitimate*.

A self-described "textualist" and "originalist" on such matters, Justice Scalia does not think his views represent simply one of several possibilities. He thinks they are the *only* possibility, entailed by the original understanding of the Constitution's text.

Thus, Justice Scalia does not think that color blindness is merely, all things considered, the best interpretation of the Equal Protection Clause. Rather, he thinks that color blindness is simply *the meaning* of the Equal Protection Clause—the only right, or even plausible, answer to the question of what the Clause entails.

Likewise, Justice Scalia does not think that the right of adults of whatever sex to engage in consensual sex is a plausible inference from the Constitution's language and history. To the contrary, he thinks the language and history *rule out* such an inference. And—crucially—he thinks that this must be obvious to any fair-minded reader of the Constitution. Again, he believes there is only one right, or even plausible, answer to what the Constitution says (or, here, does not say) on this issue.

Accordingly, when Justice Scalia dissents in abortion, affirmative action, and gay rights cases, he is not merely disagreeing with his colleagues. He is going further—and questioning the very legitimacy of, and authority for, their decisions.

Justice Scalia, it seems, believes that his colleagues in the majority are not engaged in fair-minded construction of the Constitution at all. In the face of what he regards as illegitimate substitution of policy preferences for judicial construction, Justice Scalia is not inclined to pull any of his punches—even if that makes it somewhat more likely that the results he deplores will come to pass.

POSTSCRIPT

There is an old story about a foolish father who asks each of his children how he should divide a cookie.

"Fifty-fifty. That's fair," his daughter replies.

"No," says the son. "I want the whole cookie."

"Fine," the father opines. "We'll compromise. Seventy-five, twenty-five."

I sometimes feel as though originalists hope the public reaction to their perspective will mirror the father's attitude in this allegory. Whereas the originalists denounce non-originalist legal interpretation as categorically illegitimate, the non-originalists generally acknowledge that the original understanding of the constitutional text is one legitimate tool for arriving at the best modern interpretation. To an external observer, therefore, it looks as though the only question on the table is whether originalism is wholly right or partly right. But of course the non-originalist position, like the daughter's in the story, is already a compromise.

Although most non-originalists are too polite to put the point quite this way, they actually reciprocate the originalists' wary sentiments. To say, as non-originalists do, that the original understanding is a legitimate tool of constitutional interpretation when used in tandem with other tools such as adherence to judicial precedents, examination of contemporary experience, and prudential considerations, is not to concede to the originalist his claim that originalist jurisprudence is legitimate when the original understanding is the *only* tool. A hammer is one among many useful tools for building a house, but you can't build a house using just a hammer—at least not one with modern conveniences.

NOTES

1. Concrete Works of Colo., Inc. v. City & County of Denver, 321 F.3d 950 (10th Cir. 2003), *cert. denied*, 540 U.S. 1027 (2003).
2. 539 U.S. 558, 586–605 (2003) (Scalia, J., dissenting).
3. Goodridge v. Dep't of Pub. Health, 798 N.E.2d 941 (Mass. 2003).
4. Denver, Colo., Ordinance No. 513, Series of 1990 (Sept. 4, 1990).
5. 488 U.S. 469 (1989).
6. Concrete Works of Colo., Inc. v. City & County of Denver, 540 U.S. 1027, 1027 (2003) (Scalia, J., dissenting from the denial of certiorari) (referring to the Court's affirmative action decision in Grutter v. Bollinger, 539 U.S. 306 (2003)).
7. 539 U.S. 558, 590 (Scalia, J., dissenting).

• 18 •

Is There a Constitutional Right to Sexual Privacy? Finding None, a Federal Appeals Court Upholds Alabama's Sex Toy Prohibition

August 2004

In *Williams v. Attorney General*, a federal appeals court upheld an Alabama law that makes it a crime to sell or advertise sex toys.[1] Although at some level the case—like the statute it sustains—is profoundly silly, it also raises some surprisingly deep issues.

At stake in the *Williams* case was nothing less than the proper role of courts in defining the scope of constitutional rights in the United States. To be sure, Patrick Henry never said, "give me dildos or give me death," but he did speak of liberty, as does the Constitution. And not surprisingly, how the courts go about defining that "liberty" has ramifications far beyond the legality of vibrator sales in Mobile.

In 1998 the Alabama legislature enacted the Anti-Obscenity Enforcement Act, which (among other things) prohibits the sale or barter of "any device designed or marketed as useful primarily for the stimulation of human genital organs."[2] Within a month, the American Civil Liberties Union brought a lawsuit in federal court to enjoin the law's enforcement.[3]

Joining in the ACLU's lawsuit were purveyors of sex toys, who successfully argued to the district judge that the law was irrational. After all, the statute did not actually prevent Alabamans from obtaining sex toys (which they could get by traveling to neighboring states or from anyone willing to give them away). Nor did it prohibit the commercial sale of other items used for sexual gratification, such as ribbed condoms or vibrators that were primarily intended to relieve muscle tension but could also be adapted for sexual purposes. Given these giant loopholes, the judge struck the law down as serving no rational purpose.

But in 2001, the federal appeals court reversed that ruling.[4] Citing well-established constitutional jurisprudence, the appeals court said that a law should not be invalidated as irrational simply because it does not perfectly achieve its objectives.

The appeals court remanded the case to the district court, which again ruled for the plaintiffs, but on a different ground.[5] This time, the district court held that the right to sexual privacy is "fundamental." It therefore reasoned that a law like Alabama's, which infringes on sexual privacy, could only be upheld if it was strictly necessary to serve a very important government interest. The district court then sensibly found that even if an exception-ridden sex toy sales ban is minimally rational, it's not such a vital law that it warrants overriding a fundamental constitutional right.

Then, in the summer of 2004, the federal appeals court once again reversed the federal district court. There is no recognized fundamental right to sexual privacy, the appeals court said. Hence, the law only need be minimally rational after all. And, the court noted, it had *already* concluded that the sex toy ban rationally serves the state's interest in public morals during the first round of appellate review. Accordingly, the court concluded for a second time, though for different reasons, that the law is constitutionally valid.

The practical significance of the appeals court's 2004 ruling is that a small number of Alabama stores may go out of business, and Alabamans will have to jump through some additional hoops to obtain their sex toys—or even go without. But putting its prurient interest aside, the case is probably more important for what it says about the abstract question of how to interpret the Constitution.

The text of the Constitution does not use the terms "rational basis" or "fundamental rights." So where do these legal categories come from and what is their significance? To answer these questions, we need to look at what the Constitution does say.

To begin, the Fourteenth Amendment prohibits any state from making or enforcing "any law which shall abridge the privileges or immunities of citizens of the United States." What are those "privileges or immunities"?

A good place to start looking would be the Bill of Rights, which sets forth familiar protections for speech and religion, against unreasonable searches and seizures, against cruel and unusual punishment, and so forth. Certainly, if anything in the Constitution counts as "privileges or immunities," it should be these familiar liberties.

But the Bill of Rights, the Constitution itself warns, is not an exhaustive list of constitutional protections. To the contrary, the Ninth Amendment states "the enumeration in the Constitution, of certain rights, shall not be construed to deny or disparage others retained by the people."

So it would seem that when our courts are asked to invalidate a state or federal law on the ground that it violates constitutional rights, they must engage in a two-part inquiry: First, they must ask whether the law violates any specifically enumerated right—that is, any right spelled out in the Bill of Rights or elsewhere in the Constitution. Second, they must ask whether the law violates one of the unenumerated rights to which the Ninth and Fourteenth Amendments allude, but whose content they do not specify.

And in fact, that is more or less what the courts do, but not so straightforwardly. Through a series of questionable decisions, the Supreme Court long ago concluded that the Ninth Amendment and the Privileges or Immunities Clause of the Fourteenth Amendment don't quite mean what they appear to say.[6] But meanwhile, through a different series of questionable decisions, the Court has also concluded that another provision of the Constitution—which appears to be less relevant—does justify the conclusion that the courts should enforce unenumerated as well as enumerated constitutional rights.

Which provision is that? It turns out that the Court relies, for the unenumerated rights concept, on the clause of the Fourteenth Amendment that prohibits the states from depriving "any person of life, liberty, or property, without due process of law."

This language would seem to suggest that if a state provides adequate procedures, it *can* deprive people of life, liberty, or property. But the Court has also said that laws that in their *substance* go too far in infringing liberty thereby violate the Due Process Clause.

The idea is that some deprivations are so serious, no amount of process is sufficient. Ironically, the deprivation of life is not one of them, as the Court has not struck down the death penalty, nor even subjected it to exacting judicial scrutiny. But certain deprivations of liberty are on the Court's list. These deprivations, the Justices have reasoned, are prohibited by the due process clause, under the doctrine of "substantive due process."

How do courts figure out whether a law goes too far in infringing liberty? Rather than make an ad hoc judgment in each case, they designate a relatively small number of human activities as those to which we have "fundamental rights," and they then demand that laws infringing these fundamental rights be the "least restrictive means" of furthering a "compelling interest." This test is sometimes called "strict scrutiny."

Laws that do not infringe fundamental rights, in contrast, do not have to pass strict scrutiny. They need only be minimally rational.

The effect of the doctrine is to restrict the world of strict scrutiny to the enumerated rights and the small category of unenumerated fundamental rights. By taking this approach, courts avoid having to second-guess legislatures on virtually all laws. After all, nearly every law restricts somebody's liberty in some way. But because the category of fundamental rights is very limited and the list of enumerated rights is fairly short, most laws are only subject to the deferential rational basis test.

How do the courts know which unenumerated rights, exactly, are fundamental? One might think that because these rights are not enumerated in the Constitution, that document's text is unhelpful. But that is far from true. The Supreme Court has long looked to the enumerated rights for guidance in defining unenumerated rights.

For example, the courts have extrapolated a general right of expressive association from the right of speech and the right to assemble for the purpose of petitioning the government in the First Amendment. The right to assemble together for political purposes and to speak as an individual, the Supreme Court reasoned, together imply a broader right to associate with others for expressive purposes.

Likewise, in its landmark 1965 ruling in *Griswold v. Connecticut*, the Court found a right of married couples to use contraception.[7] Certainly, this right isn't spelled out in the Constitution. So where did it come from? According to the Court, it was based on a zone of privacy that the Justices constructed from provisions of the Bill of Rights such as the Fourth Amendment prohibition on unreasonable searches and seizures, and the Fifth Amendment right against compelled testimony.

The courts have also looked to the logical implications and extensions of their prior precedents in deciding whether a right is fundamental. Thus, the abortion right recognized in *Roe v. Wade*[8] built upon *Griswold* and earlier cases that the Justices said had, even before *Roe*, already made the decision whether to become a parent was a fundamental right.

Alongside this process of extrapolation and analogy drawing, the Court has articulated a couple of verbal formulae to be used to determine whether a right is fundamental. The Court may look to whether the purported fundamental right is deeply rooted in American history and tradition; and it may also look to whether the purported fundamental right is implicit in the concept of ordered liberty.

At least in recent years, the Supreme Court has been very reluctant to recognize *new* unenumerated rights under these formulae. However, it has sometimes ruled for plaintiffs who claimed merely to be asserting new *applications* of *old* unenumerated rights.

Bedeviling the fundamental rights issue, however, is what might be called the *generality* problem: At what level of generality should a court frame a claimed right? The choice matters greatly.

Suppose, for instance, that prospective adoptive parents are rejected by their state child welfare agency on the ground that they were both previously convicted of embezzlement. The couple says they've served their time, learned their lesson, and now they are qualified to provide a loving home for a child who needs one.

Is their proffered "right to adopt" the sort of brand new right that the court will likely reject? Or is it merely a new application of an old fundamental right—the right to become a parent?

The answer makes a profound difference because of the nature of the inquiry that follows: Remember, only deprivations of a fundamental right—not deprivations of any aspect of "liberty"—trigger strict scrutiny. Moreover, whether strict scrutiny is applied makes a great deal of difference. If it does not, the government's justification for infringing a given right will almost certainly be upheld as at least minimally rational.

For a court intent on denying the fundamentality of a claimed right, it is always possible to read the prior cases narrowly—and to define the newly claimed right so narrowly that it looks ridiculous.

For example, consider the 1986 Supreme Court decision in *Bowers v. Hardwick*. There, the 5–4 majority defined the right claimed as merely (and narrowly) a right to "homosexual sodomy."[9] In 2003, when the Court decided *Lawrence v. Texas*, and overruled *Hardwick*, it did so in part because it rejected that characterization as demeaning.[10]

Conversely, it is also possible to define a right so broadly that the Court will be obliged to reject it for fear of a parade of horribles. The Supreme Court has taken this tack too when it wanted to deny a right.

For example, in the 1997 case of *Washington v. Glucksberg*, the plaintiffs sought recognition for the right "of competent, terminally ill adults to make end-of-life decisions free of undue government interference"—a characterization that sounds like a suitably small extension of prior precedent accepting a right to refuse medical treatment.[11] But the Court reformulated the issue as the much broader question of whether to recognize "a right to commit suicide which itself includes a right to assistance in doing so."[12] Not surprisingly, it then rejected that right.

The appeals court in *Williams*, the Alabama sex toy case, appeared to rely on both of these framing techniques.

In its quotation of the district court opinion, the appeals court suggested that the case posed the question whether there is an absurdly narrow (and vulgar) fundamental right to use "vibrators, dildos, anal beads, and artificial vaginas."[13] It is not difficult to imagine what the court would have said had it faced that question squarely.

The appeals court in *Williams* also raised the specter of a parade of horribles under the broader formulation. It noted that the U.S. Supreme Court has never recognized a general right of sexual privacy in so many words (although the dissent disagreed with the majority's characterization of the *Lawrence* opinion on this point). And then the appeals court majority opined that such a right should be rejected because (among other reasons) it would encompass pederasty, prostitution, and incest—which the judges believed were clearly proscribable consistent with the Constitution.

If some formulations of an asserted right are too narrow, and others are too broad, is there a formulation that satisfies the Goldilocks condition: one that is "just right?"

The answer is yes, sometimes there is—and probably there was in *Williams*, though the appeals court rejected it.

At the end of the day, both the majority and the dissent in *Williams* agreed that the proper level of generality at which to formulate the claim was as a right of sexual privacy. They just disagreed over whether to recognize that right.

Invoking the Supreme Court's *Lawrence* decision, dissenting Judge Barkett argued that the majority's parade of horribles did not follow from recognizing a right to sexual privacy. That right, Judge Barkett emphasized, need not be extended to cases involving minors, or other cases (such as adult incest) where consent may not easily be refused. The majority, by contrast, did not find these distinctions persuasive, and thought they were not compelled by *Lawrence*.

Even though the "Goldilocks condition" was satisfied in *Williams*, it will not always be satisfied. Consider a hypothetical case that raises this question: Should an asserted right to clone oneself be understood as a new right, or as an example of the familiar right to become a parent?

Or consider a case that raises this issue: Is a claimed right to use encryption technologies a new right, or an example of the familiar (enumerated) right to freedom of speech?

Questions like these do not answer themselves, of course. Reasonable minds will differ about the best characterization of the right asserted in such cases. And for this very reason, some people argue that the courts should simply defer to the legislature in such matters.

That's a plausible position, but it runs away from the most natural reading of the Privileges or Immunities Clause and the Ninth Amendment—which plainly seem to put the courts in the business of identifying unenumerated rights. And because the Supreme Court has long accepted this responsibility, albeit under the Due Process Clause, that means that judges must squarely face the generality problem when they decide which rights are fundamental.[14]

That difficult task requires reason, judgment, and humility. Merely observing that the Constitution's text nowhere mentions anal beads or artificial vaginas is both true and amusing. But it doesn't help answer the real question in a case like *Williams*.

POSTSCRIPT

In recent years, the Supreme Court's substantive due process jurisprudence has tended to result in the recognition of rights that political liberals favor—such as contraception, abortion, same-sex intimacy, and perhaps a broader right of sexual privacy. But from the late nineteenth century through the late 1930s, substantive due process was most frequently used to support economic rights of property owners and employers, including most notably, the 1905 decision in *Lochner v. New York*, which invalidated a law prohibiting bakers from working more than sixty hours per week.[15] Under today's rational basis test, that law would certainly be upheld as rationally related to the state's goal of ensuring the health and welfare of bakers and the public more broadly. At the time, however, the Court applied a much less deferential test.

Indeed, even today's "liberal" right of privacy has roots in a more conservative set of rulings. In two cases in the 1920s, the Supreme Court held that substantive due process protects the right of parents, within broad limits, to direct the upbringing and education of their children.[16] These precedents form the doctrinal foundation for modern rulings, including *Roe v. Wade*, which protect the decision whether to become a parent in the first place.

Moreover, the conservative roots of modern privacy doctrine are not merely a historical artifact. They have current force in protecting, for example, the right of parents to send their children to private schools of their own choosing or to provide home schooling if they object on religious or other grounds to the instruction offered in the public schools.[17] And *Roe* and the other substantive due process privacy cases would surely invalidate any attempt by the federal government or a state to coerce a woman into having an abortion or otherwise to limit family size, as the government of China does through its one-child policy. So it turns out that neither substantive due process in general nor even the right of privacy is especially liberal (or conservative).

If substantive due process does have a bias, it is libertarian, and libertarianism—or "classical liberalism"—does not fit neatly into today's political divisions between right and left. To say this is not, of course, to say that modern substantive due process doctrine is justified. Its critics have a point when they say that the people, through their elected representatives, are better qualified than unelected judges to say which rights not expressly spelled out in the Constitution are nonetheless sheltered by its more open-ended terms. But the defenders of unenumerated rights also have a point when they reply that it is not the judges but the Constitution itself, through the Ninth Amendment and the Fourteenth Amendment's Privileges or

Immunities Clause, that has a libertarian bias. There is thus more than a little irony in the way that self-proclaimed textualists dismiss or implausibly construe these constitutional provisions that seem quite plainly to invite all those charged with interpreting the Constitution—including judges—to look beyond the document's four corners.

NOTES

1. 378 F.3d 1232 (11th Cir. 2004) (upholding Ala. Code § 13A-12–200.2 (2004)).
2. Ala. Code §§ 13A-12–200.2(a)(1)–(3) (2004).
3. Williams v. Pryor, 41 F. Supp. 2d 1257 (N.D. Ala. 1999).
4. Williams v. Pryor, 240 F.3d 944 (11th Cir. 2001).
5. Williams v. Pryor, 220 F. Supp. 2d 1257 (N.D. Ala. 2002).
6. In *The Slaughterhouse Cases*, 83 U.S. (16 Wall.) 36, 76–79 (1872), the Court construed the Privileges or Immunities Clause of the Fourteenth Amendment as leaving state power to curtail individual rights essentially as it was before the Civil War. As for the Ninth Amendment, until the late twentieth century, it was simply ignored or read, contrary to its seemingly plain textual import, as a guarantee of state and local autonomy, rather than as a recognition of unenumerated rights. *See* Kurt T. Lash, *The Lost Jurisprudence of the Ninth Amendment*, 83 Tex. L. Rev. 597 (2005).
7. 381 U.S. 479 (1965).
8. 410 U.S. 113 (1973).
9. 478 U.S. 186, 190 (1986).
10. 539 U.S. 558, 567 (2003).
11. 521 U.S. 702, 724 (1997) (citing Brief of Respondents at 10, *Glucksberg*, 521 U.S. 702 (No. 96–110), 1996 WL 708925).
12. *Id.* at 723.
13. Williams v. Pryor, 378 F.3d 1232, 1244 (11th Cir. 2004).
14. For extended discussion of the generality problem, see Laurence H. Tribe & Michael C. Dorf, *Levels of Generality in the Definition of Rights*, 57 U. Chi. L. Rev. 1057 (1990).
15. 198 U.S. 45 (1905).
16. *See* Pierce v. Soc'y of Sisters, 268 U.S. 510 (1925); Meyer v. Nebraska, 262 U.S. 390 (1923).
17. The Supreme Court has not ruled directly on the home schooling issue, although in *Wisconsin v. Yoder*, 406 U.S. 205 (1972), it held that Amish parents were constitutionally entitled to an exemption from a state law requiring that children attend school until the age of sixteen. The Court later explained that *Yoder* was *not* simply an interpretation of the Free Exercise of Religion Clause of the First Amendment but was based in substantive due process as well. *See* Employment Div. v. Smith, 494 U.S. 872, 881 & n.1 (1990).

IV

LIBERTY, SECURITY, AND WAR

The attacks of September 11, 2001, and the U.S. military actions in Afghanistan and Iraq raised a host of legal questions. Many involve the challenge of balancing claims of liberty and equality against security. It is easy to get carried away with this sort of thinking, however. Sometimes those who favor the security side of the balance talk as though the fact that some measure threatens civil rights and civil liberties means that it must therefore enhance security. This is obviously nonsense. Repressive measures may simply be repressive. Worse, they may be counterproductive, as when they generate so much resentment among the targeted community—in our present circumstances, Arabs and Muslims—that cooperation ceases.

Still, the fact that we need not always trade off liberty and equality against security does not mean that we never face such tradeoffs. The difficulty in those cases is dealing with uncertainty.

During each of the three great international conflicts of the twentieth century, American government struck a balance that, viewed in the sober light of hindsight, was clearly insufficiently protective of civil rights and civil liberties: During the first Red Scare, which accompanied the end of World War I, Communists and other radicals were successfully prosecuted for peaceful protest; a similar fate befell dissidents during the second Red Scare of the Cold War; and in between, during World War II, our government imprisoned thousands of loyal American citizens simply on the basis of their Japanese ancestry.[1] Most readers of this book either were not yet born or were too young to have been politically active during each of these prior periods, and would therefore probably like to tell themselves that had they lived through those times, they would not have succumbed to hysteria.

Yet how does one know, in real time, that the danger is being exaggerated? A November 2001 *New York Times* article (accurately) quoted my characterization of the initial relative silence of liberals in reaction to some of the more aggressive domestic responses of the Bush Administration to the threat of terrorism. "[T]he majority position" among liberals, I said, "is, 'Well, I'm not quite sure I would go as far as the attorney general [then John Ashcroft], but I can understand why they're doing it.'" I went on to justify this reticence as follows: "The traditional way we balance these things is with the maxim, 'It's better that 10 guilty men go free than one innocent man be in jail.' I think people are a little nervous about applying that maxim where the 10 guilty men who are going to go free could have biological weapons."[2]

The chapters in this section partly reflect my own intellectual journey as the events of September 11—which inflicted their greatest damage in the city where I live and work—receded in time. The first of these, which addresses the peculiar status of "unlawful combatant," is somewhat sympathetic to the Bush Administration's position at the time. Later chapters, however, express greater skepticism toward claims made in the name of national security. Did I initially succumb to the hysteria around me, only regaining my civil libertarian moorings when it was too late? Or does that get things exactly backwards? Perhaps the better response was the initial one, with my civil libertarian relapse representing a kind of dangerous amnesia. I suspect (or perhaps I merely hope) that neither hypothesis can be confirmed for many years.

In any event, the metaphor of balancing is misleading. Although the iconic blindfolded figure of justice holds a balance in her hand, balancing has always connoted a kind of subjective decision making that seems antithetical to law. As Justice Scalia nicely made the point in a different context, balancing incommensurables such as liberty and security is "like judging whether a particular line is longer than a particular rock is heavy."[3] Sometimes people, including judges, must make such decisions, but it is hard to see how *law* figures into such an all-things-considered judgment.

Yet as you read the chapters in this section, you will find that they are chock full of law. Indeed, chapter 24, "Is the War on Iraq Lawful?," is especially illustrative. In it, I argue that the U.S.-led invasion of Iraq in March 2003 violated international law. This chapter, which received considerable play around the world when it first appeared as a column, was generally portrayed as reflecting an anti-war viewpoint. Now it happens that I thought the invasion of Iraq was misguided on policy grounds, but I didn't actually say so in the column. On the contrary, as you'll soon see, I argued that even though the war was illegal, it might have been justified anyway. That is, my column on the Iraq war, like this book as a whole, made the case for the partial autonomy of law: Simply put, it is possible to reach different conclusions about what one thinks the law requires, forbids, or permits, and what one thinks would be desirable on political, ethical, or pragmatic grounds.

NOTES

1. For an excellent account of the fate of freedom of speech during these periods, see Geoffrey R. Stone, Perilous Times: Free Speech in Wartime from the Sedition Act of 1798 to the War on Terrorism (New York: W.W. Norton & Co., 2004).
2. Pam Belluck, *Hue and Murmur over Curbed Rights*, N.Y. Times, Nov. 17, 2001, at B8.
3. Bendix Autolite Corp. v. Midwesco Enters., Inc., 486 U.S. 888, 897 (1988) (Scalia, J., concurring).

• 19 •

What Is an "Unlawful Combatant," and Why It Matters: The Status of Detained al-Qaeda and Taliban Fighters

January 2002

According to Defense Secretary Rumsfeld, the Taliban and al-Qaeda fighters being held captive at the United States Naval Base at Guantanamo Bay, Cuba, are not prisoners of war, but "unlawful combatants."[1] What's the difference?

The short answer is that a prisoner of war is entitled to the protections set forth in the 1949 Geneva Convention.[2] In contrast, an unlawful combatant is a fighter who does not play by the accepted rules of war, and therefore does not qualify for the Convention's protections.

Buried within that short answer, however, are a host of complexities and troubling implications.

First, what does it take to qualify as a prisoner of war? Article IV of the Geneva Convention states that members of irregular militias like al-Qaeda qualify for prisoner-of-war status if their military organization satisfies four criteria: "(a) that of being commanded by a person responsible for his subordinates; (b) that of having a fixed distinctive sign recognizable at a distance; (c) that of carrying arms openly; [and] (d) that of conducting their operations in accordance with the laws and customs of war."

Al-Qaeda does not satisfy these conditions. Perhaps Osama bin Laden could be considered "a person responsible for his subordinates," although the cell structure of al-Qaeda belies the notion of a chain of command. But in any event, al-Qaeda members openly flout the remaining three conditions.

Al-Qaeda members deliberately attempt to blend into the civilian population—violating the requirement of having a "fixed distinctive sign" and "carrying arms openly." Moreover, they target civilians, which violates the "laws and customs of war."

Thus, al-Qaeda members need not be treated as prisoners of war.

The question whether detained Taliban members qualify as prisoners of war under the Geneva Convention's test is more difficult—as one might instinctively think, given that the Taliban fighters resemble a traditional army to a greater extent than do the al-Qaeda fighters, who come from a variety of different nations and principally attack civilians.

The Taliban was never recognized as the legitimate government of Afghanistan by the United Nations or the United States, and only a handful of countries ever established formal diplomatic relations with the Taliban. Nevertheless, despite its lack of formal recognition, the Taliban would still be entitled to the protections of the Geneva Convention if it satisfied the four criteria listed above.

Did it? To begin, the Taliban has, or at least formerly had, a tighter command structure than al-Qaeda, suggesting it might satisfy the first criterion of "being commanded by a person responsible for his subordinates." However, Taliban members did not appear to satisfy the second and third criteria, for they did not wear uniforms that bore a "fixed distinctive sign recognizable at a distance," nor did they invariably "carry arms openly." Should these facts disqualify them from prisoner-of-war status?

Until its overthrow, the Taliban was the actual (though not recognized) government of Afghanistan, and it was attacked as such by the United States, albeit in justifiable self-defense. If Taliban members did not wear distinctive uniforms before we attacked, one might think that they should not be faulted for failing to don such uniforms immediately once the shooting started.

But in the end, this argument is unpersuasive. The requirement of a distinctive sign is no mere technicality. Its object, like many of the laws of war, is to enable the enemy to distinguish combatants from civilians, and thus to minimize civilian casualties. Yet the Taliban made clear that it was not interested in complying with the letter or spirit of the law of war.

For example, when it still controlled Kabul, the Taliban hid military equipment among the civilian population. Furthermore, as the war unfolded, it became increasingly difficult to distinguish the Taliban from al-Qaeda—which, as we have seen, clearly does not qualify to have its members treated as prisoners of war.

Even if not technically prisoners of war, al-Qaeda and Taliban captives still qualify for "humane treatment" under the Body of Principles for the Protection of All Persons under Any Form of Detention or Imprisonment,[3] a resolution adopted by the United Nations General Assembly in 1988.

Moreover, one might wonder, what is the harm in affording the captives somewhat better treatment than they are entitled to under international law? After all, the Geneva Convention hardly requires that prisoners of war be housed in four-star hotels.

The Administration's objection to affording al-Qaeda and Taliban captives prisoner-of-war status probably has less to do with the conditions in which the captives are held than with what the Administration plans to do with them in the long term.

Under President Bush's military order of November 13, 2001, al-Qaeda members and those who harbored them can be tried by military tribunals.[4] The Supreme Court approved the use of such tribunals for unlawful combatants in the 1942 Nazi saboteur case, *Ex parte Quirin*.[5]

Most of the public discussion of the President's order and the *Quirin* case has centered on the question of when a defendant can be subject to the jurisdiction of a military tribunal rather than a civilian court. But whatever the answer to that question, *Quirin* takes for granted that only *unlawful* combatants can be tried by the sort of irregular tribunals at issue in that case and contemplated by the President's order.

Lawful combatants—that is, prisoners of war—are entitled to substantive and procedural protections not contemplated by Bush's order. Accordingly, the question of whether al-Qaeda and Taliban fighters are prisoners of war or unlawful combatants turns out to matter a great deal, at least potentially.

To be sure, American courts might not have occasion to decide the question whether al-Qaeda and Taliban captives are in fact unlawful combatants. That is because another Supreme Court decision—the 1950 ruling in *Johnson v. Eisentrager*[6]—holds that enemy aliens who have not entered the United States are not entitled to access to our courts.

Accordingly, so long as the al-Qaeda and Taliban fighters are held at Guantanamo Bay and thus not deemed to have entered the United States, their only route of appeal would appear to be within the executive branch. Put more bluntly, they will have only the procedural recourse the Administration allows them.

However, the applicability of *Eisentrager* to the present circumstances is itself open to question, for two reasons. First, in that case, the Court relied on the existence of a formal declaration of war and the fact that the German petitioners were citizens of a hostile sovereign power.

In contrast, in the present conflict, whether Congress's joint resolution authorizing the use of force[7] counts as a declaration of war, and whether al-Qaeda is sufficiently state-like to count as a foreign sovereign, are open questions.

Second, while *Eisentrager* holds that the Constitution permits the government to deny enemy aliens outside the United States access to our courts, the federal habeas corpus statute can be construed to afford such enemy aliens greater court access than the Constitution alone requires.[8] Under that construction, the President's military order would be invalid. (Note that the President's order also purports to eliminate judicial review even for aliens *within* the

United States, a position clearly at odds with statutory and constitutional law, but one that is not directly relevant to the fate of the Guantanamo Bay captives.)

For these two reasons, *Eisentrager*'s application to the present circumstances is uncertain. Accordingly, it is understandable that the Administration would be eager to classify those captives it plans to try by military commission as unlawful combatants.

If the captives are unlawful combatants, they fall within the rule of *Quirin*. And if so, it does not matter whether they *also* fall within the rule of *Eisentrager*: If they do not, they are entitled to habeas corpus review, but a court entertaining their habeas corpus petitions would be obliged to uphold their convictions under *Quirin*.

There is a further reason why the Administration is eager to deny prisoner-of-war status to the al-Qaeda and Taliban fighters. Article 118 of the Geneva Convention requires that prisoners of war be "repatriated without delay after the cessation of active hostilities." Thus, if the captives are prisoners of war, they must eventually be returned to their home countries.

That prospect is troubling. At the end of a war between conventional foes, it is expected that repatriated fighters will resume their civilian lives. Individual veterans might continue to harbor ill will toward their former enemies, but for the most part, even a cold peace between nations tamps down such feelings.

But there is good reason to worry that Taliban and especially al-Qaeda fighters will not so readily have a change of heart. Members of al-Qaeda do not act out of patriotic duty to obey the commands of a military leader, but out of an ideology that instructs them to attack and kill American civilians as a means of entering the kingdom of heaven. It is doubtful that any formal cessation of hostilities would lead them to abandon what they regard as a jihad.

Moreover, unlike traditional soldiers, al-Qaeda members do not need an army in order to act. As we have learned, they can act in small groups or even individually. For this reason, too, repatriation seems far more dangerous for an al-Qaeda member than for a traditional soldier.

The truth is that whether we try them in civilian courts, courts-martial, ad hoc military tribunals, or not at all, the al-Qaeda and at least some of the Taliban captives may be too dangerous ever to be released. Assuming that many or most of them will not be subject to the death penalty, that fact commits the United States to detaining them indefinitely.

The Administration's response to this problem is to deem the Taliban and al-Qaeda fighters unlawful combatants who are not entitled to anything better than indefinite detention.[9]

As we have seen, the contention that these fighters are unlawful combatants is based upon a plausible reading of the Geneva Convention. Indeed, it would be difficult to come to any other conclusion when applying the Geneva Convention's four-part test to al-Qaeda fighters.

Nevertheless, treating the al-Qaeda and Taliban captives as prisoners of war, whether or not they are legally entitled to the status, would be less risky than it may at first appear. So long as al-Qaeda and its deadly ideology exists, we cannot say that there has been, in the words of the Geneva Convention, a "cessation of active hostilities," entitling the captives to be released. In that respect, as in others, this is a different type of war indeed.

POSTSCRIPT

In the 2004 case of *Rasul v. Bush*,[10] the Supreme Court ruled that modern jurisdictional statutes did indeed render the *Eisentrager* decision inapplicable to Guantanamo Bay. The Court thus permitted captives held there to file habeas corpus petitions—although the Justices did not specify what substantive standard would be used to evaluate the claims that these captives might eventually assert.

Meanwhile, I seem to have missed the main reason why the Administration was so set on denying prisoner-of-war status to the Guantanamo Bay captives. The Administration was not so intent on trying them before military commissions, nor was it even especially worried about repatriation. Rather, the main concern appears to have been interrogation. Under Article 17 of the 1949 Geneva Convention, prisoners of war are only obliged to provide name, rank, date of birth, and serial number. They may not be subject to torture or "any other form of coercion" to extract information. As we now know, detainees—including but not limited to those held on Guantanamo—were and continue to be subject to coercive interrogation that the International Committee of the Red Cross called "tantamount to torture."[11] That is truly shameful. Moreover, torture of anyone, even unlawful combatants, is prohibited by other international agreements to which the United States is a signatory, as I discuss in the next chapter.

NOTES

1. *See* Katharine Q. Seelye, *First 'Unlawful Combatants' Seized in Afghanistan Arrive at U.S. Base in Cuba*, N.Y. Times, Jan. 12, 2002, at A7.

2. Geneva Convention Relative to the Treatment of Prisoners of War of August 12, 1949, *opened for signature* Aug. 12, 1949, art. 5, 6 U.S.T. 3316, 75 U.N.T.S. 135 [hereinafter "Geneva Convention"].

3. G.A. Res. 43/173, UN Doc. A/RES/43/49 (Dec. 9, 1988).

4. Detention, Treatment, and Trial of Certain Non-Citizens in the War Against Terrorism, 66 Fed. Reg. 57,833 (Nov. 16, 2001).

5. 317 U.S. 1 (1942).

6. 339 U.S. 763 (1950).

7. Authorization for Use of Military Force, Pub. L. No. 107–40, 115 Stat. 224 (2001).

8. 28 U.S.C. § 2241 (2000). As discussed in the postscript to this chapter, the Supreme Court held this statute applicable to non-citizens detained on Guantanamo in *Rasul v. Bush*, 542 U.S. 466 (2004).

9. *See* John Diamond, *U.S. Rejects POW Label; War Detainees Don't Deserve Special Status, Rumsfeld Says*, Chi. Trib., Jan. 28, 2002, at 1.

10. 542 U.S. 466 (2004).

11. Although the reports of the International Committee of the Red Cross are confidential, the Committee's characterization of the United States' treatment of its prisoners was widely reported. *E.g.*, Neil A. Lewis, *Red Cross Finds Detainee Abuse in Guantanamo*, N.Y. Times, Nov. 30, 2004, at A1. The International Committee of the Red Cross maintains the confidentiality of its reports "so as to prevent humanitarian issues from becoming politicized." International Committee of the Red Cross, What Is the ICRC's Position on the Reported Abuse of Iraqi Prisoners by US and UK Forces? (May 6, 2004). Available on the ICRC website, (www.icrc.org).

• 20 •

The Justice Department's Change of Heart Regarding Torture: A Fair-Minded and Praiseworthy Analysis that Could Have Gone Still Further

January 2005

As 2004 drew to a close, the Office of Legal Counsel of the United States Department of Justice took an important step toward restoring its own integrity: It released a memorandum[1] essentially repudiating its earlier analysis of the circumstances under which someone could be found criminally liable for engaging in torture. That earlier memorandum of August 2002[2] had turned intellectual somersaults to find loopholes and excuses for the commission of what a lay observer would surely consider torture.

The new memo, in contrast, is fair-minded and reasonable. Accordingly, its author, Acting Assistant Attorney General Daniel Levin, deserves considerable praise. As I explain below, the memo definitively repudiates two of the most outrageous positions set forth in the August 2002 memo: the almost impossibly high threshold for finding an act of torture; and the contention that a torturer can escape criminal liability if he engages in torture with a noble goal in mind, such as to extract vital information from the torture victim.

In one particular, however, the new memo could have gone further. The August 2002 memo had set forth a third outrageous proposition: that Congress lacks the power to prohibit torture undertaken at the behest of the President, acting in his capacity as commander in chief. Although the new memo laudably declines to endorse this view, it does not formally repudiate the position either.

That is unfortunate, because the August 2002 memo's contentions regarding the wartime powers of the President are truly frightening. They deserve to be repudiated expressly and unequivocally.

The Office of Legal Counsel (OLC) provides legal advice to the executive branch of the federal government on important matters of public policy. Its August 2002 memo was signed by Jay Bybee, then the head of OLC and now a federal appeals court judge. Judge Bybee, who was confirmed by the Senate before the memo came to light, has refused to comment on it.[3]

Much of the political heat produced by the Bybee memo has accordingly been directed elsewhere—at the Bush Administration in general and at then–White House Counsel Alberto Gonzales, to whom the memo was addressed, in particular. Gonzales will shortly face his own Senate confirmation hearings on his nomination to become attorney general. When he does, he will likely be asked why he sought legal advice about the "standards of conduct" under the international treaty and the federal statute barring torture.

The August 2002 memo recites OLC's understanding that the torture issue arose "in the context of the conduct of interrogations outside of the United States."[4] One can reasonably infer, therefore, that the Bush Administration, with the approval of Gonzales, was interested in pushing the envelope in its treatment of suspected al-Qaeda terrorists and others detained in Afghanistan, at Guantanamo Bay, and elsewhere.

That inference receives further support from reports of the treatment of prisoners in Iraq. Together, the evidence suggests that U.S. military and civilian interrogators were given the green light to engage in practices that the International Committee of the Red Cross has described as "tantamount to torture."[5]

The Senate is thus entitled to inquire whether Gonzales knew or should have known that his request for legal advice regarding potential criminal liability for torture was part of a scheme to authorize—or at least turn a blind eye toward—torture.

In the wake of the release of the December 2004 memo, some commentators have suggested that the Administration is hoping to defuse the potentially explosive issue of the role Gonzales played with respect to the August 2002 memo.[6] If that is the Administration's hope, however, it seems a vain one; the fact that OLC has now repudiated the views it expressed earlier sheds little light on Gonzales's fitness to serve as the nation's chief law enforcement officer.

If one were to conclude that Gonzales showed poor judgment and disrespect for the rule of law by asking for the August 2002 memo, then it is hard to see how OLC's more recent change of heart would alter this conclusion. A confession of error by Gonzales himself might be relevant, but why should an about-face by OLC be relevant?

Let us put these political considerations aside for now, however, and focus on the law. What is the legal significance of the August 2002 memo and the December 2004 memo repudiating it?

OLC memos do not have the force of law in quite the way that opinions of the Supreme Court do, but neither are they mere opinion pieces about the law in the way that, say, the chapters in this book are. OLC is often asked to address constitutional issues that will never make it to court—what lawyers call non-justiciable political questions. In these circumstances, the formal advice of OLC may be the only sort of "precedent" that exists.

Moreover, although the head of OLC and the top deputies are political appointees, the office as a whole has long had a culture of independence. The dedicated and talented lawyers who work at OLC typically see themselves not as mere servants of the Administration that happens to seek their advice, but also as keepers of an inter-generational trust. Thus, one commonly sees OLC memos taking seriously the views expressed in prior OLC memos prepared for Presidents of either political party. The OLC under Republican administrations approvingly cites the memos of its predecessors in Democratic administrations, and vice-versa.

Against this background, the August 2002 memo can only be described as a serious departure from longstanding OLC practice. In content and tone, the memo reads much like a document that an overzealous young associate in a law firm would prepare in response to a partner's request for whatever arguments can be concocted to enable the firm's client to avoid criminal liability.

The December 2004 memo, however, is markedly different. Although its analysis is no less lawyerly than that contained in the August 2002 memo, it shows a sensitivity to the important role that OLC plays in shaping national policy—a sensitivity that was sorely lacking in the earlier memo.

As its title suggests, the United Nations Convention against Torture and Other Cruel, Inhuman or Degrading Treatment or Punishment[7] prohibits not only torture but also less serious forms of cruelty, inhumanity, and degradation. The United States ratified the Convention and subsequently enacted federal legislation that defines torture[8] and establishes criminal liability[9] for Americans and others found in the United States who commit torture abroad.

Significantly, however, the federal statute does not impose criminal liability for cruel, inhuman, or degrading acts. Under a reservation adopted by the Senate when it ratified the UN Convention, such lesser acts are equated with treatment that would be considered unconstitutional under the Fifth, Eighth, and Fourteenth Amendments.

The August 2002 memo seizes on the distinction between, on the one hand, torture, as defined in both the UN Convention and the U.S. implementing legislation as the infliction of "severe pain or suffering," and, on the other hand, "mere" cruel, inhuman, or degrading acts. The basic strategy of the August 2002 memo on this point is to treat all but the most horrific acts as insufficiently severe to constitute torture. Thus, the August 2002 memo sets the torture threshold at "excruciating and agonizing"[10] pain or pain "equivalent in intensity to the pain accompanying serious physical injury, such as organ failure, impairment of bodily function, or even death."[11]

Although the December 2004 memo recognizes that the plain text of the Convention and federal law do distinguish between torture and lesser degradations, it disavows the extremely high threshold advocated in the August 2002 memo.

To be sure, the new memo is not especially helpful in establishing exactly how much pain or suffering is necessary to count as "severe." For the most part, the memo simply describes cases in which the courts have and have not found torture to have occurred.

But this is probably the prudent course. Cruel, inhuman, and degrading forms of treatment are, after all, no more lawful than torture, even if they do not give rise to criminal liability in the U.S. courts. To draw sharp distinctions between torture and these "lesser" horrors, as the August 2002 memo attempted to do, could only serve to signal to potential torturers how they can avoid imprisonment while still inflicting great pain and suffering. OLC apparently now realizes that it is inappropriate to send such signals.

Perhaps the most jarring aspect of the August 2002 memo was its argument that a defendant could escape criminal liability for committing torture by presenting a defense of necessity or self-defense.

Under either defense, the torturer could argue that he tortured his victim in order to prevent some terrible harm. To use the classic example, one could claim that he had in custody a suspect believed to have planted a time bomb that, if not defused, would kill many innocents. If the defendant reasonably believed that by torturing the suspect, he would learn the location of the bomb and thus save the innocents, the argument goes, he cannot be punished for having done so.

The notion that torture is sometimes morally justified has real appeal. If one stipulates sufficiently great certainty of a catastrophe, all but the most punctilious Kantians will be tempted to say that it is better to torture the terrorist than to allow the catastrophe to occur.

The difficulty, though, is that the real world provides probabilities rather than certainties. Categorical prohibitions against torture like the one contained in the UN Convention and federal law are based on the sensible assumption that if torture is condoned in the extreme case of the *known* terrorist who has certainly planted the ticking time bomb, security officers will come to believe that they hear bombs ticking everywhere, and will use torture against people merely *suspected* of posing a security threat.

Only by prohibiting torture under all circumstances, such laws assume, can we prevent an extremely limited authorization—for torture in extreme circumstances—from becoming a license for routine torture.

It is possible that this logic is wrong. Perhaps, as Alan Dershowitz[12] and others have argued recently, careful regulation can prevent us from slipping down the slope from rare to common torture.

But if so, that is an argument for a dramatic *change* in the law, rather than an argument for reading nonexistent exceptions into the existing international and U.S. categorical bans on torture. The August 2002 memo, in proposing such exceptions, would have gutted the laws it purported to interpret.

Accordingly, the December 2004 memo states unequivocally, "there is no exception under the statute permitting torture to be used for a 'good reason.'"[13]

The principal disappointment in the December 2004 memo is its failure to condemn the view of presidential power expressed in the August 2002 memo. That earlier memo asserted that "the President enjoys complete discretion in the exercise of his Commander-in-Chief authority and in conducting operations against hostile forces."[14] It argued that Congress lacks the constitutional power to limit the President's decisions about how to treat captives.

The August 2002 memo had attempted to justify these sweeping propositions largely by presenting selective, out-of-context citations of broad language in a few Supreme Court opinions, and citing OLC's own recent post-9/11 memos.

The December 2004 memo should have unequivocally repudiated the unlimited view of presidential power espoused in August 2002. Article I, Section 8 of the Constitution commits to *Congress* the authority "to make Rules concerning Captures on Land and Water." From this language, Congress's authority to limit the President's treatment of captives is clear.

Indeed, if the August 2002 memo's view of presidential power were accepted, the President could unilaterally order discipline of U.S. service members even if that discipline clearly contradicted the Uniform Code of Military Justice, enacted by Congress. He could even order that all enemy captives be shot, notwithstanding clear treaty obligations to the contrary. These extreme examples show the absurdity of any claim that the President has an entirely free hand in the treatment of captives or the conduct of war more generally.

The December 2004 memo, by its terms "supersedes the August 2002 Memorandum in its entirety."[15] For that reason, the August 2002 assertion of the President's virtually unlimited power as commander in chief can no longer be said to constitute official OLC policy.

However, the December 2004 memo does *not* specifically disavow the August 2002 view of presidential authority. Deeming analysis of such power "unnecessary," the December 2004 memo simply declines to address the subject.

Why did the memo's author feel it was unnecessary to address this key point? The memo itself claims that "[c]onsideration of the bounds of any" presidential authority to authorize torture in violation of Acts of Congress "would be inconsistent with the President's unequivocal directive that United States personnel not engage in torture."[16]

But this explanation for the new memo's reticence as to the scope of presidential authority does not quite wash, for *none* of the OLC analysis is, strictly speaking, necessary; if the new memo had been limited to necessary analysis, there would have been no memo at all.

Given that U.S. personnel are not supposed to engage in torture or cruel, inhuman, or degrading treatment of prisoners, there is no necessity to clarify the line between the two categories of forbidden conduct; yet the December 2004 memo does just that. Similarly, with respect to the question of whether there is a good-reason exception to the torture prohibition, and a number of other issues, the December 2004 memo does not simply wash away the conclusions of the August 2002 memo; it affirmatively draws contrary conclusions.

Accordingly, one is left to worry that OLC declined to assert limits on presidential authority because OLC may continue to entertain a dangerously broad view of that authority.

Nonetheless, putting aside the legitimate worry about what the December 2004 memo does not say about presidential power, the memo is, on the whole, a most welcome development. Whatever the actual motives of the Justice Department officials who released it when they did, the memo itself should have the salutary effect of communicating to personnel overseas that the U.S. neither encourages nor tolerates torture.

POSTSCRIPT

The original OLC torture memo did indeed receive prominent attention during the Senate hearings on Gonzales, although in the end he was confirmed by a vote of 60 to 36.[17] If the OLC memo repudiating the prior condoning of torture sent a clear message condemning the practice, the confirmation of Gonzales can be read as muddying that message. For although Republican defenders of Gonzales argued that he was being made a scapegoat for policies that were largely beyond his control, fairly or not, by the time of the confirmation hearings, he was closely associated with those policies.

The Gonzales confirmation hearing, which necessarily focused on the overall qualifications and record of Mr. Gonzales, was at best a poor vehicle for examining the core issues regarding torture—namely, whether it is ever justified, and if so, how the law ought to address questions of justification.

For my part, I favor a complete ban on torture for two, seemingly contradictory, sorts of reasons. The first reason is simple. When I am in a Kantian frame of mind, I think that torture is the sort of ultimate disregard for human dignity that should be categorically renounced.

But I am not invariably a Kantian who thinks that the rightness or wrongness of a course of action can be judged regardless of its consequences, at least when those consequences are extraordinarily grave. And if we pay attention to consequences, then perhaps torture may be justified in the ticking bomb scenario or its equivalent, at least if we know to a moral certainty that the person to be tortured has committed enormous misdeeds that, absent torture, will imminently bear ghastly fruit. Those who say that an absolute prohibition is needed to prevent slippage down the slope to routine torture of possibly innocent people certainly have a point, but it is only half the story. If an absolute prohibition really prevents all torture, then it will prevent torture in the real ticking bomb cases. And if we think that torture ought to be available for the rare case of the ticking bomb that threatens thousands or even millions of lives, then an absolute prohibition aimed at routine cases may come with the unacceptably high cost of requiring a democratic society to accept its own destruction when the torture of a few terrorists could have saved it.

I am also unpersuaded by the argument that torture doesn't work. A person being tortured will say anything to make the torture stop, the argument goes, and so information obtained via torture is not reliable. This may well be true in most cases, but there is no reason to think it is always true, especially where the information obtained via torture is self-authenticating: We can actually find the ticking bomb where the tortured terrorist admits to have planted it.

Nonetheless, I still favor an absolute prohibition on torture, even when I'm in a utilitarian frame of mind. The reason is that I believe such a ban will not be fully effective. If the stakes are high enough—the destruction of a city, say—military or police personnel will almost certainly resort to torture, regardless of what the law says.

Accordingly, an absolute prohibition of torture can be justified either on the Kantian ground that torture is always wrong in itself or on the utilitarian ground that such a ban strikes just the right balance: It prevents slippage down the slope to routine torture but does not, as a practical matter, prevent torture in those rare circumstances in which it may really be necessary. For me, the truly hard question is whether someone who thinks as I do ought even to articulate the utilitarian argument. Admitting that a torture ban will not be fully effective might invite torture by those who infer from such statements that the law's prohibition is not to be taken seriously. I have chosen to articulate the argument here because I am confident that no one in power will attribute any authority to my musings.

NOTES

1. Memorandum from Daniel Levin, Acting Assistant Attorney General, Office of Legal Counsel, United States Department of Justice, to James B. Comey, Deputy

Attorney General, Office of Legal Counsel, United States Department of Justice (Dec. 30, 2004), *available at* http://www.usdoj.gov/olc/2004opinions.htm, *available in PDF format with page numbers as cited infra at* http://news.findlaw.com/hdocs/docs/terrorism/dojtorture123004mem.pdf [hereinafter "Levin memo"].

2. Memorandum from Jay S. Bybee, Assistant Attorney General, Office of Legal Counsel, United States Department of Justice, to Alberto R. Gonzales, Counsel to the President (Aug. 1, 2002), *available at* http://www.washingtonpost.com/wp-srv/nation/documents/dojinterrogationmemo20020801.pdf [hereinafter "Bybee memo"].

3. *See* Neil A. Lewis, *U.S. Spells Out New Definition Curbing Torture*, N.Y. Times, Jan. 1, 2005, at A1.

4. Bybee memo, *supra* note 2, at 1.

5. *See supra* chapter 19 note 11.

6. *E.g.*, Robert Scheer, Op-Ed., *Backing Gonzales is Backing Torture*, L.A. Times, Jan. 4, 2005, at B13 ("[P]erhaps to help Gonzales get through the hearings, the Justice Department only last week quietly slipped new guidelines onto its website redressing this stain on the country's reputation.").

7. *Adopted* Dec. 10, 1984, S. Treaty Doc. No. 100-20 (1988), 1465 U.N.T.S. 85, 113 (entered into force June 26, 1987) (entered into force for the United States Nov. 20, 1994).

8. 18 U.S.C. § 2340 (2000).

9. 18 U.S.C. § 2340(A) (2000).

10. Bybee memo, *supra* note 2, at 19.

11. *Id.* at 1.

12. *See generally* Alan M. Dershowitz, Why Terrorism Works: Understanding the Threat, Responding to the Challenge (New Haven: Yale University Press, 2002); Alan M. Dershowitz, *The Torture Warrant: A Response to Professor Strauss*, 48 N.Y.L. Sch. L. Rev. 275 (2003–2004).

13. Levin memo, *supra* note 1, at 17.

14. Bybee memo, *supra* note 2, at 33.

15. Levin memo, *supra* note 1, at 2.

16. *Id.*

17. *See* 151 Cong. Rec. S923-02 (2005).

• 21 •

Who Decides Whether Yaser Hamdi, or Any Other Citizen, Is an Enemy Combatant?

August 2002

In August 2002, a Richmond, Virginia, courtroom was the site of a dramatic confrontation between Federal District Judge Robert Doumar and the United States Department of Justice.[1] The narrow question at issue was whether Yaser Hamdi, a U.S. citizen who was captured in Afghanistan, is entitled to meet with a lawyer. Hamdi's case, however, also has much broader implications.

The government asserts that domestic courts have no authority to question the military's determination that a citizen is an enemy combatant. Yet the consequence of such a determination is that the citizen may not be entitled to all of the procedural protections of the Bill of Rights. These include the right to a lawyer, the right against self-incrimination, and the right not to be held indefinitely without being charged with a crime.

If the government's view prevails, and it alone decides who is an enemy combatant, then there is nothing to stop it from declaring anyone—you, me, or Tom Daschle—an enemy combatant who can be detained indefinitely without trial.

Our Constitution allows for such a draconian measure, but only on one condition. In wartime, Congress has the power to suspend the privilege of the writ of habeas corpus[2]—which permits a court to examine the lawfulness of executive detention. Congress clearly has not taken that drastic step. Nor has President Bush attempted, as President Lincoln did during the Civil War, to suspend habeas corpus unilaterally.

Civilian courts should grant the executive branch considerable deference in making military determinations, whether or not we are technically fighting a war—and they have a long tradition of doing so. But deference does not, and should not, mean rolling over and playing dead.

Who is Yaser Esam Hamdi? He was born in Louisiana, and therefore, under Section One of the Fourteenth Amendment, he is a citizen of the United States, even though he spent most of his life outside this country.

After being captured during the Afghanistan conflict, Hamdi was initially held at the naval base in Guantanamo Bay, Cuba. But when his American citizenship came to light, the government transported him from there to the brig at the Norfolk Naval Station.

In May 2002, the federal public defender for the Eastern District of Virginia, Frank Dunham, filed a habeas corpus petition on Hamdi's behalf. Because Hamdi was being held incommunicado, Hamdi himself had not authorized the petition to be filed. Thus, Dunham filed what is known as a "next friend" petition, a legal device that permits a third party to act on behalf of someone who is incapable of acting on his own. Dunham named himself and Christian Peregrim, a private citizen in New Jersey, as the next friends.

Judge Doumar directed the government to respond to Hamdi's petition and also ordered that Hamdi be given unmonitored access to a lawyer. The government immediately appealed to the United States Court of Appeals for the Fourth Circuit. That court issued an order staying Judge Doumar's ruling, so that it would not take effect until and unless it was affirmed at the appeals stage.

The Fourth Circuit subsequently held that Dunham and Peregrim's next friend petition was invalid.[3] It found that neither Dunham nor Peregrim had a significant relationship with Hamdi, whereas his father, Esam Fouad Hamdi, was available to file, and indeed had filed, a next friend petition before Judge Doumar.

Judge Doumar, meanwhile, ruled on Hamdi's father's petition. He found, correctly, that Hamdi's father had legal standing to act as next friend. He then ordered, once again, that Hamdi be given unmonitored access to his lawyer.

The government next went back to the Fourth Circuit, which issued another decision.[4] It agreed that Hamdi's father had legal standing to act as next friend. But it thought that Judge Doumar's decision granting Hamdi unmonitored access to an attorney was premature. Thus, it sent the case back down to Judge Doumar, so that he could rule on a threshold question relevant to deciding whether Hamdi retains the Sixth Amendment right to counsel.

Specifically, Judge Doumar has to decide whether Hamdi is, as the government has argued, an enemy combatant subject to military rather than civilian jurisdiction. If so, even though he is a citizen, he still would not be entitled to all of the protections of civilian courts.

The government makes two distinct claims regarding Hamdi, one substantive, and the other procedural. As a substantive matter, the government argues, enemy combatants captured during the course of hostilities are subject to military rather than civilian jurisdiction. This is a relatively uncontroversial proposition.

To be sure, there has been disagreement over whether Taliban members count as *unlawful* combatants—as discussed in chapter 19. But that issue should not be confused with this one. *Unlawful* combatants are defined as those who, by virtue of their failure to comply with the international law of war, cannot claim the protections of the Geneva Convention. Thus, they need not be tried before U.S. courts-martial, and can be subject to prosecution before tribunals with fewer procedural protections. (Whether the military commissions President Bush authorized in November 2001[5] provide sufficient protection to meet even this minimal standard had not yet been resolved by the Supreme Court as of late 2005, but in July 2005 a three-judge panel of the U.S. Court of Appeals for the D.C. Circuit rejected one challenge to these commissions. John Roberts was one of the three judges on the panel and accordingly recused himself from the case when it reached the Supreme Court.[6])

Lawful enemy combatants who are charged with offenses under the rules of war are entitled to the rules that obtain in U.S. courts-martial. But the military can detain lawful combatants, if it chooses, without charging them with any offense. It can simply hold them as prisoners of war until the cessation of hostilities.

There are real questions about when, if ever, the war on terrorism will end. Regarding the allegations against Hamdi, however, it is clear that hostilities have not ceased. We continue to have troops on the ground in Afghanistan who periodically come under fire from the remnants of Taliban and al-Qaeda forces. So if Hamdi was indeed a Taliban member and thus an enemy combatant, he remains one.

But was he? The "if" brings us to the critical procedural question in Hamdi's case. Hamdi says that the government has offered no evidence that he is in fact an enemy combatant. And since he is a citizen, and the privilege of the writ of habeas corpus has not been suspended, he says, the Constitution entitles him to have a civilian court examine the factual basis for his detention.

The government disagrees—putting forth a view the Fourth Circuit aptly labeled "sweeping."[7] It contends that "with no meaningful judicial review, any American citizen alleged to be an enemy combatant could be detained indefinitely without charges or counsel on the government's say-so."[8]

The Fourth Circuit did not expressly address the question of whether that sweeping view is correct when it remanded the case to Judge Doumar for him to consider whether Hamdi is an enemy combatant. But it strongly suggested that a federal district judge is entitled—indeed, required—to demand some factual showing before sustaining detention of a U.S. citizen labeled an enemy combatant.

And indeed, if the government's representation was all that was necessary to establish that a U.S. citizen was an enemy combatant, the remand would hardly have been necessary because Judge Doumar would have nothing to do in the remanded case. Thus, the Fourth Circuit has given a strong signal that it disagrees with the government's position that its combatant status determinations are unreviewable.

The question left open by the Fourth Circuit—and the question that was at the heart of the sparring in Judge Doumar's courtroom—is just what kind of a factual showing the government must make.

The government's case against Hamdi is contained in a two-page "declaration of facts" from Michael H. Mobbs, a Defense Department special adviser. In an August 16, 2002, order, Judge Doumar found the Mobbs declaration inadequate.[9]

The judge listed a number of deficiencies, including: its failure to identify exactly who Mobbs is or precisely what function he performs; the designation of Hamdi as having been "affiliated" with the Taliban without specifying the nature and degree of that affiliation; and perhaps most fundamentally, the declaration's statement of factual conclusions without setting forth most of the evidence that gave rise to those conclusions.

Accordingly, in his order of August 16, 2002, Judge Doumar required that the government produce more detailed evidence about how it determined that Hamdi is an enemy combatant and why it is holding him in solitary confinement. That evidence would be reviewed in secret by Judge Doumar, to avoid disclosing information that could be harmful to national security.

However, rather than comply, the government filed a motion[10] in the Fourth Circuit, asking that Judge Doumar's order be stayed pending appeal. As I write these words, the Fourth Circuit has not yet ruled on the government's stay application, but that court—and perhaps the United States Supreme Court as well—will likely have to face the ultimate issue soon enough.

So, should the Mobbs declaration be deemed sufficient to support classifying a citizen as an enemy combatant who is not entitled to all of the protections of the Bill of Rights applicable to civilian courts? The answer comes from a technical doctrine of federal jurisdiction that was not cited in Judge Doumar's order but lends credence to his position: the "jurisdictional fact" doctrine.

The leading decision establishing the jurisdictional fact doctrine is the important but intricate 1932 Supreme Court case of *Crowell v. Benson*.[11] Here is a somewhat oversimplified description of its holding: Suppose the law assigns certain workers' compensation cases, under certain conditions, to the executive branch, not the judiciary. Who decides whether these conditions obtain? According to *Crowell*, it is the judiciary that retains the authority to make this threshold determination.

Crowell implied that the courts *alone* have the authority to examine the facts that are necessary to trigger executive jurisdiction over a class of issues—

that is, courts get to decide "jurisdictional facts" all by themselves. Subsequent cases have made clear, however, that even with respect to jurisdictional facts, reviewing courts can be required to give substantial deference to proceedings before administrative agencies and other non-judicial bodies, such as military commissions.[12] But no case has ever held that a non-judicial body can be assigned the task of determining the facts that give rise to its own jurisdiction without *any* judicial review. *Crowell's* suggestion that courts alone decide jurisdictional facts does not accurately state the current law, but neither does the contrary position asserted by the Bush Administration—that the courts have no role in determining jurisdictional facts.

In the public debate over the legality of the military commissions that the President has authorized but not yet used, the Bush Administration has frequently invoked the Nazi saboteur case, *Ex parte Quirin*.[13] As the Administration has noted, the Supreme Court upheld the use of military tribunals for unlawful combatants. But *Quirin* also did something else: It respected the stripped-down version of the jurisdictional fact doctrine under which federal courts cannot be required to accept the jurisdictional findings of a non-judicial body without any review at all.

Granted, no civilian court heard new testimony in *Quirin*. Yet the Supreme Court did engage in substantial review of the underlying factual record as developed in the military tribunals themselves—rather than just accepting the tribunal commanders' say-so as to what conclusions should be drawn from what occurred, and their vouchsafe that the right procedures had been used.

In short, the Court itself, in *Quirin*, looked much further than the government wants Judge Doumar to look in Hamdi's case, and did not simply take the government at its word. And if the Administration is going to live by *Quirin* in defending the tribunals, then it ought to live by *Quirin* in respecting the core of the jurisdictional fact doctrine too.

Thus, *Quirin* strongly suggests that it is not enough for the military simply to tell the courts what factual conclusions it has drawn in determining that a citizen is subject to its jurisdiction. The courts must be given access to a substantial part of the evidentiary record as well.

The precedents suggest, that is, that Judge Doumar was correct in his conclusion that the Mobbs declaration is inadequate. He is entitled to see more of the evidence supporting the conclusion that Hamdi is, indeed, an enemy combatant.

At the same time, review of the factual record should accord the military substantial deference. The Fourth Circuit emphasized this point in its decision remanding the case to Judge Doumar, and it was right to do so, for Judge Doumar has not always been deferential.

For example, according to a *Washington Post* story, Judge Doumar once suggested that the government's position was tantamount to an assertion that persons designated enemy combatants could be dunked in boiling oil.[14] He even seemed to think that the peculiarity of the name "Mobbs" was a reason to be skeptical of the government's position. (Perhaps my own surname makes me sensitive to such slights.)

But even if he expressed it insensitively, Judge Doumar nonetheless had a valid point. "I do think that due process requires something other than a basic assertion by someone named Mobbs that they have looked at some papers and therefore they have determined [Hamdi] should be held incommunicado," he said. "Just think of the impact of that. Is that what we're fighting for?"[15]

POSTSCRIPT

As I discuss in the next chapter, by an 8–1 margin, the Supreme Court ultimately rejected the government's sweeping view. Writing for a plurality of the Court, Justice O'Connor rebuked the Bush Administration: "A state of war is not a blank check for the President," she explained.[16] No doubt the Justices were influenced by the fact that the Administration sought to apply its rule not only to people who, like Hamdi, were captured on a battlefield, but also to U.S. citizens apprehended in the United States itself. For the same day it decided the *Hamdi* case, the Court disposed of the case of Jose Padilla, the so-called dirty bomber. Padilla, who was apprehended in Chicago on suspicion of planning terrorist activities, was originally charged as a civilian, but the government attempted to reclassify him as an enemy combatant for reasons that remain unclear. Although the Justices ruled that Padilla had filed suit in the wrong court,[17] his case must have underscored for the Court just how far the Administration was willing to go.

NOTES

1. *See* Hamdi v. Rumsfeld, 243 F. Supp. 2d 527 (E.D. Va. 2002).
2. U.S. Const. art. I, § 9, cl. 2.
3. Hamdi v. Rumsfeld, 294 F.3d 598 (4th Cir. 2002).
4. Hamdi v. Rumsfeld, 296 F.3d 278 (4th Cir. 2002).
5. Military Order of November 13, 2001: Detention, Treatment, and Trial of Certain Non-Citizens in the War Against Terrorism, 66 Fed. Reg. 57,833 (Nov. 16, 2001).
6. Hamdan v. Rumsfeld, 415 F.3d 33 (D.C. Cir. 2005) *cert. granted*, 2005 WL 2922488.
7. *Hamdi,* 296 F.3d at 283.

8. *Id.*

9. *See* Hamdi v. Rumsfeld, 316 F.3d 450, 462 (4th Cir. 2003) (describing the district court's assessment of the Mobbs declaration).

10. Respondents' Motion for Certification of Interlocutory Appeal and for Stay, Hamdi v. Rumsfeld, 243 F. Supp. 2d 527 (E.D. Va. 2002) (No. 2:02cv439), *available at* http://news.findlaw.com/hdocs/docs/terrorism/hamdirums81902gmot.pdf.

11. 285 U.S. 22 (1932).

12. *See, e.g.*, O'Keeffe v. Smith, Hinchman & Grylls Assocs., 380 U.S. 359, 362 (1965) (per curiam); Estep v. United States, 327 U.S. 114, 142 (1946) (Frankfurter, J., concurring).

13. 317 U.S. 1 (1942).

14. *See* Tom Jackman, *Judge Skewers U.S. Curbs on Detainee*, Wash. Post, Aug. 14, 2002, at A10.

15. *Id.*

16. Hamdi v. Rumsfeld, 542 U.S. 507, 536 (2004).

17. Rumsfeld v. Padilla, 542 U.S. 426 (2004). Padilla's detention was later upheld by the United States Court of Appeals for the Fourth Circuit, 423 F.3d 386 (4th Cir. 2005), and then, in a dramatic reversal, the Justice Department indicted Padilla in a civilian court. *See* Superseding Indictment, United States v. Hassoun, No. 04-60001-CR-COOKE (S.D. Fla. Nov. 17, 2005), *available at* http://news.findlaw.com/nytimes/docs/padilla/uspad111705ind.pdf.

• 22 •

Bush Loses in the Supreme Court and America Wins

July 2004

Two rulings at the conclusion of the United States Supreme Court term in the summer of 2004 rejected the sweeping wartime powers claimed by President Bush. In the case of Yaser Hamdi,[1] the court renounced the Administration's claim that military authorities could indefinitely hold a U.S. citizen as an "enemy combatant" without ever providing him with an opportunity to contest the basis for his detention before a neutral decision maker. And in a case brought by fourteen foreign nationals,[2] the court cast aside the government's argument that because the U.S. Naval Base at Guantanamo Bay is nominally under Cuban sovereignty, American courts lack jurisdiction to entertain legal claims brought by persons who had no say in where the U.S. military chose to detain them.

Although nowhere mentioned in either case, the scandalous treatment of Iraqi prisoners at Abu Ghraib[3] and the revelations that high-level government lawyers prepared confidential memoranda authorizing torture[4] likely played a part in the Justices' reasoning. The Administration essentially said, "trust us to do what's right."[5] Clearly, the Court thought that such trust had not been earned.

Another unspoken consideration may have been at work in the Guantanamo Bay case, which has garnered considerable international attention. In recent years, a majority of the Justices of the Supreme Court have articulated a multilateralist view[6] of American law that stands in marked contrast to the unilateralism of the Bush Administration.

For example, in a 2002 Virginia case,[7] the high court ruled that the execution of the mentally retarded is forbidden by the American Constitution as "cruel and unusual punishment." While most of the Court's analysis focused on domestic considerations, the Justices also invoked a legal brief filed by the European Union that described the overwhelming disapproval of the practice in the world community.[8] Likewise, in the 2003 ruling striking down a Texas prohibition on same-sex sodomy, the Court cited a 1967 Act of the English Parliament and a 1981 ruling of the European Court of Human Rights.[9]

Significantly, the six Justices[10] in the majority in the Virginia and Texas cases also constituted the majority in the Guantanamo Bay case: the four dissenters from *Bush v. Gore*[11] plus Ronald Reagan's two relatively moderate appointees, Sandra Day O'Connor and Anthony Kennedy. These Justices regularly travel to colloquia on comparative constitutional law and see themselves as part of an international community of high court judges. It cannot have escaped their notice that to uphold indefinite detention of foreign nationals without judicial process would have made them virtual pariahs on the conference circuit.

I do not mean to suggest that the Justices decided the Guantanamo Bay case as they did so that they would be toasted at their international cocktail parties. I contend that their concern for world opinion—if that concern played the role I am suggesting it did—was for their country, not for themselves.

President Bush and his advisers have cast aside much of the longstanding bipartisan consensus under which the United States works through and with multilateral institutions like the United Nations. Alarmed by this dramatic volte-face, the majority Justices in the Guantanamo Bay case may be trying to send assurances to the rest of the world that President Bush does not speak for all Americans, not even the ones who put him in office in the first place.

Of course, neoconservative critics of the high court will see in this explanation the confirmation of their worst fears. Here are judges, they will say, who do not understand that they have no legitimate qualifications to act as agents of American foreign policy, a job committed by the Constitution to the President and (they may grudgingly admit) Congress.

Yet the high court has considered foreign policy implications before. In the most celebrated American case of the twentieth century, *Brown v. Board of Education*, the Justices were probably influenced by a government brief explaining how racial segregation in the southern United States undermined American efforts to compete with the Soviet Union for the hearts and minds of people in developing countries.[12] By holding that American apartheid violated the constitutional command of "equal protection of the laws," the court struck a blow for justice at home and American strategic interests abroad.

To be sure, the *Brown* precedent is not entirely analogous, for there the Supreme Court gave weight to foreign policy considerations in just the way that the federal executive had urged. In the Guantanamo Bay case, by contrast, the Bush Administration argued that a ruling for the detainees would undermine the war effort by diverting manpower and material from the battlefield to the courtroom.

But the majority opinion of Justice John Paul Stevens paid little heed to the Administration's parade of horribles. A decorated World War II veteran,

Justice Stevens may well have thought that he was at least as qualified as the civilians in the Bush Justice Department to forecast the impact of the court's ruling on military efficiency.

Or perhaps the Justices were simply reacting to the Administration's constant overreaching. Of course the existence of religious fanatics eager to kill large numbers of innocent American civilians warrants strong measures in response. But the Supreme Court's rulings affirm the fundamental principle that even grave dangers do not warrant the sort of blanket deference to which the Bush Administration believes it is entitled whenever it utters the words "war" and "terrorism."

POSTSCRIPT

Despite the Supreme Court's rejection of the Bush Administration positions in the *Hamdi* and *Rasul* cases, neither decision is exactly a sweeping victory for civil liberties or access to the courts. For example, the Justices did not say that Hamdi was entitled to the full panoply of rights that are afforded criminal defendants in civilian courts. Only Justices Scalia and Stevens were willing to go that far. The lead opinion by Justice O'Connor considers the question of what process is due Hamdi under a balancing test, concluding that some of the ordinary elements of a criminal trial—such as the exclusion of hearsay evidence and the presumption of innocence—need not be granted during a hearing to determine whether a given detainee is an unlawful combatant. Likewise, the *Rasul* decision permits federal courts to inquire into the lawfulness of detention at Guantanamo Bay but says nothing about the substantive test the government must meet to hold someone there.

Yet if it would be a mistake to treat *Hamdi* and *Rasul* as complete victories for civil liberties, it would be also be a mistake to evaluate them simply in terms of the particulars of the two cases. In law, as elsewhere, momentous decisions can have greater significance for what they represent than for what they actually do. Viewed as symbols, the 2004 detention cases are best seen as reaffirming a principle that is at the core of the American republic—the principle that the President is not a king, not even in matters of war.

NOTES

1. Hamdi v. Rumsfeld, 542 U.S. 507 (2004).
2. Rasul v. Bush, 542 U.S. 466 (2004).
3. *See generally* Mark Danner, Torture and Truth: America, Abu Ghraib, and the War on Terror (New York: New York Review of Books, 2004).

4. *See supra* chapter 20.

5. For example, during the oral argument in *Hamdi*, Justice Ginsburg asked Paul D. Clement, the Deputy Solicitor General, whether the government had any explanation for why some detainees were afforded the benefits of the criminal process, while others were being held indefinitely. Noting that different detainees had different "intelligence value," Clement argued that the choice between the criminal process and indefinite detention for a particular detainee "reflects the sound exercise of prosecutorial and executive discretion." *See* Transcript of Oral Argument at 23, Hamdi v. Rumsfeld, 542 U.S. 507 (No. 03–6696). When the issue of torture arose, Clement suggested that the courts were not necessary for enforcement of torture conventions because the Administration understood that torture does not produce reliable information. *Id.* at 41–42.

6. *See infra* chapter 31.

7. Atkins v. Virginia, 536 U.S. 304 (2002). For a fuller discussion of the influence of international law in the decision of this case, see *infra* chapter 30.

8. 536 U.S. at 316 n.21 (citing Brief of Amicus Curiae the European Union in Support of the Petitioner at 4, McCarver v. North Carolina, 531 U.S. 1205 (2001) (No. 00–8727), 2001 WL 648609).

9. Lawrence v. Texas, 539 U.S. 558 (2003) (citing Sexual Offences Act, 1967, c. 60, § 1 (Eng.)); *id.* (citing Dudgeon v. United Kingdom, 45 Eur. Ct. H.R. 52 (1981)).

10. Justices John Paul Stevens, Sandra Day O'Connor, Anthony Kennedy, David Souter, Ruth Bader Ginsburg, and Stephen Breyer.

11. 531 U.S. 98 (2000) (per curiam).

12. Brief of Amicus Curiae United States, Brown v. Bd. of Educ., 347 U.S. 483 (1954) (Nos. 1, 2, 4, 10).

• 23 •

Is Iraq in "Material Breach" of Its Obligations under the UN Resolution? A Geopolitical Question, Not Simply a Legal One

January 2003

As I write, the world eagerly awaits the first full report from senior United Nations weapons inspector Hans Blix on Iraq's compliance—or lack of compliance—with UN Security Council Resolution 1441.[1]

The resolution was adopted on November 8 of 2002. It states that "false statements or omissions in the declarations submitted by Iraq . . . and failure by Iraq at any time to comply with, and cooperate fully in the [resolution's] implementation" will be considered a "material breach of Iraq's obligations" under the resolution.[2]

What is a "material breach"? Resolution 1441 does not define the term—and this ambiguity could prove important both for the questions of whether there will be war with Iraq, and if there is, whether that war will enjoy international support.

Based on how the term functions in other contexts, a material breach would appear to be, very roughly, a breach that is important, not trivial—and one that is important, in particular, to the purposes the breached instrument serves. But defining a material breach in the Iraq context may be as tricky as it is significant.

Before analyzing what "material breach" is, exactly, let us take a quick look at what happens, under the Resolution, if a material breach occurs.

The Bush Administration and the news media have sometimes suggested that a finding of a "material breach" will automatically authorize war with Iraq.[3] But in fact, Resolution 1441 states that in the event of a material breach or other Iraqi interference or failures to comply with disarmament obligations, the Security Council will "consider the situation and the need for full compliance with all of the relevant Council resolutions in order to secure international peace and security."[4] That is, the resolution itself expressly considers material breach to be a trigger for further deliberation, not automatic war.

However, the resolution also "recalls that the Council has repeatedly warned Iraq that it will face serious consequences as a result of its continued violations of its obligations."[5] (There is evidence that prior UN resolutions were flouted.)

Resolution 1441 appears to speak out of both sides of its mouth because it is a compromise document. It was the result of protracted negotiations between, on the one hand, the United States and the United Kingdom, and on the other hand, other permanent members of the Security Council such as France and Russia.

Accordingly, Resolution 1441 may be seen as striking the following deal: The United States and the United Kingdom agreed that before going to war against Iraq, they would return to the Security Council for a determination by that body of whether Iraq is in material breach. Meanwhile, the other Security Council members agreed that if a material breach is found, they would authorize military action to oust Saddam Hussein from power.

With so much riding on a finding of "material breach," how should that term be understood? Even without a definition in Resolution 1441, common sense suggests the proper resolution of some obvious cases.

For example, if UN weapons inspectors find nuclear warheads stashed underneath Saddam Hussein's mattress, that fact—along with the Iraqi regime's prior failure to disclose the existence of these warheads—would constitute an obvious material breach.

Likewise, at the other extreme, if it turns out that some of the thousands of pages Iraq produced last month contain typographical errors, that would not constitute a "material breach." Indeed, it probably would not constitute a breach at all.

Of course, it is possible to imagine numerous scenarios in between these two extremes. Iraq may well have substantial stockpiles of weapons of mass destruction and an ongoing chemical and biological weapons research program, but UN inspectors, with only limited access to the most highly sensitive U.S. intelligence reports, may be unable to find direct evidence of the stockpiles and programs. If they only have circumstantial evidence, can they still conclude that a material breach has occurred? That may be the issue that, in reality, the inspectors, the Security Council states and, indeed, the world must confront.

Absent a smoking gun, when it reconvenes to consider the coming Blix report, the Security Council will have to decide whether Iraq's various omissions and misstatements (those that are more serious than typos, of course) are so grave as to constitute a material breach.

The term "material breach" was not invented in Security Council Resolution 1441. It is commonly used in contract law to denote a serious contract violation. An example illustrates the concept.

Suppose that a computer manufacturer signs a contract with another company for the latter to supply a thousand keyboards per month for three years. (This type of deal is called an "installment contract.") For five months, the keyboard maker complies with its obligations, but then in the sixth month it delivers the keyboards three days late. The delay could be costly to the computer manufacturer, and the keyboard maker would accordingly be obligated to compensate the computer manufacturer for its lost profits.

However, the delivery delay would not result in the contract's termination. The keyboard maker could continue to expect to supply keyboards at the contract price every month for the remaining two and a half years of the contract.

Put another way, the late shipment is a breach of contract but not a *material* breach. A material breach only occurs when one party so completely fails to hold up its end of the bargain that the other party is excused altogether from further performance under the contract.[6]

Contracts sometimes spell out what counts as a material breach. For example, suppose that our computer manufacturer uses low-inventory "just-in-time" production methods, so that any delay is extremely costly. Its lawyers might then have written into the contract that "time is of the essence," or more precisely still, that a delay of more than one day shall constitute a material breach. In this way, a delay that might, in another context or another industry, have seemed relatively minor, is deemed by the parties, in this context, this industry, and this contract, to be material.

When a contract does not specify whether a particular term is essential to it (and hence whether a breach of that term is "material"), courts must adjudicate the question. They do so by referring to the general terms of the contract, standard industry practice, and the course of dealing between the parties. In the end, the determination whether a particular breach was material is often a judgment call. All the law can do in the abstract is to list general factors that may prove relevant in the myriad circumstances to which contracts apply.[7]

The Bush Administration has already announced that it considers Iraq to be in material breach of Resolution 1441.[8] However, it has not yet made public the evidence showing that Iraq's declarations to date are false.

Certainly there is considerable evidence of Saddam Hussein's past weapons programs—his horrific treatment of the Kurds being the most prominent example. But that is not the main concern of Resolution 1441, which focuses not on the past, but on the present.

Thus, if the Administration does not release further evidence, and if the Blix report is ambiguous, the Security Council will be left in the position of a judge trying to decide whether there has been a material breach of a contract. It will be required, that is, to make a judgment call.

At that point, it may be useful to recall one more feature of contract law: When one party to a contract is in material breach, the other party has the option of terminating the contract, but is not required to do so. If our computer manufacturer believes that future shipments from the keyboard supplier are still a good deal, then notwithstanding a time-is-of-the-essence clause, it can continue the contract in force.[9]

If we are to continue the analogy, it becomes clear that the UN Security Council will really face two questions when it receives the Blix report: First, has there been a material breach? And second, if so, what should be done? Even in the event of a material breach, the Security Council could still decide to continue "dealing" with Iraq—sending in inspectors, trying to hold it to its obligations, and imposing sanctions other than all-out war.

Despite the implicit "deal" I described above between the U.S.–U.K. sponsors of Resolution 1441 and the other Security Council members, Resolution 1441 does not actually commit the Security Council to authorize war in the event of a material breach. That decision remains to be made. Thus, like the computer manufacturer in my simple example, the Security Council may legitimately decide that continuing the relationship—here, continuing weapons inspections—is the more prudent course.

To be sure, one of the factors the Security Council must consider in deciding whether to resort to war in response to a material breach is its own credibility. At some point, continued warnings only serve to invite defiance.

The Bush Administration argues that we have already passed that point with Iraq, and perhaps that is so. But if it is, that must be because maintaining the credibility of the UN—and, let's face it, the United States—outweighs the factors that counsel against war.

At the end of the day, the question whether a material breach of Iraq's obligations under Resolution 1441 should trigger a war requires the Security Council (and the United States, which might move forward unilaterally) to balance the benefits of war against its considerable and largely unpredictable costs.

The benefits include not just the credibility of UN and U.S. threats but also the elimination of a dangerous dictator. The costs include the loss of lives of soldiers and civilians, in Iraq and possibly elsewhere as well.

Weighing these costs and benefits is profoundly difficult. And the issue is not, despite the legalistic language of "material breach," simply a question of legal interpretation. It is a moral, practical, and political question as well.

POSTSCRIPT

Some people think that *all* of international law is not really law at all but just a matter of power and will. Whether or not they realize it, these people are thoroughgoing legal realists. What makes a proposition a legal proposition within a national or sub-national legal system, they say, is the fact that the government will back it up, by force if necessary. But there is no international law enforcement apparatus comparable to the nation-state's iron fist of force wrapped in the velvet glove of law; there is only the voluntary use of force by independent sovereign states. There is international politics, these critics say, but no true international law.[10]

I do not subscribe to this view of international law. International bodies like the World Court and the International Criminal Court *do* have the power to issue binding legal judgments. Granted, sovereign states sometimes escape sanction for their illegal conduct, but actors *within* national and sub-national legal systems sometimes escape sanction for their illegal conduct as well. At most we might say that ensuring compliance with international law can sometimes be more difficult than ensuring compliance with domestic law.

Accordingly, when I say that the question of whether Iraq was in material breach of its UN obligations was not just a narrowly legal question, I am making a particular claim about UN Resolution 1441. Some questions under international law are more clear-cut. For example, aggressive war is clearly unlawful under the UN charter. As the next chapter makes clear, that is not an idly chosen illustration.

NOTES

1. S.C. Res. 1441, UN Doc. S/RES/1441 (Nov. 8, 2002).
2. *Id.* ¶ 4.
3. For example, on November 11, 2002, President Bush stated: "The United States has agreed to discuss any material breach with the Security Council, but without jeopardizing our freedom of action to defend our country. If Iraq fails to fully comply, the United States and other nations will disarm Saddam Hussein." Remarks on the Passage of a United Nations Security Council Resolution on Iraq, 38 Weekly Comp. Pres. Doc. 2010 (Nov. 8, 2002). Subsequent events clearly showed that Bush believed it was up to the United States and other individual nations, rather than the United Nations itself, to determine whether Iraq complied fully.
4. S.C. Res. 1441, *supra* note 1, ¶ 12.
5. *Id.* ¶ 13.
6. *See* U.C.C. § 2-612(2) (2003).
7. *See* Restatement (Second) of Contracts § 241 (1981).
8. *See, e.g.*, Steven R. Weisman & Julia Preston, *Powell Says Iraq Raises Risk of War By Lying on Arms*, N.Y. Times, Dec. 20, 2002, at A1 (including statement of Secretary of State Colin L. Powell).
9. *See* U.C.C. § 2-612(3) (2003).
10. For a characteristic statement of this view, see John R. Bolton, *Is There Really "Law" in International Affairs?*, 10 Transnat'l L. & Contemp. Probs. 1, 7 (2000) ("In addition to the absence of legitimately authoritative sources of international law, there is no process to bind it to the political consent of the world's population."); *id.* at 48 ("International law is not law; it is a series of political and moral arrangements that stand or fall on their own merits, and anything else is simply theology and superstition masquerading as law.").

• 24 •

Is the War on Iraq Lawful?

March 2003

As of this writing, American and British forces are poised to attack Iraq. Questions of military strategy, geopolitics, and morality loom large, but so do questions of law.

Is the war to disarm and dislodge Saddam Hussein justified under international law? Has it been adequately authorized under U.S. law, with proper congressional approval?

It is doubtful that any court will ever address either question, but that may provide all the more reason to consider these issues in the court of public opinion.

Under international law, force is authorized in essentially two or, at most, three circumstances.

First, Articles 39 and 42 of the UN Charter permit the Security Council to "determine the existence of any threat to the peace, breach of the peace, or act of aggression" and to authorize the use of force "to maintain or restore international peace and security."

Second, Article 51 of the UN Charter recognizes "the inherent right of individual or collective self-defence" against "an armed attack."

Third, an international norm may be emerging that would permit nations to use military force to prevent genocide or other humanitarian catastrophes. However, while Saddam Hussein has, in the past, committed horrific acts against his own people, the United States has not argued that intervention is necessary to address *ongoing* crimes against humanity.

Do either of the first two grounds—based on UN Charter provisions—justify war?

In his March 17 speech, President Bush claimed that prior UN resolutions have already provided the necessary legal authority for attacking Iraq.[1]

Speaking for the Blair Administration, British Attorney General Lord Goldsmith made the same point.[2] Are they correct? The answer is no.

In November 1990, the UN Security Council adopted Resolution 678, authorizing nations "co-operating with the Government of Kuwait . . . to use all necessary means" of dislodging Saddam Hussein's troops from Kuwait.[3]

This resolution authorized force *only* for the purpose of driving the Iraqi military out of Kuwait, an objective that was fully accomplished by 1991. It would be arguably relevant now only if Saddam reinvaded Kuwait.

Then, at the conclusion of the Gulf War, the Security Council adopted Resolution 687.[4] It called for, among other things, Iraq's destruction and renunciation of various weapons, including biological, chemical, and nuclear arms. And it stated the Security Council's intention "to take, as appropriate, all necessary measures" to guarantee the inviolability of the Iraq-Kuwait border. Although that language is broad, it does not refer to the disarmament provisions. Resolution 687 makes clear that its disarmament provisions are governed by the Security Council's resolve "to remain seized of the matter and to take such further steps as may be required for the implementation of the present resolution and to secure peace and security in the area."

That last statement hardly reads as a blank check to any Security Council member or other state to act on its own to require Iraq's disarmament. Instead, it suggests, quite to the contrary, that the Security Council *itself*, acting via additional resolutions, could take "further steps."

In November 2002, the Security Council passed Resolution 1441. It warned that Iraq would "face serious consequences" if it were to remain in "material breach" of its disarmament obligations.[5] Employing the Resolution's language, the Bush Administration has argued that Iraq is in "material breach" and that war is thus justified.

However, as I explained in the last chapter, Resolution 1441 implies that the Security Council itself will decide if a material breach has occurred, and expressly states that the Security Council itself, in the event of such a breach, will "consider the situation and the need for full compliance with all of the relevant Council resolutions in order to secure international peace and security."

We know that the Security Council does not think that a serious breach warranting all-out war has occurred. Perhaps the Security Council, under veto threat from France (and possibly Russia as well), has behaved unreasonably and irresponsibly in this respect, as suggested by American and British diplomats.[6] But if so, that still does not alter the fact that the Security Council did not authorize war. At most, it bolsters the moral case for war, not the legal case.

The boldest argument for war is that the United States and other countries face the prospect of an "armed attack" by Iraq, thus justifying the sovereign right to use force in self-defense. But certainly Iraq was not about to invade the United States or even Kuwait, where thousands of American and

British troops have patrolled the border since the Gulf War. Nor have Bush and Blair pointed to any information indicating an imminent threat; instead, they have rested their arguments primarily on the fear of Saddam's future direct or indirect use of weapons of mass destruction.[7]

Thus, the argument for self-defense must be based on an expansion of that concept—from self-defense as repelling an ongoing or imminent attack, to self-defense as pre-emption of a feared future attack.

Under the pre-emption doctrine touted by the Bush Administration, an enemy that is in the process of acquiring weapons of mass destruction can be attacked before using those weapons. The underlying concern is no doubt a serious one. The doctrine, however, remains outside of international law and could potentially prove quite dangerous.

Self-defense, as it traditionally has been understood under international law, is very much like self-defense in the law governing individuals. If an aggressor is in the midst of, or just about to, attack, one need not absorb the first blow before fighting back. The attack, however, must be imminent, if not already underway.[8]

The imminence requirement is extremely important in international affairs. If the United States can take non-Security-Council authorized preemptive or preventive military action, then other countries can as well. Thus, regional powers fearing the rise of neighboring rivals could decide that it is better to act against their future enemies before the threat fully materializes.

Not every invocation of the doctrine of pre-emption will be justified. Some will be based on misjudgments, and others will simply be pretextual—justifying aggression under the guise of pre-emption. Ultimately, the doctrine allowing pre-emption of long-term threats has the potential to be enormously destabilizing.

The international law arguments in favor of the war's legality, then, are weak at best. What about the war's legality as a matter of U.S. law? There, the question is closer.

The U.S. Constitution sets no limits on the reasons for which the United States may go to war. Its primary limit is procedural. While the President is the commander in chief of the armed forces, Congress alone has the power to declare war.

Congress has not formally declared war since World War II. As I explain in the next chapter, the failure to issue formal declarations of war partly reflects the fact that such declarations are antiquated. But congressional equivocation also reflects congressional ambivalence. Members of Congress do not want to have to take the heat for a war that goes badly, but they also do not want to appear weak on national defense. Thus, they have a built-in incentive to sit on the fence.

Judged by the standards of recent American military actions, however, Congress provided President Bush with crystal clear authority to make war on

Iraq. In October 2002, Congress passed a joint resolution authorizing the President "to use the Armed Forces of the United States as he determines to be necessary and appropriate in order to (1) defend the national security of the United States against the continuing threat posed by Iraq; and (2) enforce all United Nations Security Council resolutions regarding Iraq."[9]

The constitutional problem with the congressional authorization, if there is one, is not lack of clarity; it's that Congress passed the buck. A fierce defender of congressional prerogative might argue that Congress cannot delegate to the President the power to declare war.[10] The Constitution, on this view, puts the power to declare war in the hands of Congress so that members of Congress—who must stand for frequent reelection—will make the hard decisions themselves.

This objection would be a good one if Congress had delegated something approximating its *entire* war-making power to the President. But under the circumstances, the delegation appears reasonable. If one believed that Saddam would only disarm under military pressure, then to make the threat of war credible, Congress had to delegate power to the President. It would have been premature for Congress actually to declare war in October 2002, before further planned diplomatic efforts were undertaken. The Constitution is best interpreted to permit Congress to use this type of carrot-and-stick tactic.[11]

There is one further wrinkle under U.S. law. Article VI of the U.S. Constitution makes treaties into which the United States has entered "the supreme Law of the Land." The United States is a signatory to the UN Charter, and as discussed above, under the Charter, there is no clear legal authority for war on Iraq. Accordingly, if the war violates international law—as I have suggested it does—then it also thereby violates U.S. law.

That is not to say that any court will entertain a challenge to military action. U.S. courts have long treated such questions as committed to the political branches.[12] And it is clear that Congress and the President have made their decision.

In the end, the question of whether war on Iraq is legally justified is less important than whether it is morally and practically justified. If the United States and its allies prevail in a relatively quick war with minimal loss of life, if further evidence of Saddam's malevolent intent surfaces, and if the Iraqi people welcome allied forces as liberators rather than conquerors, then quibbles about legality may be overlooked.

Nonetheless, one impact of a war of dubious lawfulness may be the continued erosion of respect for the United States as a nation committed to principles of justice under law. President Bush says that he is justified in using military might because his cause is just. To much of the rest of the world, however, it looks the other way around: that the United States and its allies act as they wish because, in the American view, might makes right.

In that respect, a bit of ancient history may be relevant. In the Melian Dialogue, a passage of his *History of the Peloponnesian War* (between Athens and Sparta in the fifth century B.C.), Thucydides recounted the reaction of the people of the small neutral island state of Melos to the invading Athenian navy. Before attacking Melos, the Athenians gave the Melians an opportunity to surrender. The Melians attempted to persuade the Athenians to leave them alone. According to Thucydides, the Athenians would have none of it. Questions of justice arise only among equals, the Athenians said, while the strong do what they will and the weak suffer what they must.[13]

The Melians refused to surrender; the Athenians prevailed militarily; they killed the adult Melian males; and they sold the women and children into slavery. But ultimately, with aid from Persia (modern-day Iran), Sparta defeated and conquered Athens, which never regained its glory.

Even as we hope that President Bush can bring the spirit of Athenian democracy to the cradle of civilization, we may fear that he has forged a different, and darker, connection to ancient Athens.

POSTSCRIPT

Suppose a member of the United States Congress or the British Parliament thought the following in the winter of 2003: that Saddam Hussein either possessed or was just about to acquire weapons of mass destruction; that he intended to use these weapons either directly or as a means of blackmailing other countries; but that the Security Council was unlikely to authorize the use of force because of French and Russian intransigence. Intelligence reports that we now know to be false but that many believed to be true at the time did in fact lead many otherwise prudent politicians on both sides of the Atlantic to draw just these conclusions.

At that point, political leaders had essentially three options. First, they might have concluded that war was not a legal option and therefore that it should be taken off the table altogether. Second, they might have concluded that war was illegal but nonetheless morally justified, and publicly so stated. Third, they might have concluded that war was necessary on moral grounds and then made weak if not wholly disingenuous arguments for its legality. When they discussed legal questions at all, American and British pro-war politicians almost universally adopted this third course.

For my part, although I opposed the war, I would have preferred the second, more honest, course from its proponents. Both the first and third options I have just described share the premise that an illegal course of conduct should not be followed. Yet that view seems to fetishize the law. To be sure, the fact that the law makes a demand of us—either as individuals or as a nation—is an important reason to comply with the demand. But equally surely, there are circumstances in which competing demands of morality or prudence should countervail the legal duty. If, as President Bush and Prime Minister Blair suggested on the eve of war, there really was good reason to believe that inaction would put millions of their fellow Americans and Britons at grave risk of annihilation, then their duty was to act, regardless of the law.

More generally, it is easy to lose sight of the fact that the law's requirements are not invariably moral requirements for right action. Domestically, the law makes legitimate demands for compliance, even on those who believe some particular law is unwise or unjust. That is because, in a democracy, each of us accepts the authority of the majority to adopt rules and principles with which some of us disagree. Moreover, even when you do not feel a moral obligation to obey the law, if the risk of detection and the penalty for violation are sufficiently great, you will comply out of prudence. But these reasons to conform your conduct to the law sometimes compete with other reasons for contrary action, and sometimes those competing reasons prevail. Our public life—both nationally and internationally—would be more honest if we frankly acknowledged these facts.

NOTES

1. Address to the Nation on Iraq, 39 Weekly Comp. Pres. Doc. 338 (Mar. 17, 2003).
2. *See* Krishna Guha & Bob Sherwood, *Lawyers Condemn Advice on Authority of 1441 Legal Position*, Fin. Times (London), Mar. 18, 2003, at 4.
3. S.C. Res. 678, ¶ 2, UN Doc. S/RES/678 (Nov. 29, 1990).
4. S.C. Res. 687, UN Doc. S/RES/687 (Apr. 3, 1991).
5. S.C. Res. 1441, ¶¶ 4, 13, UN Doc. S/RES/1441 (Nov. 8, 2002).
6. *See, e.g.*, Bob Kemper, *Bush Sets War Deadline; 'Hussein and His Sons Must Leave Iraq within 48 Hours,'* Chi. Trib., Mar. 18, 2003, at 1 ("U.S., Britain and Spain decided not to seek a vote in the UN Security Council on their resolution authorizing war in Iraq. The three nations blamed France for dooming the resolution's chances by promising to veto it.").
7. *See* Address to the Nation on Iraq, *supra* note 1, at 338–39.
8. *See, e.g.*, 720 Ill. Comp. Stat. 5/7–1 (2003) ("A person is justified in the use of force against another when and to the extent that he reasonably believes that such conduct is necessary to defend himself or another against such other's *imminent* use of unlawful force." (emphasis added)); State v. Norman, 378 S.E.2d 8 (N.C. 1989).
9. Authorization for Use of Military Force Against Iraq Resolution of 2002, Pub. L. No. 107–243, §§ 3(a)(1)–(2), 116 Stat. 1498, 1501.

10. *See, e.g.*, 148 Cong. Rec. S10247–48 (2002) (statement of Sen. Byrd).

11. As I discuss in chapter 26, in retrospect, it appears that Senator Byrd may have been right that Congress gave the President too much authority to act on his own initiative.

12. *See, e.g.*, Commercial Trust Co. v. Miller, 262 U.S. 51, 57 (1923); Holtzman v. Schlesinger, 484 F.2d 1307, 1310, 1312 & n.3 (2d Cir. 1973).

13. Thucydides, History of the Peloponnesian War 400—08 (Rex Warner trans., New York: Penguin Books, 1972).

• 25 •

Why Congressional Power to Declare War Does Not Provide an Effective Check on the President

March 2002

Among the complaints leveled against King George III in the Declaration of Independence was that he attempted to make "the Military independent of and superior to the Civil power." The framers of the U.S. Constitution sought to avoid a repetition of this evil by making the President, an elected and civilian figure, the commander in chief of the armed forces.

But the framers did not stop there. Fearful that even an elected President might overreach, they divided military authority between the commander in chief and Congress.[1] They assigned to Congress the power to declare war, to "make rules concerning captures on land and water," and—through its taxing and spending powers—the ability "[t]o raise and support armies."

In modern times, however, Congress has often been either unable or unwilling to exercise its constitutional responsibility to act as a check on the President's war-making power. In early 2002, Senate Majority Leader Daschle criticized the Bush Administration's level of consultation with Congress[2]—only to be met with a strong, adverse reaction by Republicans.[3] The hostility Daschle faced is only one recent example of the difficulties members of Congress encounter when they attempt to check executive war-making power.

Congress has not formally declared war since World War II, even though the intervening years have witnessed substantial U.S. military involvement overseas.

This is not to say, however, that Congress has played no part in the decisions to commit troops. The Tonkin Gulf Resolution[4] authorized military action in Vietnam. Similarly, Congress authorized the use of force against Iraq in 1991.[5] And in September 2001, Congress authorized President Bush "to use all necessary and appropriate force against those nations, organizations, or persons he determines planned, authorized, committed, or aided the terrorist attacks that occurred on September 11, 2001, or harbored such organizations or persons."[6]

But in each of these military conflicts, Congress stopped short of declaring war. Why?

One answer is that formal declarations of war are a relic of the eighteenth century. Modern military conflicts are too fluid, and arise too suddenly, for a declaration of war to serve any practical purpose.

Moreover, when Congress authorized military action against the perpetrators of the September 11 attacks, it did not know their precise identities. And to the extent that Congress understood al-Qaeda to be the main enemy, a question arises as to whether it can declare war on an entity other than a state.

This account does not explain Congress's failure to declare war in other recent military conflicts, however, where there were clearly identifiable state enemies: Iraq in the Persian Gulf, and Yugoslavia in Kosovo.

Indeed, in the Kosovo conflict, Congress did not even formally authorize the use of military force.[7] Although the Senate passed a resolution authorizing air attacks,[8] that resolution failed in the House of Representatives.[9] But just over a week later, the House passed a bill funding the war anyway.[10]

Congress's somewhat inconsistent actions in the Kosovo conflict illustrate the difficulty it often faces when the President uses military force. Even if Congress would be inclined against military action, once troops are in the field under enemy fire, Congress can only block such action at the cost of endangering those troops and potentially undermining the national interest. Yet Congress is virtually powerless to prevent the President from using military force in the first place.

It has long been recognized that, even absent a formal declaration of war, the President may, on his own authority, use military force to carry out the congressionally delegated power to "suppress insurrections and repel invasions."[11] Thus, for example, in *The Prize Cases*[12] the Supreme Court upheld President Lincoln's Civil War blockade of Southern ports. And no one doubts that in the event of an actual attack on the United States, the President can and should use military force even if there is insufficient time to seek congressional approval.

How long does an emergency response last? In 1973, Congress adopted the War Powers Resolution[13] in an effort to strengthen its hand vis-à-vis the President. The Resolution was enacted in response to the perception that U.S. military involvement in Vietnam escalated without proper congressional approval.[14]

The War Powers Resolution authorizes presidential use of force only in a narrow range of circumstances. Moreover, it obliges the President to report to Congress within forty-eight hours of deploying troops, and to obtain specific congressional approval for continued deployment within sixty days.

Since its adoption, the War Powers Resolution has come under criticism. Several Presidents have voiced the view that the Resolution is invalid insofar as it purports to limit a power given to the commander in chief by the Constitution.[15]

From the other side, critics who believe that Congress should have more effective checks on presidential war-making powers have observed that the War Powers Resolution does little to accomplish this goal.[16] Despite the Resolution's passage, the very same factors that made Congress reluctant to oppose presidential war-making before the adoption of the War Powers Resolution continue to operate.

After troops are in the field—whether formally authorized by Congress or not—it can appear unpatriotic to call for the abandonment of their mission. The formal need for congressional approval is superseded by the political impossibility of Congress's withholding that approval once the President has unilaterally committed troops. Thus, in practice, despite the framers' best efforts, the dice are loaded against a substantial congressional role in supervising the conduct of war.

Continued fighting in Afghanistan suggests that Senator Daschle was right when he remarked that the military action in Afghanistan had not yet "broken the back of Al-Qaeda."[17] But whether he is right or wrong is not the point. Given the political risks, it is surprising that a congressional leader would seek greater involvement in war matters. Accordingly, rather than having his patriotism questioned, Daschle should be commended for taking his constitutional obligation seriously.

POSTSCRIPT

If the allocation to Congress of the war-declaration power no longer provides an effective check on the President, one may be tempted to devise alternative checks. One such device would be reinstatement of the draft. By making all voters who are themselves draft age or who have draft-age children bear the direct cost of war, a draft would give the public a greater interest in avoiding unnecessary wars, which in turn would be felt by members of Congress.[18] In theory, the draft would also subject the sons and daughters of Senators and House members to military service, although the politically powerful usually can keep their children out of harm's way if they so wish.

Nonetheless, the reinstatement of the draft seems unlikely for the simple reason that most military experts believe that conscripts make much poorer fighters than volunteers.[19] That fact itself, however, may provide something of a check on the political appetite for war. With the armed services stretched thin by active conflicts in Afghanistan and Iraq, as well as more longstanding missions elsewhere, and with the draft deemed impractical, the inability to fight more than one or two wars at a time will require the President to pick the most pressing conflicts. Not that this limit is much consolation to those who have already lost or will lose loved ones in military conflicts that might have been avoided.

NOTES

1. *See* The Federalist No. 69 (Alexander Hamilton).
2. *See* Sheryl Gay Stolberg, *Daschle Wants President to Tell Congress More About His Plans for War*, N.Y. Times, Mar. 4, 2002, at A10.
3. *See* Dan Balz & Helen Dewar, *Daschle Defends Challenge of Bush on War; Senate Majority Leader Says GOP Response Is 'Nothing Short of Hysterical,'* Wash. Post, Mar. 2, 2002, at A13.
4. Joint Resolution of Aug. 10, 1964, Pub. L. No. 88–408, 78 Stat. 384 (1964).
5. Authorization for Use of Military Force Against Iraq Resolution, Pub. L. No. 102–1, 105 Stat. 3 (1991).
6. Authorization for Use of Military Force, Pub. L. No. 107–40, § 2(a), 115 Stat. 224, 224 (2001).
7. *See* Campbell v. Clinton, 203 F.3d 19, 20 (D.C. Cir. 2000).
8. S. Con. Res. 21, 106th Cong. (1999).
9. 145 Cong. Rec. H2441–52 (1999).
10. H.R. Res. 1664, 106th Cong. (1999); 145 Cong. Rec. H2892–96 (1999).
11. U.S. Const. art. I, § 8, cl. 15.
12. 67 U.S. (2 Black) 635 (1863).
13. War Powers Resolution, Pub. L. No. 93–148, 87 Stat. 555 (1973) (codified at 50 U.S.C. §§ 1541–1548 (2000)).
14. *See* H.R. Rep. No. 93–287 (1973), *reprinted in* 1973 U.S.C.C.A.N. 2346, 2348.
15. *See* Richard F. Grimmett, The War Powers Resolution: After Thirty Years (Cong. Research Serv., CRS Report for Congress Order Code RL 32267, Mar. 11, 2004), *available at* http://www.fas.org/man/crs/RL32267.html.
16. *See, e.g.*, John Hart Ely, *Suppose Congress Wanted a War Powers Act That Worked*, 88 Colum. L. Rev. 1379 (1988).
17. *See* Stolberg, *supra*, note 2.
18. This seems to have been Congressman Charles Rangel's motivation for proposing the Universal National Service Act of 2003, H.R. 163, 108th Cong., which would have resumed the draft and created compulsory national service for every citizen between eighteen and twenty-six years of age. *See* Charles B. Rangel, Op-Ed., *Bring Back the Draft*, N.Y. Times, Dec. 31, 2002, at A19.

19. *See, e.g.*, Letter from David J. Armor, Principal Deputy Assistant Secretary of Defense (Force Management and Personnel), to Frank C. Conahan, Assistant Comptroller General, National Security and International Affairs Division, U.S. General Accounting Office (Jan. 8, 1988), *in* Gen. Accounting Office, NSIAD-88–102, Military Draft: Potential Impacts and Other Issues (1988); Department of Defense, Office of the Undersecretary of Defense (Personnel and Readiness), Conscription Threatens Hard-Won Achievements and Military Readiness (2003), *at* http://www.defenselink.mil/news/Jan2003/d20030114avf.pdf; Doug Bandow, *Feeling a Draft?*, Cato Pol'y Rep. (March/April 1999), *at* http://www.cato.org/pubs/policy_report/v21n2/draft.html.

• 26 •

Kerry Stands by His Iraq War Vote, and with Bush, against Constitutional Law Principles

August 2004

Responding to a challenge from President Bush, during the 2004 presidential campaign Senator Kerry stated that even if he had known then what he later learned, he still would have voted to authorize the use of force against Iraq in October 2002.[1]

Bush and his supporters have pointed to Kerry's statement as evidence that the Senator is trying to have it both ways: How can he criticize the President's performance as commander in chief, if he also stands by the decision to go to war?[2]

Kerry has a good response to the charge of straddling. He says he has consistently criticized the manner in which the President has conducted the war, rather than the congressional decision to authorize force in the first place. Although Bush derides this distinction as "nuance," it is hardly a matter of hair-splitting. The President and his supporters insult the intelligence of American voters by suggesting that the distinction between means and ends is necessarily bogus.

Although Kerry's criticism of Bush's conduct of the war is fully consistent with his support for removing Saddam Hussein from power, Kerry's response to Bush's question is nonetheless problematic in a different respect. What possible justification would there have been for authorizing force against Iraq had it been known, as we know now, that Iraq had no significant weapons of mass destruction and no significant ties to al-Qaeda?

As I explain below, Kerry's reason for standing by his vote is principled and consistent. The problem is that the principle it consistently upholds is one of sweeping presidential power—a principle that he and Bush both endorse, and that the Constitution rejects.

In the leadup to the U.S.-led invasion of Iraq, President Bush offered three primary justifications for going to war. First, Bush claimed that Saddam Hussein was on the verge of possessing and using weapons of mass destruction (or "WMDs").[3] Second, Bush claimed that Saddam was supporting terrorists, including al-Qaeda.[4] Third, Bush pointed to Saddam's record as a vicious tyrant who had abused the human rights of his own citizens—a record, Bush said, that warranted intervention on humanitarian grounds.[5] Each of these justifications for war was questionable in March 2003. They are even weaker today.

U.S.-led forces in Iraq have failed to find weapons of mass destruction, and the reason appears to be that in fact, there were none.[6] Scientists who formerly worked on Iraq's biological, chemical, and nuclear weapons programs now say that these programs were largely discontinued, and the weapons stockpiles destroyed, after the first Gulf War.

Exactly why the pre-war intelligence estimates of Saddam's WMD capabilities were so far off is a matter of debate. Some blame the Central Intelligence Agency for faulty methods, while others blame the Bush Administration for puffing self-serving claims by Iraqi exiles like Ahmed Chalabi—exiles whose assertions should have received closer scrutiny.

Perhaps the strongest pre-war support for the theory that Iraq possessed WMDs derived from Saddam Hussein's own behavior. Saddam repeatedly obstructed UN weapons inspectors in a game of cat and mouse that led many observers to assume that he must therefore have had something to hide. (So why did he do it, if he didn't have something to hide? The best explanations I have heard are that Saddam was trying to scare his own people and/or that he was, and is, simply irrational.)

Thus, before the war one might have thought that Saddam either possessed WMDs or that there was a substantial probability that he did. In either event, given his past willingness to use chemical weapons against the Kurds and the Iranians, prudent planners may have thought that he posed too great a danger to be allowed to remain in power. As President Bush put the point in October 2002, in light of the risk, "we cannot wait for the final proof—the smoking gun—that could come in the form of a mushroom cloud."[7]

Accordingly, although the failure to find WMDs is embarrassing, it does not discredit the initial decision of someone who thought, based on what was known before the war, that force was justified. After all, any decision based on an assessment of risk can be the right decision even if the risk does not materialize. Policy makers—even Presidents—are asked to be prudent, not clairvoyant.

But that's a far cry from saying—as both Bush and Kerry have—that they would have supported going to war even if they knew then what we know now, namely that Saddam did not possess WMDs or even an active WMD program. They must therefore think the war was justified on other grounds.

President Bush and his supporters also justified the war by pointing to Iraq's support for terrorism. Yet the Administration's repeated invocations of the attacks of September 11, 2001, were misleading at best. Al-Qaeda is a fundamentalist Islamist terrorist movement, which disdained secular regimes like Saddam's Baath Party. A connection between the two was highly implausible, and there was scant evidence of one.[8]

The best that could be said for the terrorism argument before the war was that Saddam Hussein is an opportunist. Even if there was no evidence of active cooperation with al-Qaeda, one could have imagined that at some point, Saddam might decide to deliver a dangerous weapon to al-Qaeda or another terrorist organization in an alliance of convenience. Better to take him out before he had the chance to harm us, the Administration argued.

To the extent that this argument for preemptive action had force before the war, that force has been dissipated by subsequent events. The failure to find WMDs indicates that Saddam didn't have the dangerous weapons to deliver to the terrorists.

Thus the terrorism argument "succeeds" only in an ironic sense. As a result of the U.S. invasion, numerous foreign fighters—including known terrorists—have entered Iraq to attack U.S. forces and Iraqi civilians. So Iraq is now a hotbed of terrorism, but that is a result of the war,[9] not a justification for it.

Had they known before the war what we now know, it is hard to understand how President Bush and Senator Kerry could possibly have thought the action justified on the ground that it would reduce the terrorist threat. Indeed, it's hard to imagine how, if they knew what we know now, they could not have been convinced that the war would actually worsen that threat—by sapping resources from real anti-terror initiatives, domestic and foreign; alienating other nations; and aiding terrorist recruitment by confirming the widely held view of the United States as an imperial power.

That brings us to the third justification for the Iraq war—human rights issues. There is no doubt that Saddam Hussein was among the world's worst abusers of human rights. But the Bush Administration's invocation of this fact as a basis for war was always opportunistic at best.

How do we know that? For one thing, Saddam's worst abuses occurred in the 1980s, when he was considered a U.S. ally by members of the current Administration. And then-Governor Bush campaigned for the White House in 2000 arguing that U.S. armed forces should not be deployed for humanitarian missions if those missions will necessarily be engaged in "nation building."[10]

Did Bush and his advisers have a change of heart so that they now support nation-building exercises based on humanitarian principles? Hardly. If abuses of human rights were indeed the basis for attacking Iraq, why hasn't the Administration taken swift military action in the Sudan? There is right now an active campaign of ethnic cleansing by Arab militia or "Janjaweed" directed at the black African inhabitants of the Darfur region of that country. Great suffering is occurring; human rights abuses are rife. This campaign exceeds in scale anything that Saddam Hussein was attempting at the time of the U.S.-led invasion of Iraq.

To his credit, Senator Kerry has spoken out more forcefully than the President has regarding the need for action in the Sudan.[11] But he has also repeatedly described himself as a "realist" with respect to international relations.[12]

Kerry believes that the U.S. armed forces should generally only be used to protect vital American interests. He may allow for occasional exceptions to that principle in order to avert catastrophes of the sort now occurring in the Sudan. But he has not argued, nor could he, that Iraq falls under such an exception. Indeed, with respect to Iraq, Kerry has actually criticized Bush for departing from the realism each professes as his creed.

Although it did not receive as much attention in the pre-war period as the arguments relating to WMDs, terrorism, and human rights, there was one remaining plausible justification for war: By obstructing weapons inspectors, repeatedly entering the "no-fly" zones, and cheating on the oil-for-food program, Saddam appeared to be in breach of the UN resolutions that ended the first Gulf War. If so, then force would have been justified.

The difficulty with this argument, as I explained in chapter 23, is that the relevant UN resolutions made clear that the Security Council itself, not any individual member state, was to be the arbiter of whether a breach had occurred. Thus, if the Bush Administration wanted to rely on Saddam's failure to abide by UN resolutions, it needed a new UN resolution authorizing force. No such resolution was forthcoming.

This argument, then, does not avail Bush: He did not wait for the crucial resolution he needed. But it may work better for Kerry—who did not choose to jump the gun. Whereas the Bush Administration has been willing to rely on unilateral means or ad hoc coalitions, Kerry has repeatedly stated his strong belief in working with and through international organizations such as the UN. So Kerry may be suggesting that, knowing what he knows now, if he had been President, he would have authorized force against Iraq only if force had also been authorized by the UN.

After all, the October 2002 resolution for which Kerry, as a Senator, in fact voted, authorized force to defend the United States and "to enforce all United Nations Security Council resolutions regarding Iraq."[13] Kerry might have reasonably thought at the time that those resolutions would themselves be reasserted by the Security Council.

It's not Kerry's fault, the argument would go, that Bush went ahead without Security Council approval. And Kerry has not said that, as President, he would have done the same. On the contrary, he has strongly implied that he would not have done so.

And yet that is not exactly what Kerry said. In response to Bush's challenge, Kerry said "I believe it's the right authority for a president to have."[14] What does that mean?

Kerry appears to have been referring to an argument that economic sanctions and ordinary diplomacy with respect to Saddam had run their course. In this view, the only way to coerce Iraqi compliance with UN resolutions was to make a credible threat of war. And the only way to do that was for Congress to give the President the authority to go to war: Thus, in Kerry's argot, it—the authority to go to war—is the right authority for a President to have.

Accordingly, Kerry espouses a perfectly coherent position when he says that he voted to authorize war even as he wished to avert war. And despite President Bush's criticism, there is nothing especially "nuanced" about this view, which amounts to saying that threats are most effective when backed by the potential use of force.

But if the Bush Administration is wrong to criticize Kerry's position as equivocal, Kerry's view is nonetheless problematic for an entirely different reason: It fails to honor the spirit of the Constitution, which grants the power to declare war to Congress, not the President.

It's important to recall not just the content of Congress's resolution, but its timing. Congress voted to authorize force against Iraq before the Security Council deemed it necessary and months in advance of the moment when U.S. forces would even be in position to be deployed.

Congress thus tried to let itself off the hook. House members and Senators could tell themselves, as Senator Kerry apparently did, that they were not voting for war, but only for the threat of war to aid diplomacy. That meant that Congress effectively delegated the decision to go to war to the President.

Yet, Article I of the Constitution does not permit Congress to delegate its war-declaring power to the President. Taking that power seriously should mean that Congress only declares war (or its equivalent) when all members voting for war actually intend to take the nation to war. Otherwise, the only elected official who will really pass on the wisdom of war is the President.

Whether that President is named Bush or Kerry is not really the point. The framers of the Constitution expected the presidency to be filled by able statesmen like George Washington, the young nation's greatest war hero. They nonetheless vested the power to declare war in Congress, because it is the branch of government most closely tied to the people.

The framers expected that members of Congress would only vote to sacrifice the lives of their constituents if that was really their intent. If allowed to work as designed, this constitutional allocation of power prevents the nation from waging unnecessary wars.[15]

Senator Kerry says that he regrets having trusted President Bush not to rush headlong and unilaterally into war. The question remains why he did not trust in the Constitution.

POSTSCRIPT

One other, largely post hoc, justification has been advanced for the war in Iraq despite the absence of WMDs or al-Qaeda ties. During the 2004 campaign, President Bush repeatedly stated that by going on the "offensive," we fight the country's enemies abroad rather than at home, and thus protect the homeland.[16] This argument had some appeal for two reasons: first, the absence of any substantial terrorist attack in the United States between September 11, 2001 and the November 2004 election; and second, the inherent logic of the implicit sports metaphor. A football team that controls the clock while on offense does not permit the opposing team to score for the simple reason that it doesn't have the ball.

Whatever the reasons we were spared a terrorist strike during this period, the suggested analogy is flawed, mostly because it assumes that the enemy, like a football team, has a fixed roster of players. The worry of many hard-headed realists who opposed the war was that the American invasion and occupation of Iraq would serve to swell the ranks of terrorist organizations with new jihadists who would not otherwise have been interested in attacking the United States. Even Thomas Friedman, who supported the war, observed in an April 2005 *New York Times* column that, to the extent that the newly elected government in Iraq successfully beats back the insurgency, it may lead the jihadists that the war created to turn their attention elsewhere, including the United States.[17] On this point, as on so many others about which I take a dim view, I fervently hope to be proven wrong.

NOTES

1. *See* Jodi Wilgoren, *Kerry Says His Vote on Iraq Would Be the Same Today*, N.Y. Times, Aug. 10, 2004, at A18.

2. *See* David E. Sanger, *For Now, Bush's Mocking Drowns Out Kerry's Nuanced Explanation of His War Vote*, N.Y. Times, Aug. 12, 2004, at A22.

3. Address to the Nation on Iraq, 39 Weekly Comp. Pres. Doc. 338 (Mar. 17, 2003) ("Intelligence gathered by this and other governments leaves no doubt that the Iraq regime continues to possess and conceal some of the most lethal weapons ever devised.").

4. *Id.* at 339 ("The regime . . . has aided, trained, and harbored terrorists, including operatives of Al Qaida. . . . The danger is clear: Using chemical, biological or, one day, nuclear weapons obtained with the help of Iraq, the terrorists could fulfill their stated ambitions and kill thousands or hundreds of thousands of innocent people in our country or any other.").

5. *See* The President's Radio Address, 39 Weekly Comp. Pres. Doc. 329 (Mar. 15, 2003).

6. *See* Walter Pincus & Dana Milbank, *Kay Backs Outside Probe of Iraq Data; Ex-Inspector Again Says Forbidden Arms Probably Didn't Exist*, Wash. Post, Jan. 29, 2004, at A1.

7. Address to the Nation on Iraq from Cincinnati, Ohio, 38 Weekly Comp. Pres. Doc. 1718 (Oct. 7, 2002).

8. *See* S. Rep. No. 108–301, at 321–45 (2004); Walter Pincus & Dana Milbank, *Al-Qaeda-Hussein Link Is Dismissed*, Wash. Post, June 17, 2004, at A1.

9. *See Worldwide Security Threats: Hearing Before the S. Armed Servs. Comm.*, 108th Cong. (2004) (statement of George J. Tenet, Director, Central Intelligence Agency), 2004 WL 436313.

10. Here is what then-Governor Bush said in his debate with Vice President Albert Gore Jr. on October 11, 2000:

> Somalia. Started off as a humanitarian mission then changed into a nation-building mission, and that's where the mission went wrong. The mission was changed. And as a result, our nation paid a price. And so I don't think our troops ought to be used for what's called nation-building. I think our troops ought to be used to fight and win war. I think our troops ought to be used to help overthrow a dictator that's in our—and it's in our—when it's in our best interests. But in this case, it was a nation-building exercise. And same with Haiti, I wouldn't have supported either.

During the same debate, Bush responded as follows to a question about President Clinton's failure to intervene militarily in Rwanda:

> I think the administration did the right thing in that case, I do. . . . And that's a case where we need to, you know, use our influence to have countries in Africa come together and help deal with the situation. The administration—it seems like we're having a great love fest now—but the administration made the right decision on training Nigerian troops for situations just such as this in Rwanda. And so I thought they made the right decision not to send U.S. troops into Rwanda.

11. *See* Jon Sawyer, *Pressure Mounts for U.S. Action in Crisis*, St. Louis Post-Dispatch, July 18, 2004, at B1.

12. *See* Ronald Brownstein, *Kerry Casts Himself as Solid Realist and Bush as Dreamy Idealist*, L.A. Times, June 7, 2004, at A12.

13. Authorization for Use of Military Force Against Iraq Resolution of 2002, Pub. L. No. 107–243, § 3(a)(2), 116 Stat. 1498, 1501.

14. *See Kerry: I Would Have Backed War without WMD; Bush Touts Plan for 'Ownership Society,'* Chi. Trib., Aug. 10, 2004, at 12.

15. *Cf.* The Federalist No. 26 (Alexander Hamilton).

16. *See, e.g.*, Remarks in Toledo, Ohio, 40 Weekly Pres. Comp. Doc. 2690 (Oct. 29, 2004) ("We are staying on the offensive. We're chasing the terrorists overseas so we do not have to face them here at home.").

17. Thomas L. Friedman, Op-Ed., *The Calm Before the Storm?*, N.Y. Times, Apr. 13, 2005, at A19.

V

THE GLOBAL VILLAGE

In my experience, no two people use the term *globalization* in exactly the same way, but it generally refers to the ever-increasing interdependence of people and institutions on different parts of the globe that accompanies the ever-increasing ease of global transportation and communication. Experts argue over whether globalization is a net boon, permitting, as it does, goods and services to be produced wherever they are cheapest, or whether its dark side predominates, as nation-states must compete in a global "race to the bottom" by providing multinational corporations with relocation incentives in the form of low taxes, low wages, and lax labor and environmental standards. That is an important debate, but not the focus of this section.

The chapters in this section exemplify the related phenomenon of legal globalization: the many ways in which different legal systems collide and exert mutual influence over one another. I should confess, however, that I do not consider myself an expert in comparative or international law, or in the law of any country other than the United States. But globalization is here to stay, and it will become increasingly difficult for people to hold themselves out as really knowing anything about their own domestic legal system without knowing a fair bit about other legal systems. That, at any rate, is my view. As you will see in these chapters, the proper role of foreign and international sources is itself hotly debated.

• 27 •

When American States Execute Citizens of Foreign Countries: The Case of Gerardo Valdez

July 2001

In July 2001, Oklahoma Governor Frank Keating denied Gerardo Valdez's plea that his death sentence[1] be commuted to lifetime imprisonment. Governor Keating's decision was surprising because in this case, unlike in most others, the Oklahoma Pardon and Parole Board had recommended clemency based on mitigating evidence that was not presented at Valdez's original trial. Moreover, in denying clemency, Governor Keating rejected not only the Board's recommendation, but also a plea from Mexican President Vicente Fox.

Why was the President of Mexico interceding in an Oklahoma murder case? Because Valdez is a Mexican citizen, and it is undisputed that when he was arrested, he was not advised of his right to consult with Mexican diplomats in the United States. It is also undisputed that the failure to so advise him violated Article 36 of the Vienna Convention on Consular Relations,[2] to which both the United States and Mexico are signatories.

In a letter to President Fox, Governor Keating stated that he was nonetheless denying clemency because Valdez had not proved that consultation with the Mexican government would have averted the death penalty. In other words, according to Governor Keating, this was a case of "no harm, no foul."

Needless to say, the Mexican government does not see it that way, and may bring suit against the United States in the International Court of Justice in the Hague—known as the "ICJ" and sometimes informally called the "World Court." In June 2001, that court ruled against the United States in a very similar case, *Germany v. United States of America*.[3] That case involved Arizona's execution of Walter LaGrand,[4] a German national.

The *Valdez* and *LaGrand* cases illustrate how state and national death penalty policy in the United States have put us at odds with world opinion and international law.

Let's begin with the facts of the *LaGrand* case. In February 1984, brothers Walter and Karl LaGrand, German citizens who were born in Germany, were arrested in the United States for bank robbery and murder. They were not informed of their rights under the Vienna Convention at the time. Later that same year, they were both convicted and sentenced to death.

In the LaGrands' case, the breach of the Vienna Convention was in some sense technical and excusable. Because the LaGrand brothers had lived in the United States since early childhood, the Arizona officers who arrested them might have innocently failed to realize they were German citizens entitled to consular consultation.

Indeed, probably for this reason, although the German government learned about the case in 1992, it initially took no legal action. That changed, however, a week before Walter LaGrand's scheduled execution, when (according to its ICJ submission) Germany learned that Arizona officials in fact did know that the LaGrands were German citizens at the time they were arrested.

German diplomats then lobbied intensively with the U.S. State Department, but to no avail. On the day of the scheduled execution, Germany filed an emergency motion with the ICJ. The ICJ promptly issued an order to the United States to "take all measures at its disposal to ensure that Walter LaGrand is not executed pending [a] final decision" by the ICJ.[5]

Armed with the ICJ ruling, Germany immediately asked the United States Supreme Court to order the Arizona Governor to stay LaGrand's death sentence. That request came only two hours before the scheduled execution. In its 1999 decision in *Federal Republic of Germany v. United States*,[6] the Supreme Court rejected the request by a 7–2 vote.

The Court cited "the tardiness of the pleas" and jurisdictional barriers.[7] Arizona promptly put Walter LaGrand to death.[8]

In its June 2001 ruling in *LaGrand*, the ICJ acknowledged that, as the U.S. Supreme Court had noted, Germany could have acted in a more timely fashion. Nonetheless, the ICJ found that the United States—including the executive branch, the United States Supreme Court, and the government of Arizona—had acted in violation of its treaty obligation by failing to comply with the ICJ order.

In holding the United States accountable for conduct taken by any branch or level of government, the ICJ rejected a key U.S. argument: that the LaGrands were procedurally barred from raising their rights under the Convention.

Under U.S. law, a person held in custody by a state may challenge his conviction or sentence by seeking a writ of habeas corpus in federal court.[9] However, the prisoner is not entitled to a completely new adjudication. For example, a prisoner may not raise an objection in federal court if he has not previously raised it during his state court proceedings.

This rule is known as the doctrine of *procedural bar*, and it implements the idea that federal habeas corpus proceedings only exist to remedy state court errors. If an issue wasn't presented to a state court, or wasn't presented to a state court in accordance with the state's prescribed procedures, then the inmate is barred from raising it for the first time in federal court.[10]

The concept of procedural bar has been part of federal habeas corpus law for a very long time. Throughout the last twenty-five years, however, the Supreme Court has interpreted it with increasing strictness, narrowing the circumstances under which habeas relief can be afforded.

Thus, in 1998, in yet another case arising under the Vienna Convention, *Breard v. Greene*,[11] the Justices held that a Paraguayan national was procedurally barred from raising his treaty rights because he had earlier failed to raise them in the Virginia courts, where, by 1998, it was too late to do so.

In its ruling in the *LaGrand* case, the ICJ stated that in principle, there is nothing wrong with national and subnational courts requiring that treaty rights be raised in accordance with local procedural requirements, *so long as those requirements are fair*. But where the U.S. Supreme Court had found no unfairness in applying the procedural bar doctrine, the ICJ saw a catch-22.

According to the ICJ, the reason the LaGrands didn't raise their rights under the Vienna Convention in a timely fashion was because they did not know of those rights—which was itself because the police violated the Convention by failing to inform them of their rights.[12]

In its *LaGrand* ruling, the ICJ lauded the United States for its efforts to comply with the Vienna Convention in the future. In particular, the State Department has conducted training programs and distributed many thousands of brochures and pocket cards to federal, state, and local law enforcement officials to encourage compliance.[13] The State Department hopes that, as a result of this program, arresting officers issuing *Miranda* warnings now will also inform suspects of their right, if foreign nationals, to consular consultation.

But such warnings will not do anything for Gerardo Valdez and the nearly one hundred other foreign nationals on death rows in the United States,[14] nor for the many more foreign nationals serving prison sentences. After all, the Vienna Convention applies to *all* foreign arrestees, not just those facing possible execution.

As to foreign citizens whose rights under the Vienna Convention have already been violated, the ICJ ruling makes clear "the obligation of the United States under certain circumstances to review and reconsider convictions and sentences,"[15] notwithstanding the procedural bar doctrine.

It remains to be seen whether the United States will comply. The Supreme Court's ruling in the *LaGrand* case indicates that a majority of the Justices believe that the federal government lacks the power to enforce the Vienna Convention against unwilling states.

Yet Article VI of the U.S. Constitution states that "all Treaties made, or which shall be made, under the Authority of the United States, shall be the supreme Law of the Land." That means that there is ample federal power to enforce the Vienna Convention.

Finally, although I have discussed cases in which foreign killers invoked the Vienna Convention to escape the death penalty, it is worth remembering that the Convention also protects U.S. citizens traveling abroad.

If you were arrested while traveling in a foreign country, wouldn't you want to be informed of your right to contact the U.S. Embassy? And, more fundamentally, wouldn't you want the country to honor that right? By failing to comply with the ICJ's authoritative construction of the treaty, the United States may court a backlash, thus jeopardizing our ability to protect our own citizens abroad.

POSTSCRIPT

In March 2004, the ICJ issued a follow-up ruling entitling 51 Mexican nationals on death row in the United States to "review and reconsideration" of their convictions and sentences as the remedy for the failure to respect their rights under the Vienna Convention.[16] In a decision that treated the Supreme Court holding in *Breard* as superior to the more recent ICJ decision, the U.S. Court of Appeals for the Fifth Circuit ruled in May 2004 that the latter did not benefit one Jose Ernesto Medellin, because he had failed to raise his claims in a timely fashion—essentially the same argument the ICJ had already rejected.[17] The Supreme Court was poised to decide Medellin's case in 2005, when the Bush Administration announced that it was complying with the ICJ ruling by ordering new state court hearings for the 51 Mexican nationals.[18]

Whether that order satisfactorily resolves matters remains to be seen, for the Administration's effort at retrospective compliance with the Vienna Convention was coupled with a March 7, 2005, letter from Secretary of State Condolezza Rice indicating that the United States was prospectively withdrawing from a protocol to the Convention that gives the ICJ the power to make compliance determinations.[19] As for Medellin, in May 2005, the Supreme Court dismissed his case on the ground that resolution of his claims by the Texas courts could render judicial action at the federal level unnecessary.[20] That seemingly technical ruling proved surprisingly divisive, however, as four Justices dissented. These Justices would have sent the case back to the federal appeals court.[21] In any event, it is not implausible that Medellin's case will eventually return to the Supreme Court.

The real story in cases such as these is not consular consultation, of course. The countries invoking the Vienna Convention are not really concerned about consultation with their nationals. Given the number of foreign citizens in the United States, their respective consular and ambassadorial staff are insufficient to provide much assistance to every national who is arrested here. Foreign nations use the Vienna Convention simply as a hook by which to challenge the death penalty in the United States.

But in a world that is increasingly hostile to the United States, it may behoove us to overlook the opportunistic use of the Vienna Convention by foreign governments if that is the price we must pay to ensure that our own nationals are protected if they happen to be arrested on foreign soil.

NOTES

1. Valdez v. State, 900 P.2d 363 (Okla. Crim. App. 1995).
2. Vienna Convention on Consular Relations and Optional Protocol on Disputes, Apr. 24, 1963, art. 36, para. 1(b), 21 U.S.T. 77, 101, 596 U.N.T.S. 261, 292 (entered into force for the United States Dec. 24, 1969).
3. LaGrand Case (F.R.G. v. U.S.), 2001 I.C.J. 466 (June 27).
4. State v. LaGrand, 734 P.2d 563 (Ariz. 1987).
5. *LaGrand Case*, 2001 I.C.J. at 479.
6. 526 U.S. 111 (1999) (per curiam).
7. *Id.* at 112.
8. *See* Roger Cohen, *U.S. Execution of German Stirs Anger*, N.Y. Times, Mar. 5, 1999, at A14.
9. 28 U.S.C. § 2254 (2001).
10. *See* Baldwin v. Reese, 541 U.S. 27 (2004).
11. 523 U.S. 371 (1998) (per curiam).
12. *See* LaGrand Case (F.R.G. v. U.S.), 2001 I.C.J. 466, 488 (June 27).
13. *See id.* at 511–12.
14. *See* Raymond Bonner, *U.S. Bid to Execute Mexican Draws Fire*, N.Y. Times, Oct. 30, 2000, at A20 ("Although experts in death penalty law say they have no concrete figures, they say they believe the numbers of such cases may be growing in proportion to the number of foreign citizens on death row. At least 87 foreign citizens—from 28 countries—are on death row, in 16 states.").
15. *LaGrand Case*, 2001 I.C.J. at 514.
16. Concerning Avena and Other Mexican Nationals (Mex. v. U.S.), (judgment of Mar. 31, 2004), *available at* http://www.icj-cij.org/icjwww/idecisions.htm.
17. Medellin v. Dretke, 371 F.3d 270, 279–80 (5th Cir. 2004) (per curiam), *cert. granted* 125 S. Ct. 686 (2004), *cert. dismissed* 125 S. Ct. 2088 (2005) (per curiam).
18. The memorandum can be read in the appendices of the United States' brief to the Supreme Court. *See* Brief for the United States as Amicus Curiae Supporting Respondent at 1aa, Medellin v. Dretke, 125 S. Ct. 2088 (2005) (No. 04–5928) (per curiam), 2005 WL 504490.
19. *See* Charles Lane, *U.S. Quits Pact Used in Capital Cases; Foes of Death Penalty Cite Access to Envoys*, Wash. Post, Mar. 10, 2005, at A1.
20. *See* Medellin v. Dretke, 125 S. Ct. 2088, 2089–90, 2092 (2005) (per curiam).
21. *See id.* at 2095–2105 (O'Connor, J., joined by Stevens, Souter, and Breyer, JJ.).

• 28 •

Can One Nation Arrest the Foreign Minister of Another? The World Court Says No

February 2002

In February 2002, the ICJ (International Court of Justice) issued an important ruling in the case of *Democratic Republic of the Congo v. Belgium*.[1] While the decision was overshadowed by proceedings in a different Hague tribunal—the trial of Slobodan Milosevic in the International Criminal Tribunal for the former Yugoslavia[2]—it is nevertheless quite significant from the standpoints of international human rights law and international relations.

The case arose when Belgium issued an arrest warrant for Abdulaye Yerodia Ndombasi—the then-Foreign Minister of the Congo. The Congo argued, and the ICJ agreed, that Belgium's warrant had violated international law.

It turns out that, for reasons I explain below, the decision will not have much practical impact on the fate of Mr. Ndombasi. However, its potential long-term implications for international diplomacy and so-called universal jurisdiction to prosecute human rights violations are far-reaching.

In August 1998, Ndombasi, who was then Presidential Secretary of the Congo, made public statements denouncing the invasion of his country by soldiers from neighboring Rwanda. Ndombasi referred to the Rwandan soldiers, nearly all of whom were members of the Tutsi tribe, as "vermin" and "microbes" that "must be methodically eradicated."[3]

Given the history of tribal violence in Rwanda, Burundi, and the Congo, Ndombasi's statements were likely to inflame his countrymen, spurring them to violence. The statements did just that—causing the massacre of hundreds of Congolese citizens who happened to be Tutsi.

In April 2000, the Belgian government issued a warrant for Ndombasi's arrest on charges of war crimes and crimes against humanity arising out of his incitement of racial hatred. Belgium publicized the warrant, urging other nations to arrest Ndombasi should they find him within their jurisdiction.

What is Belgium's connection to Ndombasi's acts in the Congo? The Congo was once a Belgian colony. Indeed it was the personal property of Belgian King Leopold II. Belgian colonial rule was brutal. (Joseph Conrad's *Heart of Darkness*[4] provides a flavor of just how brutal.) As Belgium played a substantial role in creating and fueling the tribal animosities that have plagued central Africa for more than a century, one might think that Belgium bears some responsibility for the dire situation today.

However, Belgium did not seek Ndombasi's arrest out of a sense of obligation to its former colony—or at least not solely out of such a sense. Rather, Belgium sought to exercise universal jurisdiction, the asserted right of *any* nation-state to bring prosecutions in its domestic courts against persons charged with serious human rights violations *anywhere in the world*. Pursuant to that same universal jurisdiction, Belgian officials have instituted a criminal investigation against Israeli Prime Minister Ariel Sharon in connection with the 1982 massacre of Palestinian refugees by Lebanese Christian militias.

Nor is Belgium alone in asserting universal jurisdiction. Spain and Great Britain proceeded against former Chilean dictator Augusto Pinochet before he was eventually returned to Chile for health reasons.[5] And judges in several countries have begun investigations into Henry Kissinger's alleged role in human rights violations in Argentina and Chile in the 1970s.[6]

How did the *Ndombasi* case end up in the ICJ? After Belgium issued its arrest warrant for Ndombasi, the Congo sued Belgium in the ICJ, claiming that Belgium had violated a rule of international law that gives heads of state and foreign ministers immunity from arrest while they hold office. Of crucial importance, the Congo argued, was the fact that when the warrant was issued, Ndombasi was serving as Foreign Minister of the Congo.

The Congo argued that the possibility of criminal prosecution in any country in the world deters the extensive travel in which foreign ministers must engage to achieve the vital purposes of international diplomacy. Accordingly, the Congo claimed, international treaties and customary international law should be interpreted to give foreign ministers and heads of state immunity from prosecution while they serve in office.

The Congo's argument was similar, in some respects, to the argument made by President Clinton in the Paula Jones case. Clinton argued that a President should not have to defend a civil lawsuit while in office because it would interfere with his official duties.

The U.S. Supreme Court unanimously rejected Clinton's immunity claim in the 1997 decision in *Clinton v. Jones*.[7] The Justices found no merit in Clinton's prediction that permitting the *Jones* case to proceed during his tenure in office would impose an "unacceptable burden on the President's time and energy."[8] In retrospect, that judgment is subject to considerable doubt.

Ndombasi's immunity claim fared better in the ICJ than Clinton's immunity claim fared in the U.S. Supreme Court. The ICJ ruled in favor of the Congo, finding immunity. It reasoned "that the functions of a Minister for Foreign Affairs are such that, throughout the duration of his or her office, he or she when abroad enjoys full immunity from criminal jurisdiction."[9]

Under the ICJ ruling, this immunity applies regardless of whether the acts charged were committed in a private or official capacity, and regardless of whether they occurred before or after the foreign minister assumed office. Moreover, so important is the smooth functioning of international diplomacy that the ICJ rejected the Belgian suggestion that there might be an exception in the case of war crimes or crimes against humanity.

The scope of the immunity the ICJ recognized is ambiguous in two respects. First, it is unclear whether the ICJ's ruling applies to civil lawsuits. That could be significant—in part because the United States has a statute that authorizes such lawsuits.

To be more specific, America's Alien Tort Claims Act[10] confers jurisdiction on federal courts to hear civil claims by aliens alleging human rights violations by other aliens on foreign soil. For example, in *Kadic v. Karadzic*,[11] the U.S. Court of Appeals for the Second Circuit permitted a lawsuit by a group of Bosnian plaintiffs against the titular head of the self-proclaimed Bosnian Serb republic of Srpska. (Because Srpska was not a state recognized by the United States or the international community, the court rejected the defendant's claim of head-of-state immunity under U.S. law.)

After *Congo v. Belgium*, do national courts have to dismiss cases like *Kadic* if the defendant is a foreign minister? The ICJ's ruling does not speak to the question, but the rationale of the opinion—facilitating the ability of foreign ministers to travel around the world—would suggest that foreign ministers enjoy immunity against civil, as well as criminal, cases.

It is also unclear whether the immunity applies to persons other than foreign ministers and heads of state. If the goal is the protection of the institution of international diplomacy, then why not extend immunity to ambassadors? How about embassy and consular staff? Language in the ICJ opinion focuses on the concentration of power in a foreign minister, but one can also see threats to the conduct of diplomacy from legal actions against lower-level officials.

Should foreign ministers who have violated human rights think they can now trot the globe freely? The answer is no. The ICJ placed four significant limitations on its own ruling.

First, the immunity does not apply in a person's home country. If the home country permits criminal trials of the sitting foreign minister or head of state, international law is no obstacle.

Second, a state may waive the immunity, over the objection of an individual. The immunity exists to benefit states, not the persons who happen to represent states. Accordingly, it is the state, not the person, who can decide whether to assert or to waive it.

Third, a foreign minister's immunity only applies to trials by foreign *states*. Thus, where multilateral treaties and other instruments purport to supersede immunity from prosecution, the decision in *Congo v. Belgium*—which was based on customary international law, i.e., state practices deemed to have the force of law in virtue of general acceptance as such—does not override their explicit language. That means that *Congo v. Belgium* poses no obstacle to the proceedings of the International Criminal Tribunal for the former Yugoslavia, the International Criminal Tribunal for Rwanda, or the International Criminal Court.

Fourth and most importantly, immunity from prosecution only applies while a person holds the office of foreign minister or head of state. Once he leaves office, he is fair game. As the ICJ explained, "the *immunity* from jurisdiction enjoyed by incumbent Ministers for Foreign Affairs does not mean that they enjoy *impunity* in respect of any crimes they might have committed."[12]

Accordingly, because Ndombasi no longer serves as Foreign Minister of the Congo, the ICJ's ruling provides him no real protection. Belgium's original arrest warrant for Ndombasi must be revoked because it was invalid when issued. But nothing in the ICJ decision prevents Belgium from issuing a new arrest warrant for him immediately after revoking the first.

This feature of the ICJ opinion may make it seem irrelevant. Indeed, one might even think the ruling perverse. It disfavors those who hold time-limited positions within democratic regimes, as compared to those who serve lifetime or longtime dictators, who may enjoy lifetime or longtime immunity. And by making immunity turn on whether an alleged violator of human rights holds high office, the decision creates an incentive for such a person to hang on to power for as long as possible.

However, the ICJ was right not to give any serious attention to this last point. Tyrants and thugs almost invariably wish to hold on to power regardless of the rules of international law. Given the many limits on the immunity the ICJ recognized, the benefits to international diplomacy that come from *Congo v. Belgium* outweigh any competing costs to the principle of individual responsibility that is the hallmark of international human rights law.

POSTSCRIPT

The international human rights community tends to support universal jurisdiction, and I agree that it can play an important role in bringing human rights abusers to justice. Nonetheless, we should distinguish between legitimate and illegitimate uses of the concept. Where the domestic courts of a nation are unable or unwilling to institute proceedings against a human rights abuser—perhaps because his allies still hold power or the courts lack political independence—it makes sense for the world community to step in. Likewise, someone who unlawfully victimized foreign citizens should not escape justice because his countrymen and women regard the victims as enemies. But where the domestic courts of a country in which a putative defendant harmed only his own fellow citizens function independently, trial and punishment—or amnesty and reconciliation—should be left to that nation. For in such a case, a foreign country that attempted to assert universal jurisdiction would not be acting as a real surrogate for the victim country.

For this reason, I was troubled by the efforts by Spain (assisted by Great Britain) to assert universal jurisdiction over Pinochet. Pinochet had given up most of his real power in Chile under a carefully arranged agreement that—for a time anyway—ensured that he would escape prosecution in exchange for the emergence of democracy and prospective respect for human rights. In 1998, Pinochet relinquished his role as commander in chief of the Chilean military and assumed what was to be a lifetime seat in the Senate. That "deal" certainly did not amount to perfect justice; transitions from autocratic regimes rarely do. But as subsequent events in Chile illustrated, the country was capable of handling the matter internally.

Pinochet was stripped of his Senate seat in 2002 on grounds that his health made him unfit to stand trial for human rights violations and thus unfit to be a Senator as well. The charges, though not the Senate seat, were reinstated in 2004, and as this book goes to press, Pinochet awaits trial.[13] Universal jurisdiction has thus proved unnecessary in this case.

NOTES

1. Concerning the Arrest Warrant of 11 April 2000 (Dem. Rep. Congo v. Belg.), 41 I.L.M. 536 (Feb. 14, 2002).
2. *See, e.g.*, Prosecutor v. Milosevic, Case No. IT-02–54-PT, Order for Commencement of Trial (Feb. 4, 2002).
3. Doug Cassel, Op-Ed., *The World Reaches Out for Justice*, Chi. Trib., Aug. 12, 2001, at C1.
4. Joseph Conrad, Heart of Darkness (Edinburgh and London: W. Blackwood and Sons, 1902).
5. *See, e.g.*, Regina v. Bow Street Metropolitan Stipendiary Magistrate and Others, *ex parte* Pinochet Ugarte (No. 3), [2000] 1 A.C. 147 (H.L.).
6. *See Judge Seeks to Question Kissinger About Abuses*, L.A. Times, Apr. 18, 2002, at A4; Larry Rohter, *As Door Opens for Legal Actions in Chilean Coup, Kissinger Is Numbered Among the Hunted*, N.Y. Times, Mar. 28, 2002, at A13.

7. 520 U.S. 681 (1997).

8. *Id.* at 702.

9. Concerning the Arrest Warrant of 11 April 2000 (Dem. Rep. Congo v. Belg.), 41 I.L.M. 536, 550 (Feb. 14, 2002).

10. 28 U.S.C. § 1350 (2002).

11. 70 F.3d 232 (2d Cir. 1995).

12. Concerning the Arrest Warrant of 11 April 2000, 41 I.L.M. at 551 (emphasis in original).

13. *See generally* Diane F. Orentlicher, *Whose Justice? Reconciling Universal Jurisdiction with Democratic Principles*, 92 Geo. L.J. 1057 (2004); Peter Kornbluh, *Letter from Chile*, Nation, Jan. 31, 2005, at 22.

• 29 •

Should Foreigners Be Permitted to Make Campaign Contributions to U.S. Candidates? Surprisingly, the Answer May Be Yes

December 2003

Early in the 2004 election cycle, the liberal advocacy group MoveOn.org announced that it would no longer accept donations from foreign sources. Previously, a Swedish group, Democracy Aid '04, had urged Europeans to contribute to MoveOn.org as a way to defeat President Bush's reelection bid.[1]

Meanwhile, as soon as the story broke, the *Drudge Report*, the *New York Sun*, and other politically conservative news outlets reported that a group called Canadians for Clark was raising money from Canadians to support the candidacy of Democratic presidential hopeful Wesley Clark,[2] then the frontrunner for the nomination.

Foreigners who have not been admitted to the United States as permanent residents are prohibited by law from donating funds to candidates for U.S. election.[3] Accordingly, the Canadian site reportedly advised visitors to send money to MoveOn.org as a method of circumventing the prohibition. I say "reportedly" because when I visited the Canadian website[4] the day after the story broke, I found only a solicitation of funds from U.S. citizens and a statement that Canadians cannot contribute but should spread the news and hope that Americans "take notice."

But suppose that MoveOn.org, Canadians for Clark, and Democracy Aid '04 had, in fact, been soliciting foreign campaign contributions. So what? Is the law prohibiting foreign donations to American campaigns constitutional? Is it a good idea?

One might think that these are easy questions. Just as we need not permit foreigners to vote in our elections, surely we need not permit them to make campaign contributions to influence the outcomes of our elections, right?

Yet the issue is not so simple. The Supreme Court's 2003 decision in *McConnell v. Federal Election Commission*[5]—upholding most of the McCain-Feingold campaign finance reform law but striking down an obscure provision that barred minors from donating to political campaigns—suggests that the ban on foreign campaign contributions may be invalid. And even if the ban is constitutional, it's at odds with our foreign policy, as I'll explain.

A federal statute prohibits persons who are neither U.S. citizens nor permanent residents (that is, holders of green cards) from contributing any money to candidates for state or federal office, or to American political parties.[6] The provision was originally enacted in the 1970s.[7] In the 1990s, the statute received some public attention when it was alleged that fundraisers for the Democratic Party and its candidates were attempting to circumvent the law by raising money from foreign sources, including the People's Republic of China.[8]

In 2002, the law was amended with the adoption of the Bipartisan Campaign Reform Act—also known as BCRA or McCain-Feingold. [9] The amendment made clear that the foreign money ban applied to state as well as federal elections, a position that the Federal Election Commission had taken under the old wording of the statute.

The 2002 amendment also added a prohibition on the use of foreign funds for "independent expenditures" on campaign speech. As the term suggests, an independent expenditure supports a candidate (typically through advertising) but is not funded by the candidate himself or herself.

BCRA also regulates independent expenditures funded by U.S. citizens, but it falls far short of a ban. Under BCRA, American citizens who spend more than $1,000 for election-related activities within twenty days of an election need only comply with various reporting requirements. They do not face the flat ban on election speech applicable to foreigners.

The ban on campaign donations and election-related activities by foreigners has not been tested in the courts. For example, the plaintiffs in the *McConnell* case did not challenge the ban.

However, the Court's decision in that case—along with prior Supreme Court precedent—casts doubt on the ban's constitutionality.

While the Supreme Court upheld most of BCRA in the *McConnell* case, it invalidated a ban on campaign contributions by minors (that is, persons under the age of eighteen). And it did so through reasoning that would seem to apply to the foreigner ban (a neighboring provision of the same statutory scheme) as well.

The Court's brief discussion of the minor ban in *McConnell* consisted of two steps: First, the Court recited the proposition that "[m]inors enjoy the protection of the First Amendment."[10] Second, the Court found that the government had not offered a sufficiently compelling justification for a flat ban on the exercise of minors' free speech rights in the context of political contributions. Both steps of the Court's reasoning would appear to apply to foreigners as well as minors.

To begin, speech by foreigners effectively enjoys the protection of the First Amendment—thus satisfying the first step of the *McConnell* Court's reasoning.

Because the First Amendment protects "the freedom of speech," rather than the freedom of any particular speaker, the Court has held that there is a constitutionally protected right of the public to receive information, whether from a foreign or domestic source.

For example, in the 1965 case of *Lamont v. Postmaster General*,[11] the Court invalidated a federal statute that forbade the post office from delivering "communist political propaganda" that originated overseas, unless the U.S. recipient specifically indicated a desire to receive such material. Without so much as pausing over the fact that the speaker in the particular case was a foreigner, the Court proceeded directly to a discussion of the "addressee's First Amendment rights."[12]

Swedes who operate Democracy Aid '04 may not themselves have First Amendment rights while operating their website in Sweden. Nevertheless, were the U.S. government to attempt to block that website or, pursuant to the foreign campaign expenditure ban, to block the airing of Swedish-funded anti-Bush television ads during the week before the general election, the government action would infringe the right of the American public to receive information. (Blocking donations by Swedes and other foreigners to third-party organizations would be less problematic under the relevant Supreme Court precedents, which treat expenditures of one's own money as entitled to greater free speech protection than contributions to facilitate the speech of others. I'll put that distinction aside for present purposes, however.)

To say that a law *infringes* free speech is not to say that it unconstitutionally *violates* free speech. To make that further determination we must look to the second step of the *McConnell* Court's reasoning—which would ask here whether there is a sufficiently compelling justification for a flat ban on foreign campaign contributions and independent expenditures.

In *McConnell*, the defenders of the minor ban argued that it prevented adults from making campaign contributions in their children's names as a means of circumventing BCRA's individual-based dollar limits. But the Court found this justification unconvincing, given the absence of any record of such abuses, and the fact that narrower congressional options—such as household-based dollar limits, or a ban on contributions by very young children who could be presumed not to have political views—were available.

It is not entirely clear whether the ban on contributions by foreigners would survive this second step of analysis. On the one hand, the weak justification rejected by the Court for the minor ban is even weaker for the foreign ban: It is harder for Americans to circumvent BCRA's dollar limits by enlisting foreigners as channels for their donations than it is for them to enlist their own children in the same ruse.

But on the other hand, there is an interest that arguably justifies the foreigner ban that does not apply to the minor ban: The commonsense notion that elections should reflect the views of the electorate.

Although minors are not members of the electorate, they are members of our political community and will one day be members of the electorate proper. Foreigners who do not permanently reside in the United States, most people undoubtedly think, have no business trying to affect the outcome of our elections.

Is there thus a compelling government interest—one sufficiently strong to override the presumptive protection of the First Amendment—in preventing foreigners from contributing to American election campaigns? Once again, common sense might suggest that there is, but the issue is not as simple as it appears.

The very fact that the First Amendment provides presumptive protection to Americans' rights to hear foreigners' speech belies the suggestion that the government has a legitimate interest in shielding Americans from "foreign" views. For the ban on foreign speech to be constitutionally justified, something more, such as the appearance or reality of corruption, must be present.

Is that a real worry? Certainly there have been episodes in American history in which foreign powers have attempted to influence our politics. Such influence can legitimately be called corruption—not so much in the sense of a quid pro quo between American elected officials and foreign interests, as in the sense of a corruption of the core democratic ideal.

But even if there is a legitimate or compelling government interest in limiting foreign influences on our politics, it is hardly obvious that an outright ban on campaign contributions and campaign speech is a necessary means of advancing that interest.

Indeed, given the adverse public reaction to reports of foreign influence, a simple requirement that foreigners—like U.S. citizens—be subject to dollar limits in their campaign contributions, and disclosure requirements for their independent expenditures, would probably be more than sufficient to limit foreign influence to tolerable levels.

If treating foreigners on par with U.S. citizens and permanent residents would be sufficient to address the fear of foreign corruption, then the statutory ban could fail the operative test under the First Amendment. After all, the test requires that an infringement on the freedom of speech be "necessary" to the attainment of a compelling interest. And if there were other, narrower ways to address the corruption fear, then a flat ban on contributions by foreigners would be unnecessary and thus unconstitutional.

In any event, even if the ban on foreign campaign contributions and campaign speech would survive judicial scrutiny under the First Amendment, there are two further reasons to think it is problematic as a matter of policy.

First, democratic theory has always had difficulty with drawing lines that define political boundaries. In an era of globalization, decisions taken by federal and state officials in the United States have consequences all over the world. To be sure, as a practical matter, it makes sense to limit the franchise to those with the strongest ties to the relevant political community; the notion of representative government would completely unravel were we to permit everyone in the world to vote in every election in the United States.

But there are few practical obstacles to extending the same free speech rights to foreigners that we extend to Americans. And speech rights have traditionally encompassed the right to make at least some campaign contributions as well.

Indeed, we might think that precisely because foreigners are denied the right to vote in American elections that may profoundly affect them, they should have their freedom of speech rights zealously protected—as free speech is the only means they have of affecting U.S. policy. Without the right to vote, they should at least have the right to speak.

Second, the ban applies a standard of conduct to foreigners attempting to influence American policy that we do not follow when the tables are turned. As the world's preeminent economic and military power, the United States has not shrunk from seeking to influence political affairs in other parts of the world, even to the point of pursuing "regime change" through force of arms.

To be sure, whatever objections might be raised to American unilateral military action, removing a dictator from power does not amount to interfering with another country's democracy. But our foreign policy has hardly been neutral with respect to electoral outcomes either. As recently as 2002, the U.S. government was funneling hundreds of thousands of dollars to groups seeking the early ouster of Venezuela's elected President.[13]

Whether justified or not, U.S. foreign policy is in some considerable tension with a domestic election regime that forbids foreigners from spending their own resources to tell us how they think we ought to govern ourselves. That tension could—and perhaps should—be resolved by moving our foreign policy in a less interventionist direction. But at least so long as the United States and its citizens play an active role in the political affairs of foreign nations, the ban on foreign campaign contributions and electoral speech will appear hypocritical.

POSTSCRIPT

I should add a small qualification to the conclusion that the participation of the United States and its citizens in the affairs of other nations carries a reciprocal obligation that we permit foreigners to participate in American politics. In principle, some activities by the U.S. government or private citizens of the

United States (for example, George Soros) have as their aim the establishment or strengthening of democracy in countries that are in transition from autocracy. So long as they do not have a strong partisan tilt, these activities might be described as facilitating rather than interfering with other nations' democracy. They aim to help citizens of other countries make their own electoral decisions, and accordingly, one might think that they should not trigger a reciprocal duty of the United States to permit foreign countries and their citizens to influence the outcome of our elections.

That is in principle, however. In practice, it will usually be very difficult to distinguish general democracy-boosting activities from support of a particular candidate or party. That is especially true in precisely those countries in which we have the greatest interest in promoting democracy—namely, those countries in transition from autocracy, where one or more parties may have a much clearer ideological commitment to democracy than one or more of its rivals. This point was clearly illustrated by the 2004 presidential election in Ukraine, in which the United States and other Western countries supported the candidacy of the democratic reformer Viktor Yushchenko; in a real sense, his substantive platform was democracy.

NOTES

1. *See* Dana Milbank, *Gore's Hands of Stone*, Wash. Post, Dec. 14, 2003, at A4.

2. *See, e.g.*, *Campaign Cash Race Turns International; MoveOn.org Center of Intrigue; Clark Seeks Canadian Support, Website Shows*, Drudge Rep., Dec. 15, 2003, *at* http://www.drudgereportarchives.com/data/2003/12/15/20031215_223605_mattmo.htm.

3. 2 U.S.C. § 441e (2003)*; see also* 36 U.S.C. 510(c) (2003); 11 C.F.R. § 110.20 (2003).

4. The URL for the website in December 2003 was http://www.canadaforclark.com. However, by the time this book went to press, the website no longer existed.

5. McConnell v. FEC, 540 U.S. 93 (2003).

6. 2 U.S.C. § 441e (2003).

7. Federal Election Campaign Act Amendments of 1976, Pub. L. No. 94–283, § 324, 90 Stat. 475, 493.

8. *See, e.g.*, H.R. Rep. No. 105–829 (1998).

9. Bipartisan Campaign Reform Act of 2002, Pub. L. No. 107–155, § 303; 116 Stat. 81, 96.

10. 540 U.S. at 231.

11. 381 U.S. 301 (1965).

12. *Id.* at 305.

13. *See* Christopher Marquis, *U.S. Bankrolling is Under Scrutiny for Ties to Chavez Ouster*, N.Y. Times, Apr. 25, 2002, at A6.

• 30 •

The Hidden International Influence in the Supreme Court Decision Barring Executions of the Mentally Retarded

June 2002

In *Atkins v. Virginia*,[1] the Supreme Court ruled 6–3 that the Eighth Amendment's prohibition on "cruel and unusual punishments" bars states from executing mentally retarded defendants. The decision overturned the Court's 1989 decision in *Penry v. Lynaugh*.[2] There, the Justices had said that executing the mentally retarded *is* permissible.

Atkins was a rare Supreme Court victory for death penalty opponents, who have fared better recently in taking their case to governors and state legislatures. Accordingly, the decision sparked intense interest, with observers asking the following key question: Why did Justices Sandra Day O'Connor and Anthony Kennedy, both of whom routinely uphold capital sentences, change sides and join Justice Stevens's majority opinion in *Atkins*?

The opinion itself gave a straightforward answer: Between 1989 and 2002, the majority said, a "national consensus" emerged holding that it is wrong to execute the mentally retarded. But is that really the case? Although there is a trend toward prohibition, twenty of the thirty-eight states that have a death penalty still permit execution of the mentally retarded. Thus, one might reasonably think this trend has not yet reached the point of national consensus.

With the "national consensus" rationale somewhat shaky, what factors might explain the decision? The leading suspect, buried in a footnote,[3] is world opinion.

While the existence of a national consensus may be challenged, there does seem to be an international consensus that executing the mentally retarded is improper. And the Justices—who increasingly see themselves as part of an international community of high court jurists—may not have wished to remain too far out of step with their friends overseas.

How should judges decide what punishments are "cruel and unusual?" At the very least, one might think that those punishments that the framers and ratifiers of the Eighth Amendment thought cruel and unusual in 1791 are barred.

In his dissent in *Atkins*, Justice Scalia, writing for himself, Chief Justice Rehnquist, and Justice Thomas, suggested that under the historical approach, one should distinguish between idiots and imbeciles.

An *idiot*, as the term was used in the eighteenth century, was a person who would now be classified as so severely retarded that he would be unable to form the mental state necessary for a criminal conviction. That is, he would never have the mens rea (guilty mind)—typically defined by statute as intent or knowledge. Such a person could not be executed in the eighteenth century or now, simply because he could not even be convicted of a crime.

Furthermore, even if an idiot managed to form the requisite intention, he would escape capital punishment under the precursor to the modern insanity defense. By virtue of his mental defect, the idiot could not tell right from wrong.

By contrast, the term *imbecile* was applied to persons of diminished intellectual capacity who nonetheless could be held criminally responsible for their conduct. Their intent might fulfill the statutory requirement of mens rea, even if in other respects they might be woefully lacking. And it could not be assumed that an imbecile would have no ability to distinguish right from wrong.

In modern nomenclature, an imbecile would be classified as mildly or moderately retarded. In the eighteenth century, imbeciles but not idiots could be executed for capital offenses.

Justice Scalia and the other two *Atkins* dissenters also contested the majority's application of modern tests. Nevertheless, for the dissenters, the eighteenth-century understanding of the Eighth Amendment—and the ancient idiot/imbecile distinction—pretty much settled the case. Atkins claimed to be an imbecile rather than an idiot; therefore, the dissenters said, he should have lost.

For the majority of the Court however, the Eighth Amendment's meaning could not be frozen in 1791. The Bill of Rights, after all, bars "cruel and unusual punishments." It does not list specific practices that were thought cruel in 1791.

It is possible that the thumbscrew, the rack, or physical mutilation such as ear-cropping would not have been considered cruel by our forebears. Fortunately, though, the language of the Eighth Amendment invites us to decide for ourselves whether we think each of these practices is cruel—and that was what the six majority Justices in *Atkins* did.

The Court's precedents interpreting "cruel and unusual punishments" bar those punishments inconsistent with "the evolving standards of decency that mark the progress of a maturing society."[4] Under this approach, some punishments—such as burning at the stake—are categorically prohibited. Meanwhile, others—such as inflicting the death penalty on a shoplifter—are barred as disproportionate to the offense.[5]

Atkins was a case about proportionality. Conceding the legitimacy of incarcerating a mentally retarded murderer, it posed the question whether in light of his disability, execution is a disproportionate punishment.

The inquiry into society's evolving standards can be quite subjective. For that reason, the Court has sought to circumscribe its moral discretion by looking first to objective indicia of society's standards. The leading indicator is legislative action.

In his majority opinion in *Atkins*, Justice Stevens cited the one-sided trend in Congress and the state legislatures. In 1989, only two death-penalty states and the federal government barred execution of the mentally retarded.[6] By the time the Supreme Court decided *Atkins*, the federal government and eighteen states did.[7] Bills proposing bans were on the agenda in other states as well.[8]

The dissenters objected that the majority's detection of a national trend was premature. More than half of the death-penalty states, they pointed out, still permitted execution of the mentally retarded.

Who had the better of the numbers game? That depends on how you count. If one adds the states that have no death penalty at all to the states that exclude the mentally retarded from the death penalty, the result is 30–20 against the execution of the mentally retarded.

Moreover, only five states—Alabama, Louisiana, South Carolina, Texas, and Virginia—had actually carried out executions of the mentally retarded since the Court's 1989 decision in *Penry*. That calculus brings the score to 45–5.

Again, though, the numbers can be reckoned differently: For example, the five states that have executed the mentally retarded have a very substantial population.

In addition to counting legislatures, the majority rested its finding of a national consensus on public opinion polls and the opinions of a diverse set of religions.

The dissenters in turn challenged the poll results and, in a remarkable footnote by Justice Scalia, dismissed the views of religious leaders. Justice Scalia, himself a practicing Catholic, had this to say about a brief filed on behalf of the Catholic Bishops of the United States: "The attitudes of that body regarding crime and punishment are so far from being representative, even of the views of Catholics, that they are currently the object of intense national (and entirely ecumenical) criticism."[9]

Putting aside Justice Scalia's astonishing comment, let us turn to the heart of the matter, the question that is on observers' minds: Why did Justices O'Connor and Kennedy vote with the *Atkins* majority, and not with Scalia and the other dissenters?

Interestingly, they may be seen—consciously or unconsciously—as following a pattern set by prior moderate Republican Justices Lewis Powell and Harry Blackmun.

As a Justice, Powell carried out the death penalty, just as O'Connor and Kennedy have. But shortly after he retired, he announced that his experience with capital punishment convinced him that it should be abolished.[10]

Justice Blackmun had a similar change of heart. Though he often voted to overturn individual death sentences, he believed that capital punishment was not per se unconstitutional and, like Powell, O'Connor, and Kennedy, he did carry it out, at least in some cases. But in his last year on the Court, Blackmun abandoned that view—stating memorably that he would "no longer tinker with the machinery of death."[11]

Justice Blackmun's procedural objections to the death penalty, raised over the years, finally overwhelmed his belief in its abstract moral justifiability. The death penalty may have been acceptable in principle, he suggested, but the machinery used to carry out the penalty was hopelessly, irremediably flawed.

Although *Atkins* leaves the system of capital punishment intact for defendants who are not mentally retarded, it is tempting to see the journey of Justices O'Connor and Kennedy as falling within the same general pattern set by Powell and Blackmun before them: A growing dissatisfaction with carrying out the death penalty builds toward an abolitionist view based on qualms about its practical application.

More broadly, *Atkins* could be taken as evidence of what right-of-center Court watchers have dubbed the Greenhouse Effect: Conservative jurists appointed by Republican Presidents come to Washington and, the pundits charge, in an effort to impress such liberal establishment figures as *New York Times* Court reporter Linda Greenhouse, lose the courage of their convictions.

The charge may seem particularly apt in the case of O'Connor and Kennedy. While generally voting with the conservatives on issues of states' rights and affirmative action, they have disappointed the right on abortion, gay rights, and now the death penalty.

I doubt, however, that the Greenhouse Effect was at work in *Atkins*. Indeed, shortly after the ruling, Greenhouse herself observed in the *New York Times* that "it is just as likely that the decision was a singular response to a particularly unattractive feature of the death penalty in the United States" as it was a portent of future anti-death penalty decisions.[12] And although the Court again surprised analysts by its anti-death penalty ruling in another 2002 case, *Ring v. Arizona*,[13] *Ring* turned on quite different legal issues. How else to explain the fact that Justices Scalia and Thomas joined the anti-death penalty majority in *Ring*, while Justice O'Connor dissented?

But if the Greenhouse Effect was not at work in *Atkins*, what was? I would call it the Strasbourg Effect—the increasing international influence on the Justices' thinking.

Strasbourg, France, is the home of the European Court of Human Rights, or ECHR. The ECHR is the Council of Europe's principal organ for interpreting the European Convention for the Protection of Human Rights and Personal Freedoms.

In recent years, U.S. Supreme Court Justices have attended numerous international conferences with their counterparts from the ECHR, the European Court of Justice (the judicial body of the European Union), and members of constitutional courts from other nations. Notably, Justices O'Connor and Kennedy are among the most enthusiastic participants in such conferences, and for many years Justice Kennedy has taught a summer course comparing American and European approaches to human rights in Salzburg, Austria.

What happens at the international conferences? Increasingly, judges from Europe and the rest of the world have criticized the American justice system for, among other things, its reliance on the death penalty—with the execution of the mentally retarded coming in for special criticism.[14] Perhaps Justices O'Connor and Kennedy reconsidered their prior decision upholding the execution of the mentally retarded in light of the passionate view of their European colleagues.

Granted, the *Atkins* majority certainly did not rule as it did so that the Justices could avoid future awkward moments at their international cocktail parties. Yet it is not difficult to imagine that world opinion weighed on their minds.[15]

To be sure, Justice Scalia and his fellow dissenters scoffed at the idea that global practice might have some relevance to the case. The "notions of justice" of the world community, they said, "are (thankfully) not always those of our people."[16]

But unlike the dissenters, the six-Justice majority in *Atkins* was unwilling to exacerbate the worldview of the United States as a rogue nation. Indeed, a footnote in Justice Stevens's majority opinion approvingly cited a European Union friend-of-the-court brief describing overwhelming rejection by the world community of the execution of the mentally retarded.[17]

Meanwhile, in another friend-of-the-court brief, a group of former high-ranking U.S. diplomats had urged the Justices to bar execution of the mentally retarded. They argued that America's deviance from the global consensus was causing substantial friction with our allies, especially in Europe. The diplomats urged the Court to, in the words of the Declaration of Independence, show "a decent respect to the opinions of mankind."[18]

This brief—unlike the EU's brief—was not mentioned in the Court's opinion. And rightly so: It would be highly inappropriate for Justices of the Supreme Court to decide a case by trying to guess what result would advance the country's diplomatic interests.

Nevertheless, where the law invites an inquiry into "the evolving standards of decency that mark the progress of a maturing society," the Strasbourg Effect may be not only inevitable but desirable. Americans could profit from a trans-Atlantic dialogue on capital punishment. If Justices O'Connor and Kennedy did listen carefully to the opinions of their European colleagues and used them to inform their own death penalty views—not out of a naked desire to curry favor with Europe, but because they wanted to gauge the world's evolving standards of decency—they should be commended.

POSTSCRIPT

As the next chapter discusses in greater detail, not everybody thinks that it is commendable for our Supreme Court to pay attention to the opinion of the world community.

NOTES

1. 536 U.S. 304 (2002).
2. 492 U.S. 302 (1989).
3. 536 U.S. at 316 n.21 ("Moreover, within the world community, the imposition of the death penalty for crimes committed by mentally retarded offenders is overwhelmingly disapproved.").
4. *Id.* at 311–12 (quoting Trop v. Dulles, 356 U.S. 86, 101 (1958) (plurality opinion)).
5. *See* Weems v. United States, 217 U.S. 349, 367 (1910) (holding that a penalty of twelve years' imprisonment and hard labor for the falsification of public records violates the "precept of justice that punishment for crime should be graduated and proportioned to offense.").
6. Georgia and Maryland were the two states that had barred the death penalty for mentally retarded offenders at the time *Penry* was decided. Ga. Code Ann. § 17–7-131(j); Md. Code. Ann., Art. 27, § 412(f)(1). In 1988 Congress exempted mentally retarded offenders from the imposition of the death penalty under the Anti-Drug Abuse Act of 1988, Pub. L. No. 100–690, § 7001(l), 102 Stat. 4181, 4390 (codified at 21 U.S.C. § 848(l)).
7. In addition to Georgia and Maryland, *supra* note 6, the *Atkins* court listed the following sixteen states: Arizona, Ariz. Rev. Stat. Ann. § 13-703.02; Arkansas, Ark. Code. Ann. § 5-4-618; Colorado, Colo. Rev. Stat. § 16-9-401; Connecticut, Conn. Gen. Stat. § 53a-46a; Florida, Fla. Stat. Ann. § 921.137; Indiana, Ind. Code §§ 35-36-9-2 through 35-36-9-6; Kansas, Kan. Stat. Ann. § 21-4623; Kentucky, Ky. Rev. Stat. Ann. §§ 532.10, 532.135, 532.140; Missouri, Mo. Rev. Stat. § 565.030; Nebraska, Neb. Rev. Stat.

§ 28-105.01; New Mexico, N.M. Stat. Ann. § 31-20A-2.1; New York, N.Y. Crim. Proc. Law § 400.27; North Carolina, 2001-346 N.C. Sess. Laws p. 45; South Dakota, S.D. Codified Laws § 23A-27A-26.1; Tennessee, Tenn. Code. Ann. § 39-13-203; and Washington, Wash. Rev. Code § 10.95.030.

8. *E.g.*, Virginia, S.B. 497, 2002 Leg., 2002 Sess. (Va. 2002); H.B. 957, 2002 Leg., 2002 Sess. (Va. 2002); Nevada, A.B. 353, 2002 Leg., 71st Reg. Sess. (Nev. 2001). The Texas Legislature presented legislation to Governor Rick Perry, which he vetoed for procedural reasons on June 17, 2001. H.B. 236, 77th Leg., Reg. Sess. (Tex. 2001); S.B. 686, 77th Leg., Reg. Sess. (Tex. 2001).

9. *Atkins*, 536 U.S. at 347 n.6 (Scalia, J., dissenting).

10. *Compare* McCleskey v. Kemp, 481 U.S. 279, 282–320 (1987), *with* John C. Jeffries Jr., Justice Lewis F. Powell Jr. 450–53 (New York: C. Scribner's Sons, 1994).

11. Callins v. Collins, 510 U.S. 1141, 1145 (1994) (Blackmun, J., dissenting from the denial of certiorari). *Compare id. with* Gregg v. Georgia, 428 U.S. 153, 226 (1976) (Blackmun, J., concurring in the judgment).

12. Linda Greenhouse, *Hedging Bets*, N.Y. Times, June 22, 2002, at A7.

13. 536 U.S. 584 (2002).

14. For an account of the general phenomenon of "constitutional cross-fertilization" by written opinions and face-to-face meetings among the judges on the national constitutional courts of the democratic world, see Anne-Marie Slaughter, *A Global Community of Courts*, 44 Harv. Int'l L.J. 191, 194–204, 215–17 (2003).

15. In a speech to the American Society of International Law shortly before the *Atkins* case was decided, Justice O'Connor said:

> I ask myself, why does information about international law matter so much? Why should judges and lawyers who are concerned about the intricacies of ERISA, the Americans with Disabilities Act, and the Bankruptcy Code care about issues of foreign law and international law? The reason, of course, is globalization. No institution of government can afford now to ignore the rest of the world.

Sandra Day O'Connor, Keynote Address Before the Ninety-Sixth Annual Meeting of the American Society of International Law (Mar. 16, 2002), *in* 96 Am. Soc'y Int'l L. Proc. 348, 349 (2002).

16. Atkins v. Virginia, 536 U.S. 304, 347–48 (2002) (Scalia, J., dissenting).

17. *Id.* at 316 n.21 (citing Brief of Amicus Curiae the European Union in Support of the Petitioner at 4, McCarver v. North Carolina, 531 U.S. 1205 (2001) (No. 00–8727), 2001 WL 648609).

18. The Declaration of Independence para. 1 (U.S. 1776); Brief of Amici Curiae Diplomats Morton Abramowitz, Stephen W. Bosworth, Stuart E. Eizenstat, John C. Kornblum, Phyllis E. Oakley, Thomas R. Pickering, Felix G. Rohatyn, J. Stapleton Roy, and Frank G. Winser in Support of Petitioner at 6, 15, *McCarver*, 531 U.S. 1205 (No. 00–8727), 2001 WL 648607.

• 31 •

The Use of Foreign Law in American Constitutional Interpretation: A Revealing Colloquy between Justices Scalia and Breyer

January 2005

What bearing, if any, does foreign law have on the proper interpretation of the American Constitution? Speaking in January 2005 at the American University Washington College of Law,[1] Justice Antonin Scalia gave a blunt answer: none. Writers of a new constitution would be wise to pay attention to the experience of other nations, Scalia readily acknowledged, but judges interpreting our existing Constitution should pay no heed to how other countries interpret their own constitutions.

Justice Stephen Breyer disagreed. Breyer conceded, of course, that the decisions of foreign courts are not binding on American courts in the way that precedents of the U.S. Supreme Court are. Yet he nevertheless insisted that foreign judges frequently face legal problems quite similar to those that confront courts in the United States, and that the solutions the former have fashioned may be informative for American judges who are uncertain about how to resolve difficult issues.

Those contrasting positions might appear neatly to track the political affiliations of the Justices: Scalia, the conservative appointee of a Republican President, favors U.S. unilateralism, while Breyer, the centrist-to-liberal appointee of a Democratic President, favors a more global approach.

Yet the Scalia–Breyer colloquy revealed that such an ideological mapping is too neat. The real differences between Scalia and Breyer have more to do with their general views about jurisprudence: Scalia rooted his opposition to foreign law in his belief that the Constitution should be construed in accordance with the original understanding of those who framed and ratified it. In contrast, Breyer took a more pragmatic, forward-looking approach.

Perhaps most intriguing, however, was the question left unanswered by the two Justices. Both acknowledged that in an era of globalization, foreign law is increasingly relevant to numerous disputes involving the interpretation of treaties, statutes, and other sub-constitutional law. The unanswered question is how that phenomenon will ultimately affect American constitutional interpretation.

What prompted the Scalia–Breyer colloquy on foreign law? In the last several years, two controversial Supreme Court decisions involving politically charged issues made use of foreign law.

As I discussed in chapter 30, in the 2002 case of *Atkins v. Virginia*[2] the Court ruled that the Eighth Amendment's prohibition of "cruel and unusual punishments" forbids the execution of mentally retarded individuals. Under the Court's precedents, the determination whether a punishment is cruel and unusual turns on its consistency with "the evolving standards of decency that mark the progress of a maturing society."[3] In concluding that execution of the mentally retarded was out of bounds, the Court took account of practice in American states, but also invoked a brief filed by the European Union[4] which catalogued the overwhelming repudiation of the practice by the rest of the world.

Then, in the 2003 case of *Lawrence v. Texas*,[5] the Supreme Court invalidated a state law criminalizing "homosexual sodomy." As in the *Atkins* case, so too in *Lawrence*, the Court's opinion focused primarily on arguments rooted in U.S. sources. However, Justice Kennedy's majority opinion also cited a 1967 Act of the English Parliament and a 1981 ruling of the European Court of Human Rights invalidating criminal prohibitions on sodomy.[6] These developments, Justice Kennedy said, showed that, contrary to claims of supporters of the Texas law, criminal prohibition of homosexual sodomy was *not* universally accepted within Western civilization.

The Court's liberal decisions in *Atkins* and *Lawrence* unsurprisingly drew criticism from conservative pundits and politicians. Interestingly, these conservatives were not content to express disagreement with the substantive results in the two cases. In addition, they attacked the use of foreign law.

Thus, in 2004, a bill called the Constitution Restoration Act was introduced in both houses of Congress.[7] In the provision most relevant for our purposes,[8] the bill would forbid federal courts from relying upon foreign law in interpreting the U.S. Constitution. (The bill also attempts to strip federal courts of the authority to hear challenges to government action that acknowledges "God as the sovereign source of law, liberty, or government."[9])

In directing federal courts how to interpret the Constitution, the proposed Constitution Restoration Act would almost certainly violate the constitutional principle of separation of powers; Congress can no more tell federal judges what sources they may properly consult to do their job than can the courts tell Congress what witnesses to call when it holds hearings.

Accordingly, even in the unlikely event that Congress were to enact the Constitution Restoration Act, it would not be enforceable; the first court to review it would likely strike it down. Nevertheless, the mere fact that the bill was introduced illustrates the passions that the Justices' foreign law citations in *Atkins* and *Lawrence* have stirred.

In neither the *Atkins* case nor the *Lawrence* case did the Supreme Court suggest that decisions of foreign courts in any way *controlled* the outcome of American constitutional litigation. Nor did Justice Breyer indicate that he would simply *defer to* the views of foreign jurists.

Instead, in his discussion with Justice Scalia, Justice Breyer suggested that foreign opinions can be helpful in at least two ways. First, they can be the source of good ideas in much the same way that a well-crafted legal brief or scholarly article can be.

Second, the experience of a foreign nation can provide object lessons. Justice Breyer gave the example of the school vouchers question. In preparing to decide whether the First Amendment's Establishment Clause bars the use of state-funded vouchers at parochial schools, Justice Breyer said that he found it useful to study how European countries funded religious schools without sectarian strife resulting.

Given the limited and seemingly innocuous use of foreign law advocated by Justice Breyer and others, why do conservatives, including Justice Scalia, still find it objectionable?

In his colloquy with Justice Breyer, Justice Scalia made clear that he is not categorically opposed to looking to foreign law. If he were interpreting a treaty with a foreign sovereign, for example, Justice Scalia said that he would find the meaning given to the treaty by other signatories to be highly relevant.

Yet the U.S. Constitution, Scalia said, is different. How so?

Justice Scalia offered a number of objections to the use of foreign law in interpreting the U.S. Constitution, but the core of his argument derived from his professed approach to constitutional interpretation, originalism—the idea that the meaning of the Constitution was fixed when it was adopted.

It is easy to see why an originalist would eschew foreign law in interpreting the Constitution. Contemporary decisions by a European or other foreign court obviously have no bearing on what Americans thought the U.S. Constitution meant in 1789, when it was ratified. For Justice Scalia, the only foreign law relevant to that question is the pre-1789 law of England, because the framers of the American Constitution, as former English colonists, frequently used terms of art taken from the English law with which they were familiar.

Thus, for Justice Scalia, the main problem with citing modern foreign law to interpret the U.S. Constitution is not so much that the law is foreign, but that it is modern. He would (and does) object equally to citations of modern American legal trends to inform constitutional interpretation.

Fair enough, but what if one is not an originalist? What if one is persuaded by the sorts of arguments I offered against originalism in chapter 15? Or what if one is only a partial originalist? Although he did not admit it during his discussion with Justice Breyer, in many areas of constitutional interpretation, even Justice Scalia makes no effort to square his views with the original understanding.

For example, Justice Scalia has written important First Amendment opinions—such as the 1992 decision in *R.A.V. v. City of St. Paul,*[10] which invalidated a hate-speech ordinance—that appear to expand free speech protection well beyond what the framers envisioned. (Perhaps an argument could be fashioned that James Madison and his contemporaries held the view reflected in *R.A.V.*, but Justice Scalia's opinion in that case made no effort to present such an argument.)

If Justice Scalia himself is not consistently an originalist, might there be a role for foreign law in those cases in which he and other Justices employ a more modernist approach? In his January 2005 discussion, Justice Scalia said no to this question too.

Even if a judge believes in a dynamic as opposed to a static Constitution, Justice Scalia said, the judge should still be wary of foreign law. For if the meaning of the Constitution evolves, the place to look for that evolution is in the values and opinions of the American people.

Looking to foreign law, Justice Scalia argued, is simply a mask for the judge's imposing his or her own values in those instances in which American public opinion is at odds with those values—as it is, Justice Scalia claimed, on matters like the death penalty and gay rights at issue in the *Atkins* and *Lawrence* cases.

Justice Scalia pointedly noted that liberal Justices do not typically cite foreign law when, as with abortion and the rights of criminal suspects, foreign practices are more conservative than U.S. constitutional law.

Is that right? Is foreign law simply a way that judges disguise the imposition of their own values?

Justice Breyer thought not. To begin, he said that a responsible judge will cite foreign law whether it agrees or disagrees with his or her own position. More broadly, Breyer said, any interpretive method can be used dishonestly by a judge so inclined: Judges can be self-serving in the domestic authorities they cite—including their citations of the original understanding of the framers and ratifiers of the Constitution.

The Justices' attitudes towards the relevance of foreign law for constitutional interpretation are thus rooted in their respective jurisprudential philosophies. Professing originalism, Scalia wants to look at an old and narrow set of materials to discern the original meaning of the Constitution's text. Believing that the original understanding frequently cannot resolve modern, often unanticipated problems, Breyer wants as much help, and from as many sources, as he can find.

Despite that important difference, Justice Breyer observed that in numerous cases involving issues other than constitutional interpretation, foreign law is directly relevant. Contracts between parties based in different countries frequently call for the application of foreign law; treaties govern interactions between sovereigns and their citizens; and the efforts of many countries to regulate cross-border transactions of multinational corporations frequently require national courts to harmonize different laws.

Justice Scalia heartily agreed that foreign law is relevant, indeed indispensable, to resolving questions arising out of such circumstances. Accordingly, whatever the motives of those in Congress who object to Supreme Court invocations of foreign law in constitutional interpretation, it is clear that Justice Scalia, for his part, is not motivated by xenophobia or resistance to globalization.

Yet, given globalization, foreign law would appear destined to influence U.S. constitutional law. After all, throughout human history, military, commercial, and other contact with foreign peoples has invariably led to intellectual change.

Alexander the Great's expedition to India put Greek philosophers in touch with the ascetic traditions of the subcontinent; the Crusades led Christian Europeans to reencounter the lost Greek tradition, which had been preserved in the Arab world; European conquest of the New World exposed the settlers to the constitutional arrangements of the Iroquois Confederacy. In each such encounter, new patterns of thinking emerged from the cross-fertilization of cultures and ideas.

There is no reason to think that ideas about how to interpret the U.S. Constitution are immune to such forces. Concepts developed in one area of law—such as statutory interpretation or contract interpretation—frequently and logically migrate to other areas of law—such as constitutional interpretation. Thus, as foreign law plays an increasingly important role in matters outside constitutional interpretation, its substantial influence will inevitably be felt within constitutional interpretation.

Against this backdrop, it hardly seems to matter whether a Supreme Court opinion occasionally cites foreign law as non-binding authority. The real action is elsewhere. Given Justice Scalia's openness to the globalization of American law outside the context of constitutional interpretation, his resistance to the citation of foreign law in constitutional cases is ultimately likely to prove futile.

POSTSCRIPT

As I discussed in the introduction, in the March 2005 case of *Roper v. Simmons*,[11] the Supreme Court ruled 5–4 that the execution of persons for crimes they committed when they were under the age of eighteen constitutes cruel and unusual punishment. The majority opinion of Justice Kennedy stated that domestic American developments provided sufficient evidence for the conclusion that the relevant standards of decency had evolved to the point of barring the juvenile death penalty. But he buttressed that observation with evidence showing that the United States was, prior to the ruling, essentially unique in condoning the execution of juveniles.[12] A torrent of criticism ensued.[13]

The argument against this sort of invocation of foreign and international sources is plain enough: In a democracy, on starkly normative matters like the conditions, if any, that justify capital punishment, the relevant source of norms should be the values of the members of the polity in question—here, the United States—rather than the values of people elsewhere.

There is a difficulty with this argument, to be sure: Few questions are purely normative; nearly every question of value is in some way intertwined with empirical questions. That's even true with respect to the juvenile death penalty. Whether the appropriate minimum age is sixteen or eighteen may well turn on what we know about human development, and thus in *Roper* itself, the defendant and others who submitted amicus briefs on his behalf focused attention on evidence about the maturation process.[14] The extent to which adolescents are generally capable of exercising the same degree of impulse control as adults, and at what age, is largely an empirical rather than a normative question.

Nonetheless, it seems clear that the foreign materials cited by the Court in *Roper* were not thought relevant because of what they told us about the empirical question of whether teenagers have a fully developed conscience but because of what they told us about the norms of the world community. And while the majority was probably right to see those norms as relevant to a legal test that by its terms inquires into the "evolving standards of decency that mark the progress of a maturing society," the critics are also right that such norms are not going to be directly relevant to most questions of U.S. constitutional law.

But there is another kind of use of foreign materials that should be, though apparently is not, wholly uncontroversial—namely, the willingness to look at the experience in other countries to shed light on our own laws. That is what Justice Breyer was doing when he looked at European experience for insight into how school vouchers might work in the United States. More generally, as the next two chapters illustrate, such cross-national comparisons must be made with sensitivity to differences, but if undertaken in a spirit of humility, they can be quite illuminating.

NOTES

1. Discussion Between U.S. Supreme Court Justices Antonin Scalia and Stephen Breyer (Jan. 13, 2005), *at* http://www.wcl.american.edu/secle/founders/2005/050113.cfm.

2. 536 U.S. 304 (2002).

3. *Id.* at 311–12 (quoting Trop v. Dulles, 356 U.S. 86, 101 (1958) (plurality opinion)).

4. 536 U.S. at 316 n.21 (citing Brief of Amicus Curiae the European Union in Support of the Petitioner at 4, McCarver v. North Carolina, 531 U.S. 1205 (2001) (No. 00–8727), 2001 WL 648609).

5. 539 U.S. 558 (2003) (striking down Tex. Penal Code Ann. § 21.06(a) (2003)).

6. *Id.* at 572–73 (citing Sexual Offences Act, 1967, ch. 60, § 1 (Eng.)); *id.* (citing Dudgeon v. United Kingdom, 45 Eur. Ct. H.R. 52 (1981)).

7. Constitution Restoration Act of 2004, S. 2323, 108th Cong.; Constitution Restoration Act of 2004, S. 2082, 108th Cong.; Constitution Restoration Act of 2004, H.R. 3799, 108th Cong.

8. S. 2323 § 201; S. 2082 § 201; H.R. 3799 § 201.

9. S. 2323 § 101; S. 2082 § 101; H.R. 3799 § 101.

10. 505 U.S. 377 (1992).

11. 125 S. Ct. 1183 (2005).

12. *Id.* at 1198–1200.

13. *See, e.g.*, Editorial, *The Blue State Court*, Wall St. J., Mar. 2, 2005, at A16; Douglas W. Kmiec, Op-Ed., *Whose Constitution Is It Anyway?; The Execution of Minors Shouldn't Ride on the Justices' Personal Whims*, L.A. Times, Mar. 6, 2005, at M5; Jeffrey Rosen, *Juvenile Logic*, New Republic, Mar. 21, 2005, at 11.

14. *See, e.g.*, Brief for Respondent at 15–24, Roper v. Simmons, 125 S. Ct. 1183 (2005) (No. 03–633), 2004 WL 1947812; Brief of the Am. Med. Ass'n, Am. Psychiatric Ass'n, Am. Soc'y for Adolescent Psychiatry, Am. Acad. of Child & Adolescent Psychiatry, Am. Acad. of Psychiatry and the Law, Nat'l Ass'n of Soc. Workers, Mo. Chapter of the Nat'l Ass'n of Soc. Workers, and Nat'l Mental Health Ass'n as Amici Curiae in Support of Respondent, *Roper*, 125 S. Ct. 1183 (No. 03–633), 2004 WL 1633549.

• 32 •

Can Ethnic Hatred Be Eliminated by Eliminating Ethnicity? The Rwanda Experiment

April 2004

In the early to mid-1990s, the central African country of Rwanda was the scene of some of the worst ethnic violence of the twentieth century. Incited by official propaganda depicting Tutsi Rwandans as "cockroaches," radical Hutu Rwandans massacred nearly a million Tutsi and moderate Hutu.[1]

As Rwanda marks the tenth anniversary of its national catastrophe, its current government has embarked on an ambitious program to strike at the roots of ethnic hatred and violence. However, rather than campaigning for a multicultural society of mutual respect between Hutu and Tutsi, the government has gone a giant step further. It aims to eliminate distinctions between the groups entirely. As reported in the *New York Times* in April 2004, the new official policy states: "There is no ethnicity here. We are all Rwandan."[2]

To an American constitutional lawyer, that credo resonates with a famous remark by Justice John Marshall Harlan. Dissenting from the Supreme Court's infamous 1896 ruling in *Plessy v. Ferguson*, which upheld state-mandated "separate but equal" passenger railroad facilities for blacks and whites, Harlan wrote: "There is no caste here. Our constitution is color-blind, and neither knows nor tolerates classes among citizens."[3]

In recent decades, Harlan's *Plessy* dissent has served as the rallying cry for opponents of race-based affirmative action, who argue that taking account of racial differences in an effort to overcome past episodes of racial injustice is inevitably self-defeating. As Justice Scalia opined in a concurring statement in the 1995 decision in *Adarand Constructors Inc. v. Pena*, "In the eyes of government, we are just one race here. It is American."[4]

The differences among the United States, Rwanda, and other countries are, of course, substantial, so that lessons learned in one context will not neatly translate into the other. Nonetheless, thinking through the potential benefits and risks of the Rwandan effort to eliminate ethnicity may shed light on the problems confronted by other multi-ethnic societies, including our own.

The effort to eliminate ethnicity is not the whole of the Rwandan response to the genocide of 1994. Traditional community or "GACACA" courts have also been meting out justice in parallel with the United Nations International Criminal Tribunal for Rwanda. But whereas genocide trials aim to bring specific perpetrators to justice or to promote reconciliation on the individual level, the policy of ethnicity elimination is broader based and forward-looking.

Two key features of Rwanda's effort to stamp out ethnicity would be highly problematic in stable democracies: First, Rwanda is creating reeducation camps where people are trained in the "correct" way to think of their fellow citizens; second, Rwanda will prosecute those guilty of a vague crime called "divisionism."

"Divisionism" has, as its core application, the fomenting of ethnic violence. But critics charge that it can also be used as a means by which the party in power stamps out even legitimate opposition.

These means, then, are more extreme than one would expect in a democracy. Yet they are different only in degree, rather than in kind, from measures that have been taken in other parts of the world.

Although "reeducation camps" suggest images of grim conditions and totalitarian thought police, the notion of reeducation itself is perfectly appropriate in the aftermath of a horrific regime. Allied forces in Germany following World War II sought to "deNazify" the country through education, and even today, in Iraq, "deBaathification" is part of the post-war program of the U.S.-led forces and the new government.

Likewise, although the constitutional protection for freedom of speech in the United States protects even the teaching of the inferiority of some groups of persons, most constitutional democracies rule certain forms of political expression out of bounds.

Again, the German example is instructive. Article 21 of the German Constitution permits the banning of political parties that undermine "the free democratic basic order" in Germany.[5] That would include, of course, the Nazi party, as well as other groups that hold similar beliefs.

The differences between understandings of political freedom in the United States and Germany are, not surprisingly, shaped by historical context. The same is true for Rwanda.

Moreover, there is at least one reason to think that the Rwandan effort to eradicate ethnicity stands a greater chance of success than would a parallel effort with respect to race in the United States: The categories of Hutu and Tutsi are highly artificial.

Stereotypically, Tutsi are taller than Hutu, with facial features more like Ethiopians and Europeans than like those of most sub-Saharan Africans.[6] Yet these stereotypes are largely false, because intermarriage among Tutsi and Hutu has been very prevalent over the years, and the two groups were never really ethnically distinct in the first place.[7] During the 1994 genocide, Hutu extremists were able to identify Tutsi for slaughter because they knew them personally, not because they could recognize them reliably based on supposed ethnic differences.

The origin of the distinction between Tutsi and Hutu can be traced largely to the colonial period.[8] In pre-colonial times, Tutsi and Hutu were essentially class distinctions that could be changed by acquiring or losing wealth. However, Belgian rulers treated the distinction as something deeper. The Belgians thus created ethnic division among people with the same language, customs, and ancestry. If ethnic division can thus be created by government policy, perhaps it can be destroyed the same way.

Official efforts to make race disappear would face more substantial obstacles in the United States, where the cleavages among communities have often tracked differences in appearance, speech, and manner. To be sure, as a matter of science, there is no such thing as "race" that corresponds to the social distinctions one observes in the United States. There is as much genetic variation *among* persons of African descent as there is *between* persons of African and European descent[9]—meaning that this racial division is ultimately an artificial, not a natural, construct.

But the salience of race in the United States has always been cultural and social rather than scientific, even if it was sometimes falsely wrapped in the mantle of science. And given visible (if biologically unimportant) distinctions between the cultural and social groups we call races, it would take a powerful program of education indeed to make people truly blind to racial markers.

Of course, many people would object to a project of eradicating ethnic differences wholly apart from the project's likelihood of success. They would ask: Don't people have a right to identify with others of their own group?

Different societies reach different conclusions with respect to this question. France has long been willing to admit ethnically distinct immigrants and others into the political and social community on the condition that they assimilate.[10] The recent decision to prohibit French Muslim students from wearing the *hijab* (or head scarf) to public school is only the latest example of an attitude that is inclusive in its own way: Anybody, regardless of birth, can be French, so long as he or she is willing to take on French ways.

For much of the twentieth century, the French approach to assimilation stood in formal opposition to the American metaphor of the "melting pot." The American ideal was that different peoples would come to the United States, bringing with them their distinctive traditions, all of which would be thrown into the melting pot of mass culture, and out of which would emerge something new and distinct, yet nonetheless American.

But to critics of assimilation, the distinction between the French and American models was merely a formal one: In either country, critics pointed out, members of minority populations were required to give up their own culture to a much greater degree than they were able to change the mass culture.

In practice, critics charged, the price of acceptance in America was assimilation, just as it was in France. Thus, at some point, some American multiculturalists came to advocate a "salad bowl"—in which each ingredient retains its separate, distinctive flavor—instead of a melting pot. The movement for bilingual education of children whose parents' first tongue was not English was part of the shift from melting pot to salad bowl.

Bilingualism and multiculturalism themselves became embroiled in the culture wars and inspired a backlash by counter-critics who charged that the failure to assimilate held back ethnically distinct children. Accordingly, in the United States today, one again hears arguments for the melting pot, or even something closer to the French approach.

My aim here is not to take sides in the debate about multiculturalism, but simply to point out that the critique of assimilation depends upon the assumption that there is some value in preserving distinct ethnicities.

Ordinarily, that is a reasonable assumption because ethnicity is typically tied to religion, language, and culture. Most of us agree that it is unfair, or at least very burdensome, to ask someone to forego much of his or her identity as a condition of admission to the political and social community on equal terms.

But what makes the Rwandan case so peculiar is the fact that the distinction between Tutsi and Hutu does not track these other valuable distinctions among people. Tutsi and Hutu worship in the same way, speak the same language, and share a common culture. Their difference is difference *for its own sake.*

And that fact is what makes the Rwandan genocide so frightening, even compared with other horrific ethnic genocides. Students of genocide understand how a population can be whipped up to murder people whom, until literally days earlier, they regarded as neighbors and even relatives by marriage.

But usually some real distinction between the two populations—Turks and Armenians, German Christians and Jews, Orthodox Christian Serbs and Muslim Bosnians—has at least served as a pretext for the former in slaughtering the latter. Not so, however, in Rwanda.

What Rwanda teaches is that, really, any pretext for division—even violent division, and slaughter—will do. The tribal instinct runs deep in humankind.

So yes, the Rwandan government has good reason to try to tamp down ethnic divisions. But it may simply be naïve to think that any country can permanently tame the tiger of tribalism.

We can—and perhaps in some circumstances we should—seek to eradicate ethnicity, and teach color blindness. But we kid ourselves if we think that, under the right circumstances, people will not find some trivial difference to justify mass murder.

POSTSCRIPT

Article 10(2) of the European Convention for the Protection of Human Rights and Fundamental Freedoms states that the right to free speech "carries with it duties and responsibilities" that enable governments to regulate speech well beyond what would be permitted in the United States under our First Amendment. In the United States, for example, neo-Nazis, members of the Ku Klux Klan, and other groups that preach racial hatred are entitled to profess their views, so long as they do not advocate immediate violence.[11]

A number of years ago, my constitutional law class was discussing the regulation of hate speech. I asked my students whether they preferred the U.S. or the European approach. One student suggested that each approach was appropriate in its place. "We didn't have a genocide here," he said by way of elaboration.

"Well," I responded, "that depends on how you characterize the treatment of Native Americans. And," I added, "we did have slavery."

My point was not simply a matter of setting the historical record straight. In fact, I agreed with the student that the free speech regimes of the United States and Europe each fit their respective societies. But that fit is less a matter of history as such than it is an all-things-considered judgment about whether the graver danger to a given society lies in suppression of dissident views or the descent into racial, ethnic, or other violence.

In part this all-things-considered judgment is a matter of the passage of time. In Rwanda and the former Yugoslavia, the genocides are so recent that they are obviously salient to a judgment about what kinds of speech can safely be allowed. Likewise, with victims and perpetrators of Nazism still alive, that episode remains relevant in Germany.

But it is not just a matter of time. American apartheid has been illegal for just barely half a century, and it was practiced in fact for years after it was forbidden in law. Nonetheless, the sorts of hate speech restrictions one routinely sees in European countries seem out of place in the United States. Partly that's a matter of the absolutism of the First Amendment's text. Partly it's because robust interpretation of the First Amendment played an important role in the civil rights movement of the 1960s. And partly, it's a matter of culture—which may just be a fancy way of saying that most Americans have been so successfully indoctrinated in the American way of thinking that we can't imagine how we could do things any other way.

NOTES

1. *See* Emily Wax, *Journalists Sentenced In Rwanda Genocide; Prosecutor Said 'Hate Media' Urged Killings*, Wash. Post, Dec. 4, 2003, at A20.

2. Marc Lacey, *A Decade After Massacres, Rwanda Outlaws Ethnicity*, N.Y. Times, Apr. 9, 2004, at A3.

3. 163 U.S. 537, 559 (1896) (Harlan, J., dissenting).

4. 515 U.S. 200, 239 (1995) (Scalia, J., concurring in part and concurring in the judgment).

5. Grundgesetz für die Bundesrepublik Deutschland [GG] art. 21(2) (F.R.G.).

6. Jared Diamond, Collapse 314 (New York: Penguin, 2005) ("It is often stated that . . . Hutu [look] shorter, stockier, darker, flat-nosed, thick-lipped, and square-jawed, while Tutsi are taller, more slender, paler-skinned, thin-lipped, and narrow-chinned.").

7. *Id.* at 318 ("The distinction between Hutu and Tutsi is not nearly as sharp as often portrayed. . . . Hutu and Tutsi intermarried, and (before Belgians introduced [ethnic] identity cards) sometimes switched their ethnic identity.").

8. *See* Said Adejumobi, *Citizenship, Rights, and the Problem of Conflicts and Civil Wars in Africa*, 23 Hum. Rts. Q. 148, 163–67 (2001); John R. Bowen, *The Myth of Global Ethnic Conflict*, 7 J. of Democracy 3, 5–7 (1996).

9. *See* Sharon Begley, *Three is not Enough; Surprising New Lessons from the Controversial Science of Race*, Newsweek, Feb. 13, 1995, at 67; Dale E. Hammerschmidt, *It's as Simple as Black and White! Race and Ethnicity as Categorical Variables*, 133 J. of Laboratory and Clinical Med. 10, 11 (1999).

10. C. civ. arts. 21–24 (Fr.) ("Nobody may be naturalised unless he proves his assimilation into the French community, and specially owing to a sufficient knowledge of the French language, according to his condition and of the rights and duties conferred by French nationality."), *available at* http://www.legifrance.gouv.fr/html/codes_traduits/code_civil_somA.htm.

11. *See* Brandenburg v Ohio, 395 U.S. 444, 447 (1969) (per curiam).

• 33 •

What a Chinese Height Discrimination Case Says about Chinese (and American) Constitutional Law

May 2004

In May 2004, the *New York Times* reported on a disturbing phenomenon in the People's Republic of China: Otherwise highly qualified applicants for government jobs are being turned down because they are too short (and often just barely so).[1] As part of an effort to put the nation's "best face" forward in the global economy, Chinese ministries have adopted height and other aesthetic requirements.

Although the *Times* article appeared to be intended as an amusing human-interest story, the issue is in fact quite serious for those affected. Height requirements in China—for educational as well as employment opportunities—tend to be set at roughly the national average, and accordingly large portions of the population are excluded by them.

Moreover, the issue raises interesting transnational questions about the nature of equality, and the role of courts in interpreting and enforcing constitutional guarantees.

No constitutional or national statutory provision in China specifically bars height discrimination, and as a result, legal efforts to challenge minimum height requirements have invoked Article 33 of the Chinese Constitution, which makes all citizens "equal before the law."[2] However, with an important caveat, to which I'll return below, these efforts have been largely unsuccessful.

Before American readers start clucking over Chinese disrespect for human rights, it's worth noting that the situation is basically the same in the United States. Federal statutes bar discrimination in employment,[3] housing,[4] federally funded education,[5] and other areas on such bases as race, religion, and sex, but not on the basis of height.

Obviously, there are some categories of employment for which height is relevant. If I, standing exactly 6 feet tall, apply for the position of center of the

New York Knicks, clearly team president Isiah Thomas can invoke my merely average stature (along with my lazy defense and weak jump shot) as grounds for turning me down.

But the law even permits the Knicks to deny me a job as a popcorn vendor if, on purely aesthetic grounds, the team decides that it wants all of its male salespeople to be over six-foot-two. (The team would be engaging in sex discrimination if it applied the same height requirement to female popcorn vendors,[6] but no provision of federal law prohibits favoring tall men over short men, along with tall women over short women).

How about state law? New York State law goes beyond federal law in prohibiting discrimination on the basis of sexual orientation,[7] but not height. Indeed, even liberal California, which bans all arbitrary and intentional discrimination in "business establishments,"[8] does not extend that approach to employment,[9] so not only can I be prevented from selling popcorn in Madison Square Garden; I can't even sell sushi at the Staples Center (where the Los Angeles Lakers play).

Will the federal Constitution help me obtain a position as a vendor in the world's most famous arena (as the Garden bills itself)? Fat chance. The Fourteenth Amendment's Equal Protection Clause only bars discrimination by the government,[10] and the Knicks are not a state-run enterprise.

Moreover, even if the Knicks were owned by the state, they probably could still favor tall popcorn vendors. The United States Supreme Court has interpreted the Fourteenth Amendment's Equal Protection Clause as presumptively barring race,[11] national origin,[12] and sex discrimination,[13] but most other forms of discrimination are only deemed unconstitutional if they are considered "irrational."[14] And the Court's precedents make clear that almost any reason will count as rational—so the hypothetical New York State Knicks might well be able to defend a policy requiring tall popcorn vendors on aesthetic grounds.

As noted above, Chinese law does not expressly bar height discrimination, but a case brought by Jiang Tao brought the issue to public attention. In December 2001, Jiang read an advertisement for a staff position at the Chengdu Branch of the People's Bank of China. Among the other qualifications listed, the ad required that male applicants be over 168 centimeters in height (about 5 feet, 6 inches), and that female applicants be over 155 centimeters (about 5 feet, 1 inch).

Jiang sued the bank in the People's Court of Wuhou District. To the surprise of many observers, in early 2002, the court accepted the case.

Later that same year, however, the case was dismissed on what American lawyers would call "justiciability" grounds—that is, based on mootness (meaning there is no remaining controversy), standing (meaning the wrong plaintiff has sued), and ripeness (meaning the case is not ready to be resolved now) grounds.

Why was the case nonjusticiable, in the court's eyes? Shortly after Jiang's suit was filed, the bank dropped the height requirement. Because Jiang hadn't been injured by the bank's policy, he couldn't recover; if the bank reinstated the policy, the court indicated, then someone else should sue at the appropriate time.

To be sure, the court gave another reason for its decision, one that would suggest that even a plaintiff with standing in a timely case would fail. The court said that the Chinese Administrative Litigation Law only permits review of administrative action taken within the scope of the sued entity's formal regulatory responsibilities. That law further states that it does not authorize litigation involving personnel decisions. Accordingly, the court reasoned that the height requirement was not judicially reviewable.[15]

But this aspect of the decision, which seems less important than the justiciability question, may not establish a lasting precedent. Although the Administrative Litigation Law does not authorize litigation involving personnel decisions, arguably the Constitution itself does. Furthermore, pending legislative developments may clarify that Chinese courts can set aside unconstitutional administrative action, and quite apart from any new legislation, as I explain below, the Supreme People's Court may be prepared to assume this power on its own.

Thus, while Jiang's case must be judged a setback for the fight against height discrimination in China, it is hardly the last word. There will likely be further challenges to height requirements—along with challenges to other aesthetic requirements, and to the common requirement that prospective employees test negative for Hepatitis B, a not especially communicable disease that is very widespread in China.

Whether this litigation succeeds will depend in large part on whether the courts assert the power to enforce the Chinese Constitution—and if they do, on whether the leadership of the Chinese Communist Party (CCP) permits them to get away with it.

On the face of it, the Chinese Constitution does not provide for the possibility of judicial review—the power of courts to strike down laws they deem unconstitutional. Although its Article 5 declares the supremacy of the Constitution over other laws, its Articles 62 and 67 assign to the National People's Congress and its Standing Committee the powers to interpret and supervise the enforcement of the Constitution. And Article 128 specifies that "the Supreme People's Court is responsible to the National People's Congress and its Standing Committee."

Accordingly, most scholars of Chinese and comparative constitutional law have tended to classify the Chinese Constitution in the same category as the Dutch Constitution[16] and others that expressly deny to courts the power to hold legislation unconstitutional.

That classification was thrown into doubt, however, by a case that some observers have dubbed the *Marbury v. Madison*[17] of China. In the case, a woman named Qi Yuling was denied admission to a school in Shandong Province because, according to the school's records, she had already enrolled. It turned out, however, that a woman named Chen Xiaoqi had essentially committed identity theft and enrolled under Qi's name. When the school nonetheless refused to admit the real Qi, she sued, citing Article 46 of the Chinese Constitution, which guarantees a right to education.

The High People's Court of Shandong referred the question to the highest court in China, the Supreme People's Court, which ruled in July 2001 that Qi's rights had indeed been violated.[18] Although that court's terse one-paragraph opinion provides no explanation of the reasons behind the ruling, it created quite a stir, because it suggested that the Chinese courts can afford direct remedies under the Constitution. And in an article published shortly after the case was decided, Huang Songyou, Chief of the Supreme People's Court No. 1 Civil Division, endorsed this suggestion, citing the "tremendous and far-reaching importance" of his court's decision in the *Qi* case.[19]

Still, the Supreme People's Court decision in the *Qi* case is puzzling in two respects: First, as a formal legal matter, how can judicial enforcement of constitutional rights be squared with the Chinese Constitution's assignment of constitutional interpretation to the People's Congress, rather than the courts?

And second, given the reality that the People's Republic of China is a one-party state in which the CCP in fact calls the shots regardless of the formal arrangements, will the Supreme People's Court be able to follow in our own Chief Justice John Marshall's footsteps by strengthening the judiciary at the expense of the political organs of government?

The respective solutions to these puzzles are closely related to one another. As to formal power, it is worth noting that neither the *Qi* case itself, nor the challenges to height restrictions or other arbitrary employment or education conditions, call into question any law enacted by the People's Congress. The lawsuits challenge provincial, local, and administrative action on the basis of the national Constitution.

Precisely because Article 128 makes the Supreme People's Court subordinate to the People's Congress, one can understand enforcement of the Constitution by the Court as under the supervision of the Congress, as required by Article 62. Indeed, many of the strongest proponents of judicial enforcement of the Chinese Constitution argue that it is appropriate only when the Congress has failed to act—not that the courts should act in contravention of laws enacted by the Congress or its Standing Committee.

This formal reconciliation of judicial enforcement of the Constitution and Congressional supremacy may also explain the practical puzzle. It is possible that the CCP, acting through the National People's Congress and its Standing Committee, has not yet reined in the courts because it sees constitutional litigation as a useful tool for controlling provincial and local authorities.

How so? Students of American constitutional history will see an obvious parallel with the Marshall Court: Although it is true that the U.S. Supreme Court in the first half of the nineteenth century was consolidating its own power, it did so primarily as a vehicle of national power as against states' rights. Most instances of Marshall Court "activism" served a broad vision of federal power.

Likewise, the CCP is not, as it is sometimes portrayed in the West, a top-down machine able to control every aspect of life in contemporary China. On the contrary, the CCP faces more or less the same challenge that faced every imperial dynasty in China over several millenia: how to rule an enormous country in which real power is dispersed and thus corruption—or at least the opportunity for pursuing divergent agendas—is rampant?

By, in effect, delegating power to the courts to stamp out unauthorized practices, such as arbitrary employment requirements, the CCP may hope to strengthen its control over the country.

The risk—and it is one that my friends in the Chinese legal academy tell me the CCP is aware of—is that in tacitly authorizing constitutional litigation, the CCP will unleash forces it cannot control. Throughout the world today, judicial or quasi-judicial enforcement of constitutional rights is associated with constraints on all levels of government in favor of universal human rights. The CCP is gambling that just as it has encouraged economic freedom with only limited political freedom, so it can authorize constitutional litigation that does not challenge CCP authority without also authorizing constitutional litigation that does challenge the CCP.

Cases against the army or the CCP itself, the party leadership is no doubt thinking, can be readily dismissed when they arise. Indeed, one reason that the height cases have been allowed to proceed—while cases involving sex discrimination have not—may be that while height discrimination is widely unpopular, sex discrimination, which is also rampant, enjoys considerable official and public approval.[20]

Whether China's gamble succeeds remains to be seen. In the quarter century since Deng Xiaoping began transforming China's economy into capitalism in all but name, political reforms have been slow, but they have been real. Chinese people today enjoy substantially greater political freedom than they did a generation ago, including the ability to participate in contested elections—albeit elections in which the competition is *within* the CCP.

Keeping a lid on constitutional litigation will present a challenge to the CCP. In order for lawsuits against provincial, local and administrative officials to be effective, the courts must be perceived by the public as legitimate. But that means, at a minimum, that their decrees must be seen as rooted in the law, and not just the will of the CCP.

And there's the rub: To get what it wants out of the judiciary, the CCP must make real the promise of the Chinese Constitution's Article 126, guaranteeing judicial independence.

Will the result of constitutional litigation in China eventually be to hasten the emergence of real judicially enforceable restraints on the government? As Chou En-lai said when asked what he thought the significance of the French Revolution was, it's too soon to tell.[21]

POSTSCRIPT

I cannot resist taking the opportunity of this detour into Chinese constitutional law to throw one more dart at originalism in the United States. The Chinese Constitution is not unusual in setting out far-reaching guarantees that have often meant very little in practice. On paper, the constitutions of many countries—including the Soviet Union and its satellites before the fall of Communism in Eastern Europe—have been wonderful documents that bore no relation to the law as it was actually enforced. Moreover, typically the framers of these constitutions fully intended them to be only for show. Their "original understanding," if you will, was that the documents simply did not mean what they appeared to say.

What then are we to make of the efforts of lawyers asking judges to enforce the liberal constitution of an illiberal regime as written rather than as intended? I suspect that within the United States and other democracies, across the political spectrum, people would approve of this phenomenon. If a constitution says freedom of speech and political association are protected, the rulers of the regime should not be heard to make a legal argument that the constitution is a sham.

Thus, at first blush, someone who, like Justice Scalia, espouses textualism at home, should feel confident in invoking his own jurisprudence to defend constitutional litigation in China. The plaintiffs in these cases are merely asking the Chinese courts to enforce the plain language of the Chinese Constitution.

Yet on closer inspection, textualism cannot justify judicial enforcement of the Chinese Constitution because Articles 62 and 128 at least appear to assign that task to the legislature. In order to accept the argument that judicial review is consistent with Articles 62 and 128, one must first find ambiguity in those provisions. But of course most textualists—and certainly Justice Scalia—would say that when a textual provision is ambiguous, one looks to the original understanding. And here the original understanding points away from judicial review and toward one-party dictatorship. The only way for originalists to escape that conclusion is to say that the original understanding of the Chinese Constitution is illegitimate because the document itself was not adopted by democratic means.

Aha, gotcha! As I explained in the postscript to chapter 15, that is also true of the American Constitution. If the undemocratic process by which the Constitution of the People's Republic of China was adopted counts against giving controlling weight to its original understanding, then shouldn't the undemocratic process (by modern standards) by which the American Constitution, the Bill of Rights, and the Reconstruction Amendments were adopted also count against giving controlling weight to the original understanding of those texts? So perhaps the reason American originalists don't want courts to look to foreign law is not that these sources are irrelevant; perhaps they're afraid of the lessons such comparative sources yield about the flaws in their own methodology.

NOTES

1. Joseph Kahn, *Chinese People's Republic Is Unfair to Its Short People*, N.Y. Times, May 21, 2004, at A13.
2. Xianfa art. 33 (1982) (P.R.C.).
3. 42 U.S.C. §§ 2000e to 2000e-16c (2004).
4. 42 U.S.C. §§ 3601–3619 (2004).
5. *E.g.*, 42 U.S.C. § 2000d (2004); 20 U.S.C. § 1681 (2004).
6. *See* 42 U.S.C. § 2000e-2(k) (2004) (barring employment practices that have a disparate impact based on sex, absent a good justification).
7. N.Y. Exec. Law § 291(1)–(2) (McKinney 2005); N.Y. Exec. Law § 296(1)(a) (McKinney 2005).
8. *See* Cal. Civ. Code § 51(b) (West 2005); Marina Point, Ltd. v. Wolfson, 640 P.2d 115, 120–24 (Cal. 1982).
9. *See* Alcorn v. Anbro Eng'g, Inc., 468 P.2d 216, 219–20 (Cal. 1970); *see also* Cassista v. Cmty. Foods, Inc., 856 P.2d 1143 (Cal. 1993) (rejecting weight discrimination claim because weight is not listed as a forbidden ground in the California Fair Employment and Housing Act, Cal. Gov. Code §§ 12900–12996).
10. *See* The Civil Rights Cases, 109 U.S. 3 (1883).
11. *See* Palmore v. Sidoti, 466 U.S. 429, 432 (1984).
12. *See* United States v. Virginia, 518 U.S. 515, 532 n.6 (1996).
13. *See* Craig v. Boren, 429 U.S. 190, 197 (1976).
14. *See* Bd. of Trs. of the Univ. of Ala. v. Garrett, 531 U.S. 356, 365–68 (2001).
15. I have been unable to locate an official version of the opinion published in English. I rely for this description on a translation provided to me by my colleague Professor

Benjamin Liebman, Director of the Center for Chinese Legal Studies at Columbia Law School. I am especially grateful to him and to Neysun Mahboubi, currently a Fellow at the Yale Law School China Law Center, for guidance with the materials discussed in this chapter.

16. Grondwet voor het Koninkrijk der Nederlanden [Gw.] art. 120 (Neth.) ("The constitutionality of Acts of Parliament and treaties shall not be reviewed by the courts.").

17. 5 U.S. (1 Cranch) 137 (1803).

18. *See* Qi Yuling v. Chen Xiaoqi, 5 Gazette of the Supreme People's Court of the People's Republic of China 158 (2001).

19. Huang Songyou, *The Importance of Institutionalizing the Constitution in Judicial Process—On a Supreme Court Opinion*, People's Court News, Aug. 13, 2001.

20. *See* United States Dep't of State, China: Country Reports on Human Rights Practices 2004 § 5 (2005).

21. *See* Simon Schama, Citizens: A Chronicle of the French Revolution xiii (New York: Alfred A. Knopf, 1989).

VI

THE RULE OF LAW(YERS)

I once heard a story about a man on a soapbox who was urging all passersby not to vote in a coming election. "Why bother?" he said. "No matter who gets more votes, the government still wins." Non-lawyers reading this book may have a similar reaction. I have been arguing for the partial autonomy of law from other domains of value, such as economics, moral philosophy, and politics. Well that's just the problem, I can hear my lay critics saying: When liberal and conservative judges put aside their ideological divisions, what unites them is something even worse—they're all lawyers.

Indeed, something like this charge has even been made in recent years by prominent scholars and judges. Conservatives such as Harvard Law Professor Mary Ann Glendon and federal appeals court judge John Noonan have each in their own way lamented the degree to which lawyers and judges in general, and the U.S. Supreme Court especially, have hijacked public discussion of our most pressing national questions.[1] Prominent liberal legal academics have also joined in the attack. Stanford Dean Larry Kramer, Georgetown Law Professor Mark Tushnet, and my Columbia Law School colleague Jeremy Waldron have all written books condemning the Supreme Court for much the same sin.[2] Likewise, a spate of articles and op-eds blamed the Democrats' electoral defeat in the 2004 presidential and congressional elections on liberals' over-reliance on the courts, especially on the question of same-sex marriage, which sparked a popular backlash.[3]

Whether the critics are correct is impossible to say with confidence. One would need to perform an experiment in which history were re-run without certain critical judicial rulings. My own suspicion is that the critics overstate the case. They are right to observe that courts alone cannot bring about lasting social change over a determined opposition, and given our commitment to democracy, courts generally should not even make the attempt. But courts can and sometimes should play an important role in catalyzing and prodding social change. That is probably the best account of the role the Supreme Court and lower federal courts played in the civil rights movement in the 1950s and 1960s.[4]

In any event, the critics—and here I include populist voices as well as judicial and academic ones—are undoubtedly right to observe a gap between the views and methods of ordinary people and the views and methods of legal elites on critical issues. Some such gap is probably inevitable and perhaps even desirable in a constitutional democracy in which courts are supposed to act as a check on popular passions, but too wide a gap will eventually lead to instability.

Accordingly, the chapters in this section try to make the lawyer's perspective legible to the layperson, focusing both on the internal workings of the legal profession and the public's perception of lawyers and the law. Three of these chapters make use of data collected from random telephone surveys conducted in 2002. Columbia Law School commissioned the surveys, which I designed. The surveys and summary results appear in the appendix.

NOTES

1. *See* Mary Ann Glendon, A Nation Under Lawyers: How the Crisis in the Legal Profession is Transforming American Society 167–69 (New York: Farrar, Straus, and Giraux, 1994); John T. Noonan Jr., Narrowing the Nation's Power: The Supreme Court Sides with the States 4–6 (Berkeley: University of California Press, 2002).

2. Larry D. Kramer, The People Themselves: Popular Constitutionalism and Judicial Review 227–33 (New York: Oxford University Press, 2004); Mark Tushnet, Taking the Constitution Away from the Courts 174, 182 (Princeton, N.J.: Princeton University Press, 1999); Jeremy Waldron, Law and Disagreement 289–91 (Oxford: Clarendon Press; New York: Oxford University Press, 1999).

3. *See, e.g.*, David von Drehle, Op-Ed., *Take the Issues to the People, Not the Courts*, Wash. Post, Nov. 14, 2004, at B4; John Leo, *What Now, Democrats*, U.S. News & World Rep., Nov. 15, 2004, at 82; Burt Neuborne, *Courting Trouble; Liberal Overdependence on the Courts, Combined with an Obsessive Preoccupation with Church-State Symbolism, Has Reached Its Limit*, Am. Prospect, Jan. 2005, at A16; Jeffrey Rosen, *Courting Disaster*, N.Y. Times Mag., Dec. 5, 2004, at 29; Paul Starr, Op-Ed., *Winning Cases, Losing Voters*, N.Y. Times, Jan. 26, 2005, at A17; Neil Gorsuch, *Liberals'n'Lawsuits*, Nat'l Rev. Online, Feb. 7, 2005 (LEXIS, Magazine Stories Combined); *cf.* Benjamin Wittes, *Letting go of Roe; the Democratic Party's Commitment to Preserving Roe v. Wade Has Been Deeply Unhealthy for the Cause of Abortion Rights, for Liberalism More Generally, and Ultimately for American Democracy*, Atlantic Monthly, Jan. 1, 2005, at 48.

4. *Compare* Gerald N. Rosenberg, The Hollow Hope: Can Courts Bring About Social Change? 156 (Chicago: University of Chicago Press, 1991) ("While it must be the case that Court action [in mid-twentieth-century civil rights cases] influenced some people, I have found no evidence that this influence was widespread or of much importance to the battle for civil rights."), *with* Neal Devins, *Judicial Matters*, 80 Cal. L. Rev. 1027, 1041 (1992) ("[B]oth the promise and failure of *Brown* were lightning rods to the civil rights movement" because they "spurred black activism" and "influenced legislative deliberations over the 1964 Civil Rights Act and the Elementary and Secondary Education Act."), *and* Malcolm M. Feeley, *Hollow Hopes, Flypaper, and Metaphors*, 17 Law & Soc. Inquiry 745, 751–52 (1992) ("Rosenberg could have drawn more extensively on the work of Stuart Scheingold" who "develop[ed] the intriguing hypothesis that courts can facilitate the placement of issues on the public agenda and thus can serve as catalysts for significant social change.").

• 34 •

Debate over an American Bar Association Legal Ethics Rule Underscores Lawyers' Competing Obligations to Keep Secret and to Disclose

August 2001

At the 2001 annual meeting of the American Bar Association (ABA), the House of Delegates approved a number of amendments to the Model Rules of Professional Conduct. Although the Model Rules have no binding force, they are nonetheless important, because most state bars' disciplinary bodies have adopted them in one form or another. Changes approved by the ABA are likely to become official policy in many states.

The most attention-grabbing of the changes prohibits attorneys from having "sexual relationships with a client unless the sexual relationship predates the formation of the client-lawyer relationship."[1] Take that, Arnie Becker and Ally McBeal!

Another change, while less sexy, is perhaps of greater symbolic importance because of what it says about the legal profession's understanding of how to balance its obligations to clients and the public. This change amends Model Rule 1.6, governing disclosure of a client's confidential information.

The basic injunction of Model Rule 1.6 is clear: Absent the client's consent, a lawyer must keep the client's secrets. The old version of the rule makes a limited exception, however, permitting attorneys to disclose information without the client's consent, in order "to prevent the client from committing a criminal act that the lawyer believes is likely to result in imminent death or substantial bodily harm."[2]

So suppose one day your client Ralphie drops by to thank you for helping him with a big public construction contract. As he's leaving your office, Ralphie mentions that he's planning to "whack that punk Jackie." Let's say you have a twinge of conscience. No problem. Model Rule 1.6 lets you warn Jackie, or better yet for your own safety, place an anonymous call to the FBI.

But now suppose your client is the Nukem Corporation. The Nukem CEO tells you that his employees Larry, Curly, and Mo accidentally spilled some leftover plutonium in an open field behind the main power plant. You tell him that he's obliged to notify the Environmental Protection Agency and immediately start a massive cleanup and containment effort. "Gee, I wish I could," the CEO replies. "But that would really hurt our quarterly statement. Who's going to know, anyway?" You use all of your persuasive skills but to no avail. The company will do nothing about the spill.

Your conscience bothers you again. You know that improperly discarded plutonium will eventually find its way into groundwater, where it will have terrible effects on plants, animals, and humans. However, the contamination process may take years to occur, and so the death or substantial bodily harm that will result from Nukem's dumping is not "imminent." Under the old version of Model Rule 1.6, you can't disclose.

The ABA to the rescue! The new version of Model Rule 1.6 eliminates the imminence requirement, so that an attorney can disclose client information "to prevent reasonably certain death."[3] If you practice law in a state that has adopted the amendment, you can stop the poisoning—since the deaths you foresee eventually resulting from the spill are, while not "imminent," still "reasonably certain" to occur in the future. The official commentary on the new Model Rule even gives the toxic waste example (minus the fanciful names) I've described.[4]

Despite the obvious moral appeal of broadening the scope of permissible disclosure under Model Rule 1.6, critics worry that it will undermine the attorney–client relationship. The core confidentiality requirement of Model Rule 1.6—like its counterpart in evidence law, the attorney–client privilege[5]—is based on the premise that in the long run, the public benefits when clients can speak frankly with their lawyers, even if in some situations secrecy leads to injustice or harm.

Confidentiality serves the public interest, it is said, because most clients are basically law-abiding. As the official commentary to the new version of Model Rule 1.6 notes: "Almost without exception, clients come to lawyers in order to determine their rights and what is . . . deemed to be legal and correct. Based upon experience, lawyers know that almost all clients follow the advice given, and the law is upheld."[6] If that is so, the critics of the amendment to Rule 1.6 charge, the attorney's confidentiality obligation should not be watered down.

Their argument goes as follows: Permitting disclosure in the small number of cases in which disclosure is necessary to prevent future death or substantial bodily harm may seem like the right thing to do if one only thinks about those cases, but it does greater harm in the long run. Faced with uncertain and thus unreliable protection for their confidences, people will hesitate to seek legal advice; then, not knowing their legal obligations, they will violate laws with which they would have complied had they sought legal counsel. The end result will be more harm to the public, not less.

Supporters of the expanded disclosure provision respond that these fears are overstated. For one thing, both the old and new versions of Model Rule 1.6 concern the circumstances under which an attorney is *permitted* to disclose client information. There are very few circumstances in which a lawyer is required to disclose client information.[7] Clients worried about disclosure will generally be able to find attorneys who place a much greater value on client loyalty than on satisfying contrary twinges of conscience.

Moreover, supporters of the amendment contend, the complexity of the law means that people will continue to seek legal advice despite the rule change. Even relatively modest modern businesses must negotiate a tangle of laws and regulations concerning anti-competitive behavior, the environment, handicapped access, labor relations, workplace safety, and many other features of their operations. It is a practical impossibility to do so without consulting legal experts.

Indeed, even individuals embroiled in the legal system quickly discover that it is far too complex for the typical amateur. If a lawyer who represents himself has a fool for a client, one can only imagine what kind of client a layman who represents himself has.

In short, neither corporations nor individuals, supporters of the new version of Rule 1.6 suggest, will truly be deterred from consulting lawyers by the amendment.

The arguments concerning the amendment to Model Rule 1.6 purport to be about an empirical question: How will clients act under the new rule? Yet neither side puts forward evidence about how clients respond to different confidentiality rules—suggesting that the true root of the debate is philosophical, not empirical.

To be sure, as the Supreme Court noted in a 1998 case, the handful of empirical studies of the issue that have been conducted are largely inconclusive.[8] And more conclusive studies might change the minds of some—especially if they had dramatic results, demonstrating that in the wake of an amendment, there would either be wide-scale shunning of legal advice, or no change at all in the frequency with which lawyers are consulted. Still, one senses that few of the principals in this debate would change their positions even were they confronted with hard data.

At bottom, the debate over Model Rule 1.6 is a debate between which of two competing roles of the lawyer to emphasize: zealous advocate versus officer of the court.

In our legal system, lawyers play both of these roles. A lawyer must help his client to put on as strong a case as possible, but a lawyer may not suborn perjury. A lawyer must help the client achieve the client's goals, but a lawyer may not assist a client in committing a crime. A lawyer must keep his client's secrets but not . . . what exactly?

That is the particular question at stake in the debate over Model Rule 1.6, which has now moved to the states. Short of making the confidentiality rule absolute or abolishing it entirely, any qualification of the rule's secrecy requirement will necessarily reflect a compromise. As a result, any resolution of this debate will be open to the charge that it goes too far—as well as the converse charge that it does not go far enough. And so lawyers, as a group and as individuals, will continue to struggle to reconcile the irreconcilable.

POSTSCRIPT

State bars, often under the supervision of state supreme courts, set ethics rules, and it is up to each of them to decide whether to adopt the ABA proposals in whole or in part. Whatever the precise rules, the clash between the professional duties and the personal conscience of the lawyer invariably makes for good drama. Films and TV shows routinely show sympathetic characters wanting to do the right thing by disclosing a client confidence, but struggling to overcome a rule that works an injustice in the particular case.

The conflict is real and acute, but it is not unique to lawyers. In other circumstances as well, people must decide whether to take an action that seems justified in the particular instance but which, in the long run, may lead to greater harm. The question of whether to pay ransom to kidnappers is a classic case. Paying the kidnappers may secure the release of the hostage but it will also encourage future kidnappings. Given the tragic nature of the choice, it is difficult to say that either course of action is clearly right or wrong.

But if actors in other fields must sometimes choose between seemingly right conduct in the particular case and acting in accordance with a rule that, in the long run, supposedly leads to beneficial results, this sort of dilemma is endemic to law. In the next chapter, I suggest that it may also play some role in the public's persistent dislike of lawyers.

NOTES

1. Model Rules of Prof'l Conduct R. 1.7 cmt. 12 (2002); *see also* Model Rules of Prof'l Conduct R. 1.8(j) (2002).
2. Model Rules of Prof'l Conduct R. 1.6(b)(1) (2001).

3. Model Rules of Prof'l Conduct R. 1.6(b)(1) (2002).
4. *See* Model Rules of Prof'l Conduct R. 1.6 cmt. 6 (2002).
5. *See* Upjohn Co. v. United States, 449 U.S. 383, 389 (1981).
6. Model Rules of Prof'l Conduct R. 1.6 cmt. 2 (2002).
7. One such exceptional circumstance is singled out by section 261.101 of the Texas Family Code, which imposes upon attorneys an affirmative duty to report cases of known or suspected child abuse, notwithstanding any claim of attorney–client privileges. *See* Camile Glasscock Dubose & Cathy O. Morris, *The Attorney as Mandatory Reporter*, 68 Tex. B.J. 208 (2005).
8. *See* Swidler & Berlin v. United States, 524 U.S. 399, 409 n.4 (1998).

• 35 •

Can the Legal Profession Improve Its Image? Americans Believe Lawyers Are Necessary but Dishonest, Survey Finds

April 2002

A nationwide survey[1] commissioned by Columbia Law School contains some disheartening news for lawyers. Americans think lawyers are dishonest and overpaid. Moreover, although roughly half of the people asked thought that lawyers perform a useful function, almost as many said that lawyers do more harm than good.

In light of these findings, can the legal profession improve its image with the public? Or is the problem more than just a matter of appearances, one going to the heart of what lawyers do?

In the Columbia Law survey, a representative sample of a thousand Americans was asked a series of questions about the legal profession. (A final question, which I shall discuss in the next chapter, asked people about the role of the Supreme Court.)

The first question concerned honesty. Respondents were asked whether they thought that lawyers were "especially honest, somewhat honest, about average, somewhat dishonest, or especially dishonest."

The good news is that lawyers fared better than politicians. Sixty-one percent of respondents thought politicians especially dishonest or somewhat dishonest; 39 percent thought the same of lawyers. Only 16 percent thought politicians especially honest or somewhat honest; yet 31 percent thought the same of lawyers.

But this is good news only if one is grading on a curve—and a generous one at that. Comparing public perceptions of lawyers to those of police leads to a much less flattering picture of lawyers.

Fifty-eight percent of respondents rated police above average for honesty—a figure sharply higher, of course, than the 31 percent who thought the same of lawyers. And while, as noted above, 39 percent believed lawyers dishonest, only 12 percent thought the same of police.

Interestingly, despite the widespread perception that public opinion about the criminal justice system is racially polarized, African Americans rated police only slightly less honest than white Americans did. Moreover, both groups thought police substantially more honest than lawyers.

The news relating to perceptions of attorney compensation is also grim. The survey asked: "Given the level of compensation of other professions in society, such as doctors or corporate executives, overall, do you believe most lawyers are overpaid, fairly compensated, or underpaid for the work they do?" A full 60 percent of respondents said lawyers are overpaid, compared with a mere 2 percent who thought lawyers underpaid.

Overpaid compared with doctors or corporate executives? Clearly, when Americans envision attorneys, few of them think of public defenders, legal aid lawyers, or district attorneys earning annual salaries insufficient to pay off their college and law school loans.[2]

Instead, they must have in mind the lawyers who represent large corporations for handsome hourly rates, or the handful of plaintiffs' attorneys who earn enormous contingency fees from judgments against those same corporations.

Plaintiffs' lawyers will be relieved to learn that despite the sustained efforts by proponents of tort reform and other measures aimed at curtailing legal remedies, Americans continue to think our justice system worth keeping—albeit just barely.

The survey asked: "Do you believe that lawyers do more harm than good by filing lawsuits that may raise the cost of doing business, or do they perform a beneficial role by holding big companies accountable to the law?" By a 50 to 41 percent margin, the respondents thought lawyers perform a beneficial role.

That view was more or less consistent across the country, although the margin was largest among African Americans, who more frequently expressed the opinion that lawyers perform a beneficial role.

Only the wealthiest Americans thought lawyers do more harm than good, and then only by a very slight margin of 48 percent to 46 percent.

What do the results of the Columbia Law survey tell us? They do not necessarily reflect negative experiences with attorneys. Most of the respondents were not basing their answers on recent experience. Fewer than one-third of them reported having used the services of a lawyer within the previous year.

Perhaps then the survey results simply reflect deep-seated stereotypes. After all, the fact that Americans think lawyers dishonest and overpaid is hardly surprising. Negative portrayals of lawyers have been a staple of Western culture at least as far back as ancient Athens. For example, in his play *The Clouds*,[3] Aristophanes mercilessly ridiculed the proto-lawyers of his day—who specialized, he claimed, in making arguments for injustice triumph over arguments for justice.

But it would be too simple to dismiss public dissatisfaction with the legal profession as the product of uninformed prejudice. Certainly, contemporary popular culture offers alternative, positive images of lawyers. Real-life plaintiffs' representatives Jan Schlictmann and Erin Brockovich were portrayed sympathetically by, respectively, John Travolta[4] and Julia Roberts.[5] (True, Brockovich lacked a law degree but the lawyerliness of her actions was exactly what made them heroic.)

Granted, the explosion of law-related television shows in the nearly two decades since the premier of *L.A. Law* has not always portrayed lawyers in the most sympathetic light. Yet these shows have tended to depict lawyers, especially criminal defense attorneys, as complex human beings struggling to do the right thing within a framework of rules that sometimes sacrifices justice in particular cases in favor of systemic objectives.

Why then does the negative view of lawyers persist? One possibility, of course, is that lawyers in fact are overpaid and less honest than members of other professions. If so—and even if not—law schools, the organized bar, and all concerned members of the profession should redouble their efforts to set and live by the highest ethical standards.

Yet such efforts are, I suspect, destined to be of limited utility. The root cause of distrust of lawyers may be a distrust of the law itself.

Law, in the sense of rules and principles that govern human conduct, is a blunt instrument. Sometimes, for the law to work properly, it must impede rather than further the aims of justice.

Consider a standard target of popular critiques of the legal system: the so-called exclusionary rule, under which courts refuse to admit evidence obtained in violation of the Fourth Amendment right of a suspect to be free of unlawful searches and seizures.

The point of the rule is to deter the police from violating suspects' rights.[6] If police know that illegally obtained evidence will not be admitted, they will follow the correct procedures—thereby protecting the freedom and privacy of everyone, innocent and guilty alike. But these long-term consequences are not often visible, and the fact that the rule often lets the guilty go free is plain to every observer.

The limited empirical evidence we have suggests that the exclusionary rule is reasonably effective.[7] Since the Court applied it to the states in the 1961 case of *Mapp v. Ohio*,[8] police procedures have become more professional with no documented decline in the effectiveness of police work. But, again, these facts are not highly visible.

The same is true of the parallel exclusionary rule of *Miranda v. Arizona*.[9] Aiming to prevent coercive interrogation of suspects in violation of the Fifth Amendment, *Miranda* renders the confessions of suspects who have not been properly read their rights inadmissible for most purposes in court.

Again, the long-term consequences of *Miranda* are beneficial—suspects are now apprised of their rights—but not widely appreciated by the public, because they seem to benefit criminals. And the costs of *Miranda*, in sometimes letting the guilty go free, are both more visible and deeply felt.[10]

Film and television dramas, in particular, routinely portray the exclusionary rules of the Fourth and Fifth Amendments as posing serious costs to law enforcement. Fictional defense attorneys are constantly invoking these "technicalities" to free their dangerous clients.

Although these dramas take aim at defense attorneys and, in some instances, judges, their real target is the law itself. The dramas fault the law because, as a body of rules and principles, it sometimes aims to achieve a long-term goal—such as deterring illegal police activity—over justice in the immediate case.

The failure of justice in a particular episode is all too visible and easy fodder for dramatic treatment; the long-term institutional benefit, in contrast, is invisible and undramatic.

No wonder Americans think lawyers untruthful. In a real sense, whenever the law subordinates truth to some long-term institutional interest, it requires lawyers to dissemble.

Consider, for instance, the lawyer who tells a jury that his client should be acquitted because the government has failed to prove its case beyond a reasonable doubt—when he knows that excluded but reliable evidence would provide just such proof. That lawyer may not technically be lying, but only in the same sense that Bill Clinton may not technically have been lying when he denied having sex with Monica Lewinsky.

More generally, if one imagines the job of the lawyer as using the law's technicalities and ambiguities—its loopholes—to benefit a client, it is difficult to see how *any* compensation for lawyers would not be too much.

Perhaps, then, hostility to lawyers follows logically from hostility to the law's tendency to pursue social goals indirectly. Modern representative governments do not establish councils of elders to choose, on an ad hoc basis, what they consider to be a just resolution to whatever social conflicts may arise. Instead, we prescribe general rules and principles in advance of their application, knowing that this will sometimes mean that faithful adherence to such rules and principles leads to undesirable results.

We consider such occasional undesirable results an acceptable price to pay to avoid a system of government in which all-important decisions are committed to the unguided discretion of a few designated wise elders. But when the undesirable results are visible, and the long-term benefits obscure, public resentment and distrust can predictably result.

I suspect that most people, if pressed on the subject, would accept that it sometimes makes sense to choose law over justice. But that doesn't mean that people have to like it.

In sum, lawyers may serve as a lightning rod for the public's understandable hostility to law-as-the-occasional-enemy-of-justice. If so, then the real news in the Columbia Law survey may not be so bad for the legal profession.

If lawyers indeed are faulted for the perceived flaws in the law itself, then it is hardly surprising that more people thought lawyers dishonest than honest, or that many more people thought them overpaid than fairly compensated. The surprising news—and it is good news—is that so many Americans think, on balance, that lawyers play a beneficial role.

POSTSCRIPT

If the problem with disobeying a general rule or standard is that doing so will create the wrong sorts of incentives prospectively, then we have a genuine dilemma: If you pay the ransom, you encourage future kidnappings; if a judge admits illegally seized evidence, she encourages police to commit additional violations of constitutional rights against unreasonable searches and coercive interrogation.

But not every choice between ad hoc decision making and rule following must trade present and future goods against one another. Sometimes lawmakers deliberately choose clear bright-line rules that they know will be both over- and under-inclusive because they do not trust the people subject to, or charged with applying, the rules to make appropriate judgments on an ad hoc basis. In these circumstances following the rule makes good sense even if one thinks the rule could occasionally be skirted without adverse consequences.

Speed limits are the paradigmatic case. A law that said, "drive at a speed that is safe, all things considered," would be disastrous. Even though a very skilled driver might safely be able to drive 75 miles per hour on a clear day, giving each driver the discretion to decide how fast he can safely drive would lead to numerous accidents; many drivers would overestimate their driving skill and, without a fixed speed limit to keep all of the traffic moving at roughly the same speed, even those drivers who fairly evaluated their skills would have difficulty coordinating their speed with that of other drivers. So here a fixed rule makes eminent sense.

But sometimes a fixed rule is simply wrong, both in the particular case and prospectively. Lawmakers are not omniscient or clairvoyant, and thus they frequently write rules that lead to undesirable results when applied to unanticipated circumstances. The canonical example is an ordinance prohibiting "vehicles in the park." Is a bicycle a vehicle? How about a skateboard? If, as seems true under our standard linguistic conventions, an ambulance is a vehicle, can courts read an emergency vehicle exception into the ordinance? The endless debate in the jurisprudence literature over this set of examples focuses on the extent to which judges should read laws as written and if not, on whether and how to gauge legislative purpose.[11]

Yet there may be a way to circumvent much of that debate. Let us assume that everybody agrees that had the city council given the issue any thought at all, it would have written the ordinance so as to ban "vehicles except for emergency vehicles such as ambulances and fire engines." Now the only justification for keeping the ambulance out of the park pursuant to a literal reading of the ordinance that does not contain the exception would be a worry that if judges can fashion their own exception for the seemingly clear case of ambulances, they will fall down the slippery slope to making exceptions for not-so-clear cases, such as skateboards and bicycles, as well. The courts will end up interpreting the law in ways that are at odds with the actual goals of the elected representatives on the city council. Better, the textualist says, for the judge to read the law just as written, and leave any changes for the legislature to enact prospectively.

But there is a problem with the textualist's approach. It requires courts to interpret the law sub-optimally until the legislature (or city council in our example) acts—and for a host of reasons, legislatures are slow to act.

If we could somehow find a way for our laws to be subject to very frequent revision, then the problem would largely go away. A judge could confidently permit ambulances or even bicycles in the park if he thought that reading best served the public interest, knowing that the city council or some other democratically accountable body would step in to correct any errors. Thus, if our laws were easily changeable, then as we encountered new circumstances, we could have the best of both worlds: The people, through their elected representatives or otherwise, would make the laws, and those laws would be constantly subject to revision to improve their efficacy.

Consider a dramatic analogy drawn from the private sector. The Toyota Motor Company is one of the most successful manufacturers of automobiles in the world. Floor workers at Toyota car plants follow a highly detailed set of rules about all of their production processes. But, by contrast with the image of the assembly plant from the days of Henry Ford, these rules are not unchangeable mandates written by top managers or engineers. When a manufacturing problem arises, any worker on the factory floor has the discretion to pull a cord (called the "andon") that brings production to a halt and initiates deliberation about what went wrong. The product of such deliberation is often a change in the rules and procedures by which the cars are made. In this way, the Toyota manufacturing process combines the virtues of rules with the virtues of discretion.[12]

Can we have, in the phrase of my colleague William Simon, a "Toyota Jurisprudence"?[13] The answer, perhaps surprisingly, is yes. During the last decade,

I have been working with a group of law professors and social scientists on specifying mechanisms by which legal and other institutions can in fact learn from experience in order to engage in continual updating of their rules and procedures.[14] But the full idea will require another book to elaborate. Look for such a volume (tentatively titled "Learning to Govern") by yours truly, Archon Fung, Bradley Karkkainen, James Liebman, Dara O'Rourke, Charles Sabel, and William Simon, in a bookstore near you or online in the not-too-distant future.

NOTES

1. *See infra* appendix.
2. *See* Jonathan D. Glater, *High Tuition Debts and Low Pay Drain Public Interest Law*, N.Y. Times, Sept. 12, 2003, at A1.
3. Aristophanes, The Clouds (Alan H. Sommerstein ed. & trans., Warminster: Aris and Phillips, 1982).
4. A Civil Action (Touchstone Pictures 1999); *see also* Janet Maslin, *Lawyer Errs on the Side of Angels*, N.Y. Times, Dec. 25, 1998, at E1.
5. Erin Brockovich (Universal Pictures 2000); *see also* Michael Wilmington, *Roberts Rules: Julia Roberts and 'Erin Brockovich' Are a Perfect Fit*, Chi. Trib., Mar. 17, 2000, at A.
6. *See* Elkins v. United States, 364 U.S. 206, 217 (1960).
7. *E.g.*, Myron W. Orfield Jr., *The Exclusionary Rule and Deterrence: An Empirical Study of Chicago Narcotics Officers*, 54 U. Chi. L. Rev. 1016, 1017 (1987) ("This study—based on extensive, structured interviews with Chicago narcotics officers—documents the exclusionary rule's significant deterrent effects. On an institutional level, the rule has changed police, prosecutorial, and judicial procedures; on an individual level, it has educated police officers in the requirements of the fourth amendment and has punished them when they have violated those requirements."); *see also* Donald Dripps, *The Case for the Contingent Exclusionary Rule*, 38 Am. Crim. L. Rev. 1, 14–18 (2001) (reviewing the arguments and empirical support for an exclusionary rule and concluding that "these arguments lead to the conclusion that the rule has had a significant impact on police behavior, although the magnitude of that impact is open to reasonable disagreement.").
8. 367 U.S. 643 (1961).
9. 384 U.S. 436 (1966).
10. *See, e.g.*, Report of the U.S. Dep't of Justice, Office of Legal Policy, to the Attorney General, on the Law of Pre-trial Interrogation (1986) (advising that "the Department of Justice should seek to persuade the Supreme Court to abrogate or overrule the decision in *Miranda v. Arizona*" because, among other reasons, "*Miranda* is damaging to public confidence in the law." In cases where serious criminals are acquitted because of violations of their *Miranda* rights, the perception "by members of the public must be that the system has become deranged, treating their lives, their security and their deepest sensibilities as pawns in an inscrutable game"), *reprinted in* 22 U. Mich. J.L. Reform 437, 542, 545 (1989).

11. The "no vehicles in the park" example first appeared in a 1958 issue of the *Harvard Law Review* in a debate between H.L.A. Hart and Lon Fuller, and has since been a fixture in the literature on rules and standards. *See* H.L.A. Hart, *Positivism and the Separation of Law and Morals,* 71 Harv. L. Rev. 593, 607–08 (1958) (introducing the example); Lon L. Fuller, *Positivism and Fidelity to Law—A Reply to Professor Hart,* 71 Harv. L. Rev. 630, 663 (1958); *see also, e.g.*, William N. Eskridge, Jr. & Judith N. Levi, *Regulatory Variables and Statutory Interpretation*, 73 Wash. U. L.Q. 1103, 1103–11 (1995); Brian Leiter, *Beyond the Hart/Dworkin Debate: The Methodology Problem in Jurisprudence*, 48 Am. J. Juris. 17, 21 (2003); Frederick Schauer, *Exceptions*, 58 U. Chi. L. Rev. 871, 893 (1991); Cass R. Sunstein, *Problems with Rules*, 83 Cal. L. Rev. 953, 991 (1995). The example appears to be based in part on the case of *McBoyle v. United States*, which held that an airplane was not a "motor vehicle" within the definition of a federal statute that prohibited the transporting of stolen vehicles in interstate or foreign commerce. 283 U.S. 25 (1931) (interpreting the National Motor Vehicle Theft Act, ch. 89, 41 Stat. 324 (1919)).

12. *See* Paul Adler, *Flexibility versus Efficiency: A Case Study of Model Changeovers in the Toyota Production System*, 10 Org. Sci. 43, 54 (1999); John Paul MacDuffie, *The Road to Root Cause: Problem-Solving at Three Auto-Assembly Plants*, 43 Mgmt. Sci. 479, 95 (1997).

13. *See* William H. Simon, *Toyota Jurisprudence: Legal Theory and Rolling Rule Regimes* (Columbia Law Sch. Pub. Law & Legal Theory Working Paper Group, Paper No. 04–79, 2004), *available at* http://papers.ssrn.com/sol3/papers.cfm?abstract_id=602626; *see also* William H. Simon, *Solving Problems vs. Claiming Rights: The Pragmatist Challenge to Legal Liberalism*, 46 Wm. & Mary L. Rev. 127, 191–92 (2004).

14. *See, e.g.*, Michael C. Dorf, *After Bureaucracy*, 71 U. Chi. L. Rev. 1245 (2004); Michael C. Dorf & Charles F. Sabel, *Drug Treatment Courts and Emergent Experimentalist Government*, 53 Vand. L. Rev. 831 (2000); Michael C. Dorf & Charles F. Sabel, *A Constitution of Democratic Experimentalism*, 98 Colum. L. Rev. 267 (1998).

• 36 •

Americans' Faith in the Supreme Court—and in the Constitution: Survey Shows *Bush v. Gore*'s Effect Was Limited

May 2002

In the immediate aftermath of the United States Supreme Court's ruling ending the contested presidential election of 2000,[1] commentators complained that the Court had squandered its hard-earned capital as a non-partisan referee by making what appeared to many to be a political decision.[2]

The criticism was not confined to talking heads or legal experts. Even one of the Justices, John Paul Stevens, wrote in dissent that as a result of the majority's decision, the clear loser of the election was "the Nation's confidence in the judge as an impartial guardian of the rule of law."[3]

Yet it now appears that, whatever the short-term effects of *Bush v. Gore* were, the decision has not done the lasting damage that we commentators and Justice Stevens feared. On the contrary, the same survey I discussed in the last chapter finds Americans still overwhelmingly satisfied with the Supreme Court exercising the extraordinary power that it does.

That result may be surprising coming less than a year and a half after *Bush v. Gore*. But it should not be surprising given the quasi-religious status that Americans have long accorded to the Constitution. Americans' confidence in the Supreme Court, moreover, stands as a challenge to those who criticize the Court from both the right and, increasingly, the left.

In the previous chapter, I described a Columbia Law School survey that asked a representative sample of a thousand Americans how they viewed the legal profession. The final question of the survey asked about the Supreme Court. Respondents were asked whether they agreed or disagreed with the following statement: "Even though I sometimes disagree with or dislike the rulings of the United States Supreme Court in particular cases, the fact that the Supreme Court can strike down unconstitutional laws is a good feature of the American system of government."

By setting aside the Court's rulings in particular cases, the survey question asked Americans to think about what lawyers call the power of "judicial review" over the long run.

The survey revealed that Americans are quite happy with the Court's role in our constitutional system. A full 83 percent of Americans agreed with the statement, with only 13 percent expressing disagreement. (The remainder had no opinion.) Support for judicial review was strong in every demographic group.

Support was weakest among African Americans. That is understandable in light of the Court's constitutional as well as statutory jurisprudence on civil rights issues over the last generation,[4] and the fact that African Americans, as the most loyal Democratic constituents, may have been the group that felt most aggrieved by the Court's performance in the 2000 presidential election. Yet even among this group, general support for judicial review was strong, with 74 percent agreeing with the statement.

For much of American history, politicians have campaigned against the Supreme Court. Abraham Lincoln denounced the Court's 1856 pro-slavery decision in *Dred Scott v. Sandford.*[5] Franklin Roosevelt wanted to pack the Court with New Dealers who would uphold his legislative program.[6] Southern Senators denounced the Court's 1954 decision in *Brown v. Board of Education*[7] invalidating mandatory racial segregation in public schools.[8]

Continuing the pattern, Richard Nixon took aim at Justices who he thought were soft on crime.[9] Then Ronald Reagan[10] and both Presidents Bush[11] echoed new Right criticisms of the Court's recognition of a constitutional right to abortion in *Roe v. Wade.*[12] And recently, Democratic Senators have decried the current Supreme Court's repeated invalidation of Acts of Congress in the service of states' rights.[13]

Politicians' attacks on the Court have typically been motivated by what the Columbia Law survey question calls results in "particular cases." Yet their rhetoric has often gone much further. When politicians say that judges should "interpret the law rather than make the law," or that judges should not engage in "judicial legislation,"[14] the politicians call into question the very practice of judicial review.

The Constitution, after all, is a magisterially vague document. It prohibits "unreasonable searches and seizures." It forbids denials of "the equal protection of the laws." It speaks of "powers . . . reserved to the States." None of these or the many other open-ended provisions of the Constitution is self-defining.

Therefore, except in cases of extraordinarily clear and blatant violations of the Constitution, whenever the Supreme Court decides that a challenged government action violates the Constitution, it makes a somewhat controversial judgment. And precisely because it is controversial, that judgment, from the perspective of those who disagree, can be always characterized as judicial legislation.

Indeed, it is for just this reason that constitutional scholars have long wrestled with their own version of the politicians' complaint, what Yale Law School professor Alexander Bickel called "the counter-majoritarian difficulty."[15] This is simply a fancy term for the fact that judicial review substitutes the views of unelected judges for the views of elected legislatures, and thus often for the views of a majority of Americans. That fact is troubling in a democracy, in which political issues are generally resolved by majority rule.

The Supreme Court and its defenders have at least two answers to the counter-majoritarian difficulty. First, they justify judicial review on the ground that the Constitution's language and structure assume the practice, even though the Constitution nowhere expressly mentions judicial review. In providing for a federal judiciary with the power to decide cases "arising under this Constitution," the argument goes, the Constitution implicitly also provided for judicial review—for that is the very business of the courts.[16]

Second, judicial review can be defended by challenging the premise that our system of government always favors majority rule. The very point of a constitution, according to this argument, is to protect the rights of the minority against the tyranny of the majority. Justice Brennan stated the point well in his dissent from a 1987 decision that held the Georgia death penalty was not administered in a racially discriminatory manner. As Brennan wrote: "It is the particular role of courts to hear" the faint voices of those in the minority, "for the Constitution declares that the majoritarian chorus may not alone dictate the conditions of social life."[17]

To these answers to the counter-majoritarian difficulty, the Columbia Law survey suggests that we may now add a third: At the most fundamental level, judicial review is not counter-majoritarian because an overwhelming majority of the people endorse the practice of judicial review.

In other words, even though judicial decisions "in particular cases" sometimes substitute the Justices' views for those of national, state, or local majorities, these particular decisions are taken in the name of the people as a whole, in the sense that the people prefer having the Court decide constitutional matters than leaving such issues entirely to elected representatives.

Put another way, just as democracy is no less democratic because it is representative and not direct, democracy is no less democratic because some of the officeholders the people have approved are judges and not legislators.

Why would the people want to refer constitutional questions to the unelected Supreme Court, rather than to their own elected representatives? One possibility is that, like Justice Brennan, Americans generally value minority rights as much as majoritarian decision making.

However, I would suggest that this is only a partial explanation. In addition, Americans have long been in the thrall of what may justly be called a cult of the Constitution. For example, for most of the pre–Civil War period, it was a commonplace that the new American republic owed its prosperity to the wisdom of the founding fathers. The Philadelphia Convention of 1787 was often described as divinely inspired.[18]

Even when the original Constitution's chief flaw—its compromises over slavery—was tearing the country apart in the decades leading up to the Civil War, no less an abolitionist than Frederick Douglass could insist that the *true* Constitution supported his cause.[19] Reverence for the Constitution, even as particular decisions come in for criticism, remains a staple of our public culture today.

One might think that people could revere the Constitution while despising the Supreme Court, and indeed, that attitude too has been a standard leitmotif in American history. But it is very much an undercurrent. To a much greater degree, the main current has been one of *equating* the Constitution with the Supreme Court.

The Court itself bears substantial responsibility for this association. Consider, for example, the 1958 decision in *Cooper v. Aaron*[20]—the only opinion ever signed by all nine Justices. There, the Court affirmed what it called "the basic principle that the federal judiciary is supreme in the exposition of the law of the Constitution."[21] It also added that since the early nineteenth century, this principle has "been respected by this Court and the country as a permanent and indispensable feature of our constitutional system."[22]

The actual result in the *Cooper* case was clearly right. Arkansas Governor Orval Faubus had resisted the desegregation of public schools, and the Court told him in no uncertain terms that willful disobedience of a judicial order would not be tolerated. However, recent cases have relied on *Cooper*'s "basic principle" not only to put down outright defiance but to deny Congress *any role* in interpreting the Constitution. Using *Cooper*'s precedent that way takes the Court's rhetoric out of context.

Since 1997, the Court has extended *Cooper*'s reasoning in decisions striking down provisions of the Religious Freedom Restoration Act,[23] the Age Discrimination in Employment Act,[24] the Violence Against Women Act,[25] and the Americans with Disabilities Act.[26] In these rulings the Court has asserted a doctrine of judicial exclusivity—under which the judiciary, and never the legislature, says what the Constitution means—rather than a doctrine of judicial supremacy—under which the Court invalidates political actors' decisions denying minority rights but grants some deference to the legislature when the latter seeks to expand rather than to contract constitutional rights.

As noted above, Democratic Senators have begun to question the Court's efforts to freeze Congress out of constitutional interpretation entirely in decisions like these. Whether these Senators succeed will depend in substantial measure on just why it is that Americans trust the Supreme Court.

To the extent that trust in the Court is based on the view that the Court will protect minority rights, the public may eventually grow tired of the Court's invalidation of civil rights laws. After all, a broad cross-section of Americans was adversely affected by this series of decisions: religious believers, older Americans, women, and the disabled.

On the other hand, to the extent that the Justices have successfully fostered the view that they alone speak for the Constitution, the Democratic Senators' complaints will likely fall on deaf ears. If the public respects the Court not just as the ultimate expositor of the Constitution, but as its sole expositor, the current Court's judicial exclusivity doctrine will likely prevail.

POSTSCRIPT

Americans who claim to support judicial review despite disagreeing with particular Supreme Court decisions may see the Court as a kind of hedge against political outcomes they regard as undesirable in just the way that, according to public opinion polls, Americans like divided government.[27] By striking down legislation it deems unconstitutional, the Court acts as a check on the ability of any one party to dominate the agenda of government. Judicial review is simply another of the checks and balances that Americans associate with the Constitution they so revere.

But if this account is right, we are left with a puzzle: Why do politicians ever phrase their arguments as attacks on the popular institution of judicial review by decrying "judicial activism" as such, rather than strictly limiting their criticism to particular unpopular decisions? Wouldn't they be more effective in rallying support for their causes by paying respect, even if only lip service, to judicial independence and the dignity of the courts, while decrying what they deem specific abuses of judicial power?

The answer, I suspect, is that politicians who attack the courts are not really interested in mass public opinion. Most of the public pay scant attention to the courts. They vote on the economy, national security, education, and other issues on which they see government making concrete differences in their lives. Those who have strong views on social issues like abortion, gay rights, or school prayer often do care about the courts, but what they care about is how the people who end up being judges will resolve questions concerning the particular social issues that concern them. It is probably too much to expect that—excepting readers of this book!—most people who are busy with work and family would take the time to ponder, and then vote based upon, abstract institutional questions like the proper functioning of judicial review in our democracy.

A chilling confirmation of my hypothesis was on display in April 2005 at a Washington meeting of political conservatives dubbed "Remedies to Judicial Tyranny." Justice Anthony Kennedy came under attack for authoring the Court's 2003 decision invalidating the Texas sodomy law and the Court's 2005 decision invalidating the juvenile death penalty.[28] After stalwarts such as Phyllis Schlafly called for Kennedy's impeachment, one Edwin Vieira opined that Kennedy "upholds Marxist, Leninist, satanic principles drawn from foreign law." Accordingly, Vieira claimed, Stalin's maxim, "No Man, no problem" should apply. As the *Washington Post* story from which these facts are drawn observed, Stalin's full quotation reads: "Death solves all problems: No man, no problem."[29]

Even if Vieira was calling only for Kennedy's impeachment rather than his assassination, and apart from the irony of a Red-baiter approvingly quoting Stalin, the general public can only be put off by this sort of hyperbole. But of course Schlafly, Vieira, and the politicians who express similar sentiments are not interested in reaching the general public. This sort of "red meat" aims to energize political activists, the sorts of people who despise the idea of divided government. As the Columbia survey shows, the average Americans paying scant attention to politics hold more moderate, and I might add, more sensible, views.

NOTES

1. Bush v. Gore, 531 U.S. 98 (2000) (per curiam).
2. *E.g.*, Alan M. Dershowtiz, Supreme Injustice: How the High Court Hijacked Election 2000 3 (New York: Oxford University Press, 2001) ("[T]he unprecedented decision of the five justices to substitute their political judgment for that of the people threatens to undermine the moral authority of the high court for generations to come."); Bruce Ackerman, *The Court Packs Itself*, Am. Prospect, Feb. 12, 2001, at 48.
3. 531 U.S. at 128–29 (Stevens, J., dissenting).
4. *See, e.g.*, Alexander v. Sandoval, 532 U.S. 275 (2001) (finding no private right of action to enforce regulations barring actions of recipients of federal funds that have a disparate racial impact); City of Richmond v. J.A. Croson Co., 488 U.S. 469 (1989) (discussed *supra* chapter 17); McCleskey v. Kemp, 481 U.S. 279 (1987) (upholding the death penalty despite statistical evidence that suggested that its application depends on race); *see also* Mark Tushnet, Taking the Constitution Away from the Courts 173 (Princeton, N.J.: Princeton University Press, 1999) ("[I]n 1999 . . . maintaining judicial review harms African-Americans.").
5. *E.g.*, Abraham Lincoln, The Dred Scott Decision: Speech at Springfield, Illinois (June 26, 1857) (discussing *Scott v. Sandford*, 60 U.S. 393 (1856)), *in* Abraham Lincoln: His Speeches and Writings 352, 355–59 (Roy P. Basler ed., Cleveland and New York: The World Publishing Company, 1946).
6. *See generally* Robert H. Jackson, The Struggle for Judicial Supremacy (New York: Octagon Books, 1941).

7. 347 U.S. 483 (1954).

8. *See* Robert Young, *Pupil Segregation Banned*, Chi. Trib., May 18, 1954, at 1 (reporting the reactions of Senator Eastland: "[T]he south will not abide by nor obey this legislative decision by a political court . . . integrated schools are not desired by either race in the south," and Senator Russell, who characterized the ruling as "a flagrant abuse of judicial power").

9. *See* Peter Arenella, *Rethinking the Functions of Criminal Procedure: The Warren and Burger Courts' Competing Ideologies*, 72 Geo. L.J. 185, 192 (1983).

10. *E.g.*, Proclamation No. 5761, 53 Fed. Reg. 1464 (Jan. 19, 1988) (signed on January 14, 1988) (suggesting on National Sanctity of Human Life Day that *Roe* is inconsistent with the Declaration of Independence's recognition of an inalienable right to life).

11. Remarks to Participants in the March for Life Rally, 25 Weekly Comp. Pres. Doc. 110 (Jan. 23, 1989) ("I think the Supreme Court's decision in Roe versus Wade was wrong and should be overturned."); Telephone Remarks to the March for Life, 41 Weekly Comp. Pres. Doc. 82 (Jan. 24, 2005) ("The America of our dreams, where every child is welcomed in law—in life and protected in law may still be some ways away, but even from the far side of the river . . . we can see its glimmerings. We're making progress in Washington. I've been working with Members of the Congress to pass good, solid legislation that protects the vulnerable and promotes the culture of life.").

12. 410 U.S. 113 (1973).

13. *See, e.g.,* Editorial, *Federalism and Guns in School*, Wash. Post, Apr. 28, 1995, at A26 (quoting Senator Herb Kohl describing the Court's decision in *United States v. Lopez*, 514 U.S. 549 (1995), as "a piece of judicial activism that ignores children's safety for the sake of legal nit-picking"); Linda Greenhouse, *The Supreme Court: The Court on Federalism; Women Lose Right to Sue Attackers in Federal Court*, N.Y. Times, May 16, 2000, at A1 (quoting Senator Joseph R. Biden Jr.'s reaction to the Supreme Court's decision in *United States v. Morrison*, 529 U.S. 598 (2000): "The damage done to the act is not as bad as the damage done to American jurisprudence.").

14. *E.g.*, Remarks at a Fundraiser for Senatorial Candidate John Cornyn in Dallas, Texas, 38 Weekly Comp. Pres. Doc. 533 (Mar. 28, 2002) ("[W]e've got to get good, conservative judges appointed to the bench and approved by the United States Senate. I want people on the bench who don't try to use their position to legislate from the bench. We want people to interpret the law, not try to make law and write law.").

15. Alexander Bickel, The Least Dangerous Branch: The Supreme Court at the Bar of Politics 16 (Indianapolis: Bobbs-Merrill, 1962).

16. *See* Marbury v. Madison, 5 U.S. (1 Cranch) 137, 178–79 (1803).

17. McCleskey v. Kemp, 481 U.S. 279, 343 (1987) (Brennan, J., dissenting).

18. *See* Michael Kammen, A Machine That Would Go of Itself 3 (New York: Knopf, 1986) (reporting that "[s]choolbooks of that era [the 1840s] often stated that the Constitution had been divinely inspired. Their authors could not refer to the Constitution without a choral vocabulary of 'revered,' 'glorious,' and 'sacred'").

19. *See* J.M. Balkin, *Fidelity in Constitutional Theory: Does the Constitution Deserve Our Fidelity: Agreements with Hell and Other Objects of Our Faith*, 65 Fordham L. Rev. 1703, 1709–10 (1997).

20. 358 U.S. 1 (1958).

21. *Id.* at 18.

22. *Id.*

23. Religious Freedom Restoration Act of 1993, Pub. L. No. 103–141, 107 Stat. 1488. The Court struck down the act in *City of Boerne v. Flores*, 521 U.S. 507 (1997).

24. Age Discrimination in Employment Act of 1967, Pub. L. No. 90–202, 81 Stat. 602 (codified as amended at 29 U.S.C. §§ 621–634 (1997)). The Court struck down provisions of the act in *Kimel v. Fla. Bd. of Regents*, 528 U.S. 62 (2000).

25. Violence Against Women Act of 1994, Pub. L. No. 103–322, Title IV, 108 Stat. 1902, 1902–55. The Court struck down provisions of the act in *United States v. Morrison*, 529 U.S. 598 (2000).

26. Americans with Disabilities Act of 1990, Pub. L. No. 101–336, 104 Stat. 327. The Court struck down provisions of the act in *Bd. of Trs. of the Univ. of Ala. v. Garrett*, 531 U.S. 356 (2001).

27. *See* Bruce Bartlett, Op-Ed., *Longing for Good Old Gridlock*, N.Y. Sun, Nov. 26, 2003, at 8 ("In the latest survey by Hart/Teeter for the Wall Street Journal and NBC News, 62 percent of Americans said they preferred Congress and the presidency to be controlled by different parties. Only 29 percent said that it would be better if one party controlled both."); John F. Harris, *In '04, GOP Is a Target Missed; Democrats Seldom Aim at Accountability Issue, Strategists in Both Parties Say*, Wash. Post, Oct. 31, 2004, at A17 ("When asked in surveys, said Democratic pollster Mark Penn, a majority of voters say they prefer a divided government as the best way to ensure centrist policies."); Patrick O'Connor, *Bush May Have Shorter Coattails*, Hill, Aug. 30, 2004, at 33 ("In a national survey conducted by American Research Group in March, 44 percent of the 770 respondents said they preferred a split government, with the president from one party and the congressional majority from another, while 38 percent said they wanted the president and congressional majority to be from the same party.").

28. Roper v. Simmons, 125 S. Ct. 1183 (2005) (invalidating the juvenile death penalty); Lawrence v. Texas, 539 U.S. 558 (2003) (invalidating Tex. Penal Code Ann. § 21.06(a) (2003)).

29. *See* Dana Milbank, *And the Verdict on Justice Kennedy Is: Guilty*, Wash. Post, Apr. 9, 2005, at A3; *see also* Jason DeParle, *In Battle to Pick Next Justice, Right Says Avoid a Kennedy*, N.Y. Times, June 27, 2005, at A1.

• 37 •

Whose Constitution Is It Anyway? What Americans Don't Know about the Constitution—and Why It Matters

May 2002

"From each according to his ability, to each according to his needs"—one of Karl Marx's most famous maxims—describes what Marx believed to be the proper means for distributing resources in a communist society.[1] With the fall of communism in eastern and central Europe, and the increasingly market-oriented policies of nominally communist countries like Vietnam and China, one might have thought Marx's adage a quaint relic.

Astoundingly, however, a recent survey of a representative sample of over a thousand Americans conducted by Columbia Law School shows that Marx's slogan is alive and well—right here in the United States.[2] The survey found that 69 percent of respondents either thought that the United States Constitution contained Marx's maxim, or did not know whether or not it did.

The survey result cannot be dismissed as anomalous, for it parallels the outcome of a survey conducted by the Hearst Corporation in 1987.[3]

These results, taken together, are troubling for a constitutional democracy in which popular consent underwrites the government's legitimacy. How can Americans be said to tacitly ratify the Constitution over time when so many of them have a deeply erroneous idea of what it contains?

The Columbia Law Survey asked Americans five yes-no questions designed to test their knowledge about the American Constitution. For each question, respondents were also given the option of answering "don't know." In response to the question whether the Constitution contains the Marxist maxim, 35 percent said yes, 31 percent said no, and 34 percent said they did not know the answer.

That pattern indicates that the number of people who actually *knew* the right answer is substantially less than 31 percent. After all, more than half of the people who believed they knew the right answer—the 35 percent who erroneously answered yes—were wrong.

We can infer that some substantial fraction of the people who did not answer "don't know" were actually guessing. It is therefore safe to assume that some portion of the people who correctly answered "no" were also guessing, but they happened to guess right. In short, the fraction of survey respondents who really knew the right answer, and weren't just lucky guessers, is probably less than a quarter.

The survey respondents did better in answering three other questions. When read the first sentence of the Fourteenth Amendment, an impressive 83 percent stated that it is part of the Constitution. Moreover, 64 percent of respondents correctly answered the question of whether Supreme Court Justices serve for renewable twelve-year terms. (They do not; they serve for life.)

And 60 percent correctly disagreed with the statement that "In time of war or other declared national emergency, the President may suspend the Constitution's Bill of Rights." (Only the privilege of the writ of habeas corpus, not the entire Bill of Rights, may be suspended, and notwithstanding some bold assertions of presidential power by Abraham Lincoln, only by congressional action, not by the President acting alone.[4])

Even if some of the people who answered this question correctly were only guessing, the fact that they guessed that the Constitution does not grant completely unchecked, sweeping power in times of crisis demonstrates important support for the rule of law.

Nonetheless, the Columbia Law Survey revealed substantial ignorance about fundamental issues. In addition to confusion about whether the Constitution contains a Marxist manifesto, Americans showed little understanding of how constitutional adjudication works. Respondents were read the following statement and asked whether it is true or false: "If the Supreme Court were to overrule *Roe vs. Wade*, abortion would be illegal throughout the United States." Fewer than one-third correctly answered "false."

Roe v. Wade established that there is a constitutional right to abortion. If the case were overruled, abortion *could be made illegal* in those states that wished to prohibit it—but it would remain legal in other, more liberal states. To be sure, perhaps following a decision overturning *Roe*, abortion *could* be made illegal throughout the United States by an Act of Congress pursuant to its power to regulate interstate commerce; abortion is a medical procedure that would likely be deemed the sort of economic activity that the Court's precedents permit Congress to regulate; and under the Constitution's Supremacy Clause, such a federal prohibition would trump any state laws permitting abortion. But the passage of such a federal statute would not follow *automatically* from *Roe*'s demise. As a legal matter, overruling *Roe* would simply mean that the Constitution does not prohibit a category of laws—anti-abortion laws. It would not mean that the Constitution would require that such laws be passed.

The distinction between what is constitutionally permitted and what is constitutionally required might be considered a rather technical point. However, it is at the very heart of the constitutional debate about abortion, and that debate is hardly an obscure one.

Indeed, to judge by the rhetoric of political campaigns, one might think that abortion is the only issue for which our courts have responsibility. Pro-choice and pro-life politicians alike hammer away at the significance of judicial appointments for the abortion issue. And yet it turns out that two-thirds of Americans do not fully understand what is at stake.

In lamenting public ignorance of our constitutional system, I do not mean to play the scold. People are busy with work and family obligations, and given the complexity of the world, it is impossible for even the most conscientious citizen to be fully informed about everything that affects his or her life. After all, who among us would not provide erroneous answers to some pretty basic questions about science, history, or economics, to name just a few subjects about which the Columbia Law survey did not ask?

Yet even as ignorance about the Constitution may be completely understandable, it remains cause for concern. To see why, it may help to go back to basics.

The fundamental challenge of government is one of balance. On the one hand, the state needs sufficient tools to meet the great challenges that can only be solved by collective action: national defense, combating private violence, safeguarding public resources, and so forth. On the other hand, a government that is powerful enough to do its job properly can itself become a threat to the very people it is meant to protect. Constitutions attempt to resolve this tension by both empowering and constraining government.

How so? As James Madison wrote in the *Federalist Papers*, "A dependence on the people is, no doubt, the primary control on the government; but experience has taught mankind the necessity of auxiliary precautions."[5] In other words, the first and most important check on abuses is regular elections. However, Madison knew that even democratically elected officials can become despotic without the sort of "auxiliary precautions" one finds in a constitution that limits government.

These are not mere abstract propositions. They are as pressing today as they were when Madison set them down in the eighteenth century. What is the proper role for government in combating terrorism and protecting the natural environment? To what extent should the government be limited in pursuing these aims by, respectively, rights of privacy and property? In our system of government, such questions raise urgent political as well as constitutional issues.

It is tempting to think that responsibility for resolving such questions can be neatly divided between elected officials—who answer their "political" aspects—and the courts—which address matters of constitutional interpretation.

Tempting, perhaps, but mistaken. Although the framers of our Constitution anticipated that the courts would invalidate unconstitutional laws, they also expected that "primary" responsibility for setting constitutional limits would belong to elected representatives and thus, ultimately, to the people.

As I explained in the last chapter, Justices of the Supreme Court sometimes speak as though they alone are responsible for interpreting the Constitution. But in truth the public plays a substantial role. For one thing, there are some constitutional issues—what lawyers call "non-justiciable" questions—that courts simply do not touch. A prominent example in the late 1990s was whether the offenses for which President Clinton was impeached constituted "high crimes and misdemeanors." That was a constitutional issue to which Congress was the sole authority.[6]

Most constitutional questions are capable of resolution by courts. Yet that does not mean that the public plays no role in deciding such questions.

For one thing, numerous constitutional tests expressly incorporate public understandings. Is a search "unreasonable" within the meaning of the Fourth Amendment? Do sexual materials offend "community standards," so that they may be banned despite the First Amendment?[7] Does a given form of punishment violate society's "evolving standards of decency," so that it violates the Eighth Amendment?[8] These are all constitutional questions that can only be answered with reference to public views.

In addition, public attitudes shape constitutional law through the judicial appointments process. Political battles in the Senate over Supreme Court and other judicial nominations can take the form of referenda on methods of constitutional interpretation.

Moreover, in cases of contested nominees, Senators pay close attention to the views of their constituents. For this and other reasons, it would therefore seem essential that those constituents have some fairly clear sense of what the Constitution contains.

At the conclusion of the Constitutional Convention in 1787, Benjamin Franklin was reportedly asked what form of government had emerged, to which he replied, "A republic, if you can keep it."[9] More than two centuries later, though we face serious national security and other dangers, we are unlikely to lose our republican form of government.

But that is no reason to take what the Constitution calls "the blessings of liberty" for granted. Thus, the results of the Columbia Law survey should be a call to action to those of us—including journalists, politicians, and especially teachers—responsible for informing the public about the law.

The late Chief Justice Warren Burger understood this last point very well. When he oversaw the bicentennial celebration of the Constitution in the late 1980s, Burger distributed copies of the Constitution to schoolchildren throughout the nation. Now that those children have grown up, they appear to have misplaced their Constitutions. So, to make my own small contribution to public knowledge about the American Constitution, I'll let you know how you can get your own free copy of the Constitution. Just log onto the Internet and point your browser to findlaw.com/casecode/constitution.

POSTSCRIPT

Critics of judicial review sometimes argue that the courts' willingness to invalidate laws they deem unconstitutional discourages politicians from paying attention to constitutional questions. An opponent of a proposed bill who charges that it would violate some constitutional guarantee can be met with the rejoinder that if so, the courts will strike it down. The politicians' job, in this view, is to enact legislation deemed useful, with questions of constitutionality left to the courts.[10] And, the argument could easily be extended, when politicians do not focus attention on constitutional issues, the public follows suit. Could judicial review itself be responsible for Americans' ignorance of what the Constitution says and how it works?

These are complex and ultimately empirical questions for which more research is required. One way to test whether judicial review encourages constitutional apathy on the part of legislators would be to compare legislative debates in the United States with those in constitutional democracies that lack judicial review, such as the Netherlands. There are, however, at least two difficulties with any direct comparison between systems that have, and systems that lack, judicial review.

First, there are vanishingly few constitutional democracies that do not practice something like judicial review. The Netherlands and Great Britain formally avow the doctrine of parliamentary supremacy, but the laws of both countries are subject to judicial review by the European Court of Justice and the European Court of Human Rights. Even Israel, which lacks a constitution that was adopted by super-majority, has judicial review under its so-called basic laws, which the Supreme Court of Israel has used to invalidate acts of the Knesset.[11]

Second, any comparison of systems with and without judicial review would have to distinguish between real and disingenuous arguments about constitutionality. A politician who opposes some proposed law on policy grounds would not hesitate to offer constitutional grounds to oppose the law as well. Thus, the burden for the critics is to show more than a handful of instances in which, in a system without judicial review, a politician favors some proposed law on policy grounds but nonetheless votes against it because he thinks that the law is unconstitutional. No doubt this sort of thing happens where the constitutional issue is extraordinarily clear-cut, but of course, the debate about judicial review is about cases in which the relevant provisions are ambiguous.

Furthermore, the impeachment of President Clinton provides a reason to think that the critics are mostly wrong. As noted above, there is no judicial review of impeachment decisions. Accordingly, the House and Senate were acting in this matter as though they were a legislature in a constitutional system without judicial review. Perhaps true to the critics' observation, members of both bodies repeatedly invoked constitutional arguments both for and against the proposition that Clinton's misdeeds constituted impeachable offenses. On the whole, the arguments were thoughtful and sophisticated. But they were largely disingenuous. In the House, 224 out of 228 Republicans voted for at least one article of impeachment, while 200 out of 205 Democrats voted against all of them. In the Senate, 50 out of 55 Republicans voted to convict Clinton on one or more charges, while every Democrat voted to acquit him entirely.[12] These stark figures strongly suggest that the constitutional arguments were mostly self-serving.

So the critics may be right that politicians do not take constitutional arguments seriously, but that fact does not appear to be a consequence of judicial review. And if one thinks that the Constitution ought to be taken seriously, then its shabby treatment by politicians seems like a reason to favor, rather than oppose, judicial review. True, as the legal realists argue, the constitutional analysis of judges can sometimes serve as a mere cover for political bias—as some argue occurred in *Bush v. Gore*.[13] But on the whole, the voting pattern of the courts on constitutional questions is not nearly so clearly partisan as the congressional pattern in the Clinton impeachment was.

NOTES

1. Karl Marx, *Critique of the Gotha Programme, in* Justice 159, 162 (Alan Ryan ed., New York and Oxford: Oxford University Press, 1993).
2. *See infra* Appendix.
3. *See* Ruth Marcus, *Constitution Confuses Most Americans; Public Ill-Informed On U.S. Blueprint*, Wash. Post, Feb. 15, 1987, at A13.
4. U.S. Const. art. I, § 9, cl. 2 ("The Privilege of the Writ of Habeas Corpus shall not be suspended, unless when in Cases of Rebellion or Invasion the public Safety may

require it."); *see also Ex parte* Merryman, 17 F. Cas. 144, 149 (C.C.D. Md. 1861) ("I can see no ground whatever for supposing that the president, in any emergency, or in any state of things, can authorize the suspension of the privileges of the writ of habeas corpus, or the arrest of a citizen, except in aid of the judicial power. He certainly does not faithfully execute the laws, if he takes upon himself legislative power, by suspending the writ of habeas corpus, and the judicial power also, by arresting and imprisoning a person without due process of law.").

5. The Federalist No. 51 (James Madison).

6. *See* U.S. Const. art I., §§ 2–3; *Cf.* Nixon v. United States, 506 U.S. 224 (1993).

7. *See* Miller v. California, 413 U.S. 15, 24 (1973).

8. *See* Trop v. Dulles, 356 U.S. 86, 101 (1958) (plurality opinion).

9. Fred Barbash, The Founding: A Dramatic Account of the Writing of the Constitution 207 (New York: Linden Press/Simon & Schuster, 1987).

10. Mary Ann Glendon, A Nation Under Lawyers: How the Crisis in the Legal Profession is Transforming American Society 168 (New York: Farrar, Straus, and Giraux, 1994) ("Elected officials have offered little resistance to judicial inroads on their powers. On hot issues, they are often . . . only too happy to be taken off the hook by the courts."); Mark Tushnet, Taking the Constitution Away from the Courts 55, 57–58, 173 (Princeton, N.J.: Princeton University Press, 1999) ("Judicial review may serve politicians' interests, not their constituents.' Political leaders often find judicial review a convenient way to hand off hard decisions to someone else.").

11. C.A. 6821/93, United Mizrahi Bank Ltd. v. Migdal Coop. Vill. 49(4) P.D. 221.

12. *See* Chart, *The Votes for Impeachment*, N.Y. Times, Dec. 21, 1998, at A25; Richard L. Berke, *Impeachment: The Motivations; Democrats Stand by Clinton, but It Isn't Personal*, N.Y. Times, Dec. 21, 1998, at A22; Graphic, *The End of Impeachment; How They Voted*, Atlanta J. & Const., Feb. 13, 1999, at 12A; Alison Mitchell, *The President's Acquittal: The Overview; Clinton Acquitted Decisively: No Majority for Either Charge*, N.Y. Times, Feb. 13, 1999, at A1.

13. 531 U.S. 98 (2000) (per curiam). *See supra* chapter 2.

• 38 •

Unsolicited Advice to Law School Applicants: With Prospects Newly Limited, Be Sure You Want to Become a Lawyer

November 2002

As I write, the short-term picture for law school graduates has rarely been grimmer. Firms that lavished meals and Broadway show tickets on their numerous summer recruits just a few years ago have recently laid off quite a few of those same recruits—now associates. Meanwhile, they have drastically cut back on the number of new associates hired.[1] Graduates of elite schools have far fewer options than in the recent past, while graduates of other schools must struggle to find any gainful employment. Yet law schools around the country continue to set records for the number of applicants.[2]

These two phenomena seem contradictory. Why would people apply to law schools in record numbers at precisely the moment when law jobs have become scarce? Can thousands of law school applicants be wrong?

In a word, yes. Applicants should think carefully before they follow the current stampede.

To be sure, the rise in applications is no great mystery. In the immortal words of our forty-second President, it's the economy, stupid. Simply by writing "web designer" on his or her resume, a college graduate of the class of 1998 could expect a large salary, stock options, and the ability to come to work wearing Birkenstocks and carpenter pants. The only people applying to law school then were the risk-averse and those with a genuine interest in the subject.

With their other opportunities dramatically curtailed, more recent college graduates reason: "I'll go to law school for three years, increase my marketability, and by the time I get out, the economy will be booming again. Best of all, because there are no prerequisites for law school, my major in accounting, which I had hoped to parlay into a job with Arthur Andersen, won't be a problem."

There is a certain logic to this approach. It's fortified by the often-heard claim that you can do anything you want with a law degree. Here's one version of that claim, which I found on the website of an elite law school touting its program in international law: "A . . . degree [from us] has the prestige that allows you to do anything you want, anywhere in the world."[3]

Sounds pretty good, doesn't it? And in a way—but a very limited way, unfortunately—it's true.

Lawyers do indeed end up running Fortune 500 companies; holding elected and appointed positions in federal, state, and local governments; writing murder mysteries; and performing countless other responsibilities that never require them to say, "May it please the court, my client is innocent."

But guess what? Most law school graduates become lawyers, at least for several years, and usually for their entire careers. That's why it's called law school rather than learn-to-do-anything-you-want-anywhere-you-want school.

Okay, that's not quite fair. We don't actually teach students how to be lawyers in law school. Mostly we teach them how to "think like a lawyer," which, as I explain in the next chapter, simply means teaching people how to think clearly and precisely. That ability is obviously useful in business, government, fiction writing, and other endeavors besides law.

Still, even if clear thinking is useful in chess, you're not going to figure out how to defeat Gary Kasparov by studying the law of contracts. And even though lawyers sometimes make the leap from general counsel to CEO, an MBA is a more direct ticket to the boardroom.

Moreover, it's not just that law school trains students in thinking about the law; law school placement offices channel graduates into jobs in the law. And students who come to law school simply because they couldn't think of anything better to do are likely to follow the path of least resistance when it comes to choosing a career as well. Thus, the very students who most need guidance may be the least likely to receive it.

When the law firms show up to recruit—as they do even in a soft economy—a student without clear direction is likely to start wondering about which firm in which city best suits her. But she probably won't ask the logically antecedent, and more important question: Should I work for a law firm at all?

To be sure, enterprising students can find unconventional jobs, even right out of law school. And most schools provide assistance, in the form of placement services and loan forgiveness, for public interest jobs.

But those positions, too, are typically law jobs. With the exception of the odd investment bank or consulting firm, recruiters for non-law positions do not come to law school campuses. Students interested in those jobs must go out on their own. It's possible, but again, what are the odds that someone who goes to law school out of inertia will take that initiative?

For the most part, when people say that you can do anything with a law degree, what they have in mind is doing something other than practicing law after a long stint of practicing law. A fairly common career path goes from working in a law firm for a client, to working in-house in that client's office of general counsel, to working in that enterprise's main line of business.

David Stern and Paul Tagliabue, the lawyers who run the National Basketball Association and the National Football League, respectively, are good examples. Each labored many years as an attorney before moving to the front office.

Don't get me wrong. I'm thrilled that so many talented young people—not to mention people who have been out of college for many years—are applying to law school. Outstanding students are always a joy to teach.

And a great many of the finest lawyers came to law school by default, only to discover that they had a knack and passion for the job. Despite perennial lawyer jokes, a legal education offers the opportunity to grapple with issues of justice and, in the words of Oliver Wendell Holmes Jr., to "live greatly in the law."[4]

But college students and recent graduates who see law school as a haven for generalists should be forewarned: The great life you choose by embarking on a legal education will most likely be in the law, rather than business, the arts, or sports.

If that appeals to you, by all means, come. If not, well, I hear medical school applications have been down lately.

POSTSCRIPT

The number of people applying to law school continued to rise, albeit at a somewhat slower pace, through 2003–2004, the last academic year for which data are available.[5] For the first time ever that year, more than 100,000 people applied to law school. Although not all of these applicants end up attending law school, roughly half of them do,[6] and nearly all of these eventually pass the bar.[7] Any way you slice it, that's a lot of lawyers. Some people argue that quite apart from the career satisfaction of the lawyers themselves, all these lawyers are bad for society as a whole. In the language of economics, lawyers simply impose "transaction costs" on otherwise useful activity—a kind of tax on dispute resolution—whereas actors in other fields, such as scientists and engineers, "create value."[8]

There is certainly something to this criticism. The tort system, for example, is a notoriously inefficient means of delivering compensation to victims of medical malpractice and other forms of negligence, with one study showing roughly half of the money spent on tort litigation going to lawyers.[9]

But even this number is not so bad as it may at first appear. The tort system is not merely a means of compensating accident victims; it also serves to deter harmful conduct; and in the absence of much more extensive regulation of the sort that American's tend to dislike, the fear of litigation may serve to improve overall health and safety. To the extent that this is so, even tort lawyers "add value."[10]

Moreover, most of what lawyers do involves avoiding, rather than resolving, disputes. The lawyers who hammer out a contract that anticipates potential disputes and resolves them in advance, grease the wheels of commerce by making it that much easier for parties with adverse interests to trust one another. This too adds value.

The real issue, it seems, is the disappearance of good jobs in fields other than law. Given the degree to which our law requires a detailed knowledge of American society and culture, law is one of the few fields that is likely to remain resistant to outsourcing. (The monopoly power of state bars helps too.) Competition from highly skilled but relatively poorly paid workers in China, India, and elsewhere means fewer and fewer high-paying jobs in the United States for engineers, financial analysts, and others whose expertise is not country-specific. So if many of our most talented young people now choose to enter law rather than to pursue careers in one of these other fields, that may well be an effect, rather than a cause, of the declining overall competitiveness of the U.S. economy.

NOTES

1. *See* Carlyn Kolker, *Tightening the Spigot*, Am. Law., Aug. 30, 2002, at 19.
2. According to the Law School Admission Council, the organization that administers the Law School Admission Test, ABA applicants increased by 17.6 percent from the 2000–2001 school year to the 2001–2002 school year, from 77,200 to 90,900. The following year, there were 99,500 ABA applicants, an increase of 9.5 percent. Law School Admission Council, LSAC Volume Summary, *at* http://www.lsacnet.org.
3. Stanford Law School, Studying International Law at Stanford, *at* http://sils.stanford.edu/SILSstudy.html.
4. Oliver Wendell Holmes Jr., Collected Papers 30 (New York: Harcourt, Brace & Howe, 1920).
5. *See* Law School Admission Council, LSAC Volume Summary, *at* http://www.lsacnet.org.
6. *See id.*
7. *See* Linda F. Wightman, LSAC National Longitudinal Bar Passage Study, *at*

http://www.lsacnet.org/LSAC.asp?url=lsac/research-reports/NLBPSExecutiveSummary.htm (finding that by 1998, 95 percent of students who began law school in 1991 had passed the bar).

8. *See, e.g.*, Derek C. Bok, *A Flawed System of Law Practice and Training*, 33 J. Legal Educ. 570 (1983); Kevin M. Murphy et al., *The Allocation of Talent: Implications for Growth*, 106 Q.J. Econ. 503, 503 (1991) (reporting the results of an empirical study and stating that "[o]ur evidence shows that countries with a higher proportion of engineering college majors grow faster; whereas countries with a higher proportion of law concentrators grow more slowly"). For a critique of these studies, see Frank B. Cross, *Lawyers, the Economy, and Society*, 35 Am. Bus. L.J. 477 (1998); Frank B. Cross, *The First Thing We Do, Let's Kill All the Economists: An Empirical Evaluation of the Effect of Lawyers on the United States Economy and Political System*, 70 Tex. L. Rev. 645 (1992).

9. *See* Deborah L. Rhode, *Frivolous Litigation and Civil Justice Reform: Miscasting the Problem, Recasting the Solution*, 54 Duke L.J. 447, 464–65 (2004); *see also* Tillinghast-Towers Perrin, U.S. Tort Costs: 2003 17 (2003) (reporting somewhat lower transaction costs).

10. *Cf.* Carl Bogus, Why Lawsuits Are Good for America 138 (New York: New York University Press, 2001) ("[L]awsuits are good for America because the common law serves an essential regulatory function.").

• 39 •

How to "Think Like a Lawyer": Advice to New and Prospective Law Students

August 2001

Each August, at law schools all across the country, thousands of first-year students begin studies that will, for most of them, culminate in their joining the legal profession a few years later. The start of any new venture is always a time of excitement and anxiety, but such classic works of fiction and memoir as *The Paper Chase*[1] and *One L*[2] have contributed to a mythology of law school as a kind of extended hazing ritual. As a result, the anxiety can dominate the excitement.

To try to calm the fears of new and future law students, I offer a few words of advice that I wish someone had given to me when I was a 1-L in 1987. I hope what I have to say will also be of interest to those readers who have finished their legal studies, as well as to those who have no intention of ever beginning such studies.

First-year law students come to law school after twelve years of primary and secondary school, four years of college, and in many cases some additional years in the workforce or in graduate school. Why, then, should another three years of school be frightening? The answer is surely the mystery surrounding the Socratic method.

Here is an example of the Socratic method based on the first day of my course in constitutional law:

Me: Ms. Yavlinsky, suppose the New York state legislature passes a statute banning "the making of any statements critical of the New York government." You write an editorial for the student newspaper in which you state that the members of the legislature who voted for the statute thereby violated their oath to support the Constitution. You are prosecuted for violating the statute. Do you have a constitutional defense?

Ms. Yavlinsky: Yes.

Me: What is your defense?

Ms. Yavlinsky: It violates the First Amendment.

Me: But the First Amendment says that "*Congress* shall make no law . . . abridging the freedom of speech, or of the press." Is the New York legislature the same body as Congress?

Ms. Yavlinsky: No.

Me: So is the prosecution permissible?

Ms. Yavlinsky: I don't think so?

Me: Why not?

Ms. Yavlinsky: I think the First Amendment has been applied to the states.

Me: Very good. Indeed it has. Later in the semester, we will study a series of cases in which the Supreme Court ruled that when the Fourteenth Amendment prohibits any state from denying a person "liberty" without "due process of law," it implicitly includes within "liberty" most of those rights that are spelled out in the Bill of Rights.[3] But I'm troubled by something else today. Why should a New York court have to pay any attention to what's in the federal Constitution?

Ms. Yavlinsky: Because of Article VI.

Me: I assume you are referring to the portion of Article VI that says: "This Constitution . . . shall be the supreme Law of the Land; and the Judges in every State shall be bound thereby, any Thing in the Constitution or Laws of any state to the Contrary notwithstanding."

Ms. Yavlinsky: Yeah, that's it.

Me: Well, that seems rather circular doesn't it? I have here in my pocket another document, also labeled the "Constitution of the United States." It has the following provisions:

> Article I: The form of the government of the United States shall be a dictatorship.
>
> Article II: The dictator shall be all-powerful.
>
> Article III: The dictator shall be Columbia Law School Professor Michael Dorf, unless and until he appoints a successor.
>
> Article IV: This Constitution shall be the supreme law of the land; and everybody shall be bound by it, any thing in the constitution or laws of any state or other body to the contrary notwithstanding.

Tell me Ms. Yavlinsky, why is the Constitution printed in the front of your casebook more authoritative than the "Dorf is Dictator" constitution?

Ms. Yavlinsky: Because the real Constitution was ratified by the people.

Me: Did you ratify it?

Ms. Yavlinsky: No.

Me: Did any of your ancestors ratify it?

Ms. Yavlinsky: No.

Me: What were your ancestors doing in 1789, when what you call the real Constitution was ratified by the people?

Ms. Yavlinsky: They were serfs in Russia.

Me: I see. Well perhaps the so-called real Constitution is binding because it was democratically chosen by the people who lived here at the time?

Ms. Yavlinsky: Okay.

Me: If you had been living in the United States in 1789, would you, as a woman, have been permitted to vote for the people who decided whether to ratify the Constitution?

Ms. Yavlinsky: No.

Me: Did enslaved African Americans vote for ratification?

Ms. Yavlinsky: No.

Me: How about most Native Americans?

Ms. Yavlinsky: No.

And so it goes. For every answer it seems there is another question, until the exasperated students begin to feel like the point of the Socratic method is to show how much smarter the professor is than they are.

It's true that the Socratic method can be used to confuse and humiliate students. It can also be misused in other ways—for example, when the professor asks the students in effect to try to read his mind, rejecting perfectly intelligent answers because they are not exactly what was expected.

When used well, however, the Socratic method teaches law students a vital skill: critical thinking.

In *The Paper Chase*, Professor Kingsfield (memorably portrayed by John Houseman in the film version) tells his students: "You come here with minds full of mush—and leave thinking like a lawyer." But, what exactly does it mean to think like a lawyer?

The answer—the secret to law school success—is nothing. There is no such thing as thinking like a lawyer. There is only clear thinking and confusion.

To be sure, the law often requires much greater precision than is needed in other spheres of life. A person's ability to avoid going to prison or to keep her fortune can turn on exactly what a word in a statute or contract means, and accordingly lawyers must learn to pay careful attention to nuance. But there is nothing different in kind about lawyerly precision that distinguishes it from any other type of clear thinking.

To paraphrase the first President Bush, for at least a generation, most law professors have practiced a *kinder, gentler*[4] form of the Socratic method. These days, one would be hard pressed to find an example of the archetypal, Kingsfieldian Socratic law professor who never utters a declaratory statement and gives the impression that everything any student says is wrong.

Nevertheless, the myth of the bullying Socratic law professor persists as a staple in fiction and in the fearful imaginations of new and prospective law students. Why?

In part, the myth persists because it glorifies the legal profession. Those of us who hold law degrees have an interest in the general public believing that we have some distinctive skill by virtue of our special, and especially arduous, training. Thus, there is a tendency among current lawyers to exaggerate how much they suffered when they were law students.

But the self-interest of legal professionals is only part of the story. The public also has an interest in believing that lawyers think differently from everybody else.

In his 1930 book, *Law and the Modern Mind*, attorney (and later federal appeals court judge) Jerome Frank explained why the lay public had always been hostile to lawyers as a class. According to Frank, most people believe that the law itself is clear, but that hair-splitting lawyers introduce uncertainties as a means of manipulating the law to serve their clients' and their own interests. Law school, in the public mind, aims to displace common sense with legalistic pedantry.[5]

The public's view, Frank argued, is mistaken. In most instances, the law cannot be certain, because life is simply too complex for a lawmaker to anticipate all of the circumstances to which a legal norm might be applied.

To return to the famous example I cited in the postscript to chapter 35, suppose the city council enacts an ordinance prohibiting "vehicles in the park." Whether the ordinance should be construed to bar ambulances or bicycles depends on a host of factors, including the statute's purpose, the tools used to infer that purpose, and the role the particular judge thinks the legislative purpose properly plays in legal interpretation.

Although most lawyers would probably side with Frank and against the myth of legal certainty, law school does pose a real danger for those students who absorb the wrong lesson—and come to resemble not Socrates, but the Sophists (at least as they are ordinarily portrayed these days. The actual Sophists of ancient Athens were more than philosophical wise guys).

The point of the Socratic method is to encourage students to question assumptions they did not even realize they were making. That is an essential element of legal training, but it can be taken too far.

For example, in the above hypothetical dialogue, I was trying to induce Ms. Yavlinsky and the other students in the class to ask themselves why the Constitution is binding law. A clear answer to that question will be useful to students in figuring out how the Constitution should be interpreted. By using the Socratic method to elicit an answer, or a range of answers, rather than simply telling them what I think in a lecture, I am helping them sharpen their own analytical skills.

But a student who comes away from the class thinking, as a result of the Socratic give-and-take, that the law has no rightful claim to authority and that he can therefore ignore it, has missed the point of the lesson. Even if he is right as a matter of political theory, he will not be an effective lawyer if he treats the law as wholly illegitimate.

More generally, in exposing students to the law's inevitable ambiguities, the Socratic method risks inducing cynicism—the view that the law can mean anything or nothing. But this view is no better than its opposite: the naïve view that law always has a single, undebatable meaning.

Cynicism is an unwarranted and unintended consequence of the use of the Socratic method. While there is some uncertainty in some areas of law, that is a far cry from saying there is no certainty anywhere in the law. The existence of dusk does not call into question the distinction between day and night.

POSTSCRIPT AND CONCLUSION

Thus we return to the thesis I laid out in the introduction: Neither formalists nor legal realists fully capture the way the law works in practice. But what about my claim just now that there is nothing about thinking like a lawyer that distinguishes it from precise thinking in other fields? Is this claim consistent with the other formulation of my thesis, what I called the partial autonomy of law? For if law is even partially autonomous from other disciplines, then surely thinking about that autonomous part *is* distinct from ways of thinking in other fields.

The tension is merely rhetorical. Law, understood as a body of norms, is distinct from the normative implications, if any, one can draw from other fields whose insights may seem relevant to law—economics, history, moral philosophy, etc. To figure out what the law forbids, permits, or mandates often requires a synthesis of, among other things: the linguistic meaning of some authoritative text; the different ways that text may have been understood and acted upon over the course of history; the ways in which other, related questions have been resolved that may be analogous or disanalogous to the particular question; and the desirability or undesirability of the likely consequences of one or another decision. To say that law is relatively autonomous of other disciplines is thus to say that no other field of human knowledge puts these materials together in quite the same way.

Learning to synthesize such diverse materials does take time and practice. Moreover, the process is more art than science. In that respect, the legal realists are literally correct. Many of the most powerful legal realist writings took aim at the claims of the arch-formalist Christopher Columbus Langdell, who claimed that law is a science.[6]

Accordingly, if what is meant by "thinking like a lawyer" is synthesizing the distinctive sorts of data that go into figuring out what the law means, then perhaps the term is not mere empty verbiage. But too often lawyers and non-lawyers alike speak and act as though the lawyer's art can only be practiced by the initiates who have received a legal training. Anyone willing to think clearly about the often-vexing conundrums the law presents can think like a lawyer. And as I use that phrase, it is no insult, but one of the highest forms of praise.

NOTES

1. John Jay Osborn, The Paper Chase (Boston: Houghton Mifflin, 1971); The Paper Chase (Twentieth Century Fox 1973).
2. Scott Turow, One L (New York: Putnam, 1977).
3. *See, e.g.*, Duncan v. Louisiana, 391 U.S. 145, 147–48 (1968).
4. *See* Thanksgiving Address to the Nation, 27 Weekly Comp. Pres. Doc. 1737 (Nov. 27, 1991).
5. *See* Jerome Frank, Law and the Modern Mind 28–30 (New York: Brentano's, 1930) ("To the layman this circumlocutory mode of speech [used by judges and lawyers] seems at times unnecessarily strained, artificial and almost dishonest.").
6. *E.g.*, Grant Gilmore, The Ages of American Law 41–67 (New Haven: Yale University Press, 1977); Felix S. Cohen, *Transcendental Nonsense and the Functional Approach*, 35 Colum. L. Rev. 809 (1935); Roscoe Pound, *Mechanical Jurisprudence*, 8 Colum. L. Rev. 605 (1908); *see generally* Thomas C. Grey, *Langdell's Orthodoxy*, 45 U. Pitt. L. Rev. 1 (1983).

Appendix

As discussed in chapters 35, 36, and 37, in 2002, Columbia Law School conducted a series of surveys of representative samples of Americans on law-related subjects. The questions (which I wrote), and a summary of the answers given to two of those surveys, are provided below. Complete results, including sampling methodology, statistical significance, and breakdowns by age, education, income, race, region, and sex, can be found on the web at http://www2.law.columbia.edu/news/surveys/index.shtml.

SURVEY I: LAWYERS AND THE LEGAL PROFESSION (APRIL 2002)

For question 1, respondents were asked to rate lawyers, politicians, and police officers for honesty. (Due to rounding, answers to this and other questions do not necessarily total 100 percent.)

Occupation	*Especially or Somewhat Honest*	*About Average*	*Especially or Somewhat Dishonest*	*Don't Know*
Lawyers	31%	30%	39%	1%
Politicians	16%	21%	61%	1%
Police	58%	29%	12%	1%

2. Have you used the services of a lawyer within the past twelve months?

Yes	32%
No	68%

3. Do you believe that lawyers do more harm than good by filing lawsuits that may raise the cost of doing business, or do they perform a beneficial role by holding big companies accountable to the law?

More Harm Than Good	41%
A Beneficial Role	50%
Don't Know	9%

4. Given the level of compensation of other professions in society, such as doctors and corporate executives, overall, do you believe most lawyers are overpaid, fairly compensated, or underpaid?

Overpaid	60%
Fairly Compensated	36%
Underpaid	2%
Don't Know	2%

5. Please tell me if you agree or disagree with the following statement: "Even though I sometimes disagree with or dislike the rulings of the United States Supreme Court in particular cases, the fact that the Supreme Court can strike down unconstitutional laws is a good feature of the American system of government."

Agree	83%
Disagree	13%
Don't Know	3%

SURVEY II: AMERICANS' KNOWLEDGE OF THE U.S. CONSTITUTION (MAY 2002)

1. Does the Constitution include the following statement about the proper role of government: "From each according to his ability, to each according to his needs."

Yes	35%
No	31%
Don't Know	34%

(Correct Answer: No)

2. True or False: The U.S. Constitution states the following: "All persons born or naturalized in the United States, and subject to the jurisdiction thereof, are citizens of the United States and of the State wherein they reside."

True	83%
False	10%
Don't Know	7%

(Correct Answer: True)

3. True or False: In time of war or other declared national emergency, the President may suspend the Constitution's Bill of Rights.

True	32%
False	60%
Don't Know	9%

(Correct Answer: False)

4. True or False: A Justice of the Supreme Court serves for a term of twelve years, at the conclusion of which, he or she may be appointed to a second twelve-year term by the President.

True	24%
False	64%
Don't Know	12%

(Correct Answer: False)

5. True or False: If the Supreme Court were to overrule *Roe v. Wade*, abortion would be illegal throughout the United States.

True	57%
False	32%
Don't Know	11%

*(Correct Answer: False)**

*The statement is false because a decision overturning *Roe* would leave the question of whether to prohibit abortion to the state legislatures. However, if, following such a decision, Congress were to enact a nationwide federal abortion ban, and if the Supreme Court were to uphold the ban as a valid exercise of congressional power to regulate interstate commerce, then abortion would be illegal throughout the United States. It is also conceivable, though extremely unlikely, that a decision overturning *Roe* would be based on the supposition that failure to prohibit abortion either denies to fetuses the equal protection of the laws or deprives them of life without due process; in either case, the overruling decision would require all states to prohibit abortion. Despite these possibilities, it is reasonable to suppose that most respondents who answered "true" were simply mistaken about what *Roe* itself held and what its overruling would likely entail.

Table of Cases

Index

About the Author

Michael C. Dorf is the Michael I. Sovern Professor of Law at Columbia University School of Law. He is the editor of *Constitutional Law Stories* (2004) and coauthor, with Laurence H. Tribe, of *On Reading the Constitution* (1991). A *magna cum laude* graduate of Harvard College and Harvard Law School, he served as a law clerk to Judge Stephen Reinhardt of the U.S. Court of Appeals for the Ninth Circuit and for Justice Anthony M. Kennedy of the U.S. Supreme Court. Professor Dorf has written dozens of scholarly articles on constitutional law and related subjects and since 2000 has written a bi-weekly column on the website writ.FindLaw.com. A 2002 study found that the scholarship of no American law professor to have entered legal academia in the previous decade was more widely cited.* He lives in New York City with his wife and two daughters.

*The study, Most Cited Law Faculty: 50 Most Cited Faculty Who Entered Teaching Since 1992, was conducted by Professor Brian Leiter of the University of Texas School of Law, and is available at http://www.utexas.edu/law/faculty/bleiter/rankings02/50_most_cited.html.